Christmas 1960-Present

A Collectors Guide to Decorations and Customs

Robert Brenner

Schiffer Publishing Ltd

4880 Lower Valley Road, Atglen, PA 19310 USA

Dedication

It is to my parents, Bernard and Jeanette Brenner, and to Sharon's parents, Al and Carmen Thiel, that I dedicate this book. Both of us were very fortunate to be born into German families richly steeped in old world traditions. Our parents sacrificed their personal needs and wants at Christmas to ensure that Santa Claus would bring to their children everything for which they asked (within reason, of course). Both sets of parents passed not only their love of family tradition on to the next generation, but modeled parenting skills which continue today in their grandchildren and great-grandchildren.

Libraryof Congress Cataloging-in-Publication Data

Brenner, Robert.
    Christmas: 1960-present: a collectors guide to decorations and customs/by Robert Brenner.
        ISBN 0-7643-1484-X (Paperback)
    1. Christmas--Collectibles. 2. Christmas decorations--Collectors and collecting. I. Title.
    NK4696.4 .B689 2002
    394.2663'075-dc21
                                2002007579

Designed by "Sue"
Type set in Americana XBd BT/Lydian BT & Aldine 721

ISBN: 0-7643-1484-X
Printed in China
1 2 3 4

Published by Schiffer Publishing Ltd.
4880 Lower Valley Road
Atglen, PA 19310
Phone: (610) 593-1777; Fax: (610) 593-2002
E-mail: Schifferbk@aol.com
Please visit our web site catalog at www.schifferbooks.com
We are always looking for people to write books on new and related subjects. If you have an idea for a book please contact us at the above address.

This book may be purchased from the publisher.
Include $3.95 for shipping.
Please try your bookstore first.
You may write for a free catalog.

In Europe, Schiffer books are distributed by
Bushwood Books
6 Marksbury Ave.
Kew Gardens
Surrey TW9 4JF England
Phone: 44 (0)20-8392-8585
Fax: 44 (0)20-8392-9876
E-mail: Bushwd@aol.com
Free postage in the UK. Europe: air mail at cost

Contents

Acknowledgements 4
Introduction—Our Return to the Past 5
    1850-1859 5
    1860-1869 5
    1870-1879 5
    1880-1889 5
    1890-1899 5
    1900-1909 5
    1910-1919 5
    1920-1929 6
    1930-1939 6
    1940-1949 6
    1950-1959 6
The 1960s—A Return to Simplicity in Our Decorating 7
    Historical Perspective on Our Return to Simplicity 7
    Our Cards and Books 13
    Our Trees 16
    How We Decorted Our Homes and Trees 17
    A Closer Look at Our Tree Decorations 26
    Under Our Trees 34
    Indoor Electric Lighting of Our Trees and Homes 41
    Outdoor Electric Lighting 45
The 1970s—The Return to the Home-Crafting of Decorations .. 48
    Historical Perspective of This Decade—We Delve into the Past ... 48
    Our Cards 50
    Our Trees 52
    How We Decorate Our Homes and Trees 53
    American Influences on Glass Ornaments 56
    European Influences on Our Glass Ornaments 57
    Candy Containers 61
    Tinsel Icicles and Tinsel Garlands 62
    Plastic Decorations 63
    A Closer Look at Christmas Ornaments and Decorations For Our Trees ... 64
    Under Our Trees 66
    Indoor Electric Lighting of Our Trees and Homes 70
    Outdoor Electric Lighting 73

The 1980s—A Return to the Past Traditional Look of Christmas 75
    Historical Perspective—Return to European Traditions 75
    Our Trees 77
    Our Cards 79
    How We Decorated Our Homes and Trees 80
    American Influences on Glass Ornaments 82
    European Influences on Glass Ornaments 83
    American Importers and Manufacturers of the Decade 91
    A Closer Look at Tree Decorations of This Decade 98
    Under Our Trees 101
    Indoor Electric Lighting of Our Trees 103
    Outdoor Electric Lighting 104
The 1990s—The Designers Influence our Christmas Decorating 105
    Historical Perspective—Designers and Their European Designs 105
    Our Trees 107
    How We Decorated Our Homes and Trees 110
    Our Cards 110
    American Influences on Glass Ornaments and Tree Decorations 114
    European Influences on Glass Ornaments and Tree Decorations 114
    Italy Gains New Prominence in Manufacturing Glass Ornaments 122
    Czechoslovakia 128
    Poland Gains Prominence in the Creation of Glass Ornaments 130
    American Importers and Manufacturers of Tree Ornaments 132
    Santa Claus Figures and Ornaments 153
    Candy Containers 153
    Paper and Cardboard Ornaments 153
    Clay Ornaments 153
    Wooden Ornaments 153
    Tinsel Icicles and Garlands 154
    Under Our Trees 154
    Indoor Electric Lighting of Our Trees 157
    Outdoor Electric Lighting 157
References Cited 160

Acknowledgments

Without the generous understanding, motivation, and help of countless individuals, this book would never have been possible. I especially wish to thank Bruce Waters for his photography expertise, which is very evident. Hours upon hours of careful handling and delicate maneuvering were necessary to photograph the hundreds of Christmas items contained herein. His patience is beyond belief. Special thanks go also to Fred Studach, a personal close friend who spent countless hours helping Bruce with the intricacies of photography work here on site in Princeton. Eric Stensrud also helped with sorting and categorizing. Thanks go to Jeff Snyder, "editor extraordinaire," who spent hours upon hours working with me on the editing of this book and Bonnie Hensley who also spent countless hours doing a magnificent job of creatively planning the layout of this book.

Equally important is my wife Sharon, who spent hours upon hours helping with various aspects of this book. Her editorial skills and suggestions were of tremendous help in this project. Special thanks to my first mom, Jeanette, and my second mom, Carmen, who help manage our collection: sort, categorize, and catalog the many Christmas items photographed from our collection for this project. Moms are the best!

Certain individuals from Europe were extremely instrumental in helping me with information and wonderful images. First of all, I wish to thank Ulrike Bohm-Beck of Lauscha who served as a translator of never-before read material on the period in Germany between World War II and the Reunification of Germany. Of special help in Germany was Helena Horn, the director of the marvelous glass museum in Lauscha. What a wonderful gift to Germany this museum curator is. Ms. Horn has transformed this museum into a spectacular display of not only Christmas tree ornaments and interpretative exhibits revolving around their manufacturing but a stupendous display of German glass blown in this region. Also of great help in Germany were Helmut Krebs, Harald Wohlfahrt, Sandra Brehm, and Michael Krebs.

From Italy, I would like to acknowledge the unselfish contributions of time, research material, and photographs from Enrico Scaletti, Luca Terruzzi, and Fausto and Fiorenzo Di Gilardoni.

From the Czech Republic, I would like to thank Filip Brogowski. From Poland, I would like to thank Marek Palowski, Glen Lewis, and Patricia and Eric Breen.

Thanks go to the following friends and associates who provided so much help in many different ways: Jim and Roberta Fiene, Laura and Craig Beane, Mike Makurat, Mike Garvey, and Eric Stensrud. Eric has been instrumental in helping with our collection. Having been a Christmas collector since the age of ten; at twenty-three, Eric has been our mainstay in helping to decorate and undecorate at Christmas and has built an unbelievable collection of those items which fit into these decades.

Finally, I wish to thank all those who have produced these creative and colorful Christmas items for so many years. Thanks also go to the countless collectors like you who collect these items, serving as caretakers so future generations might continue to enjoy their beauty.

Introduction—Our Return to the Past

While this book deals with American Christmas from 1960 to 1999, it is helpful for the reader to delve into the past in order to fully understand just how we arrived at our fashions and trends for these decades. All of our decorating and celebrating customs have evolved from past traditions, our rich cultural heritage, and our ethnic backgrounds. All of these help mold our vision of what Christmas decorations should be like and how we ought to celebrate this holiday.

For anyone, who remembers Christmas decorations before 1960, they can perhaps remember some pretty interesting fads. We ended the 1950s with a trendy novelty: the Aluminum Christmas tree! Americans were ready to return in the 1960s to a more simplistic celebration. We flocked our trees white, decorated them with one or two colors of simple glass ornaments, and lit them with blue or clear flood lights. Thus, we veered from trend setting decorating and turned to a more mainstream, almost "non-controversial" style.

By briefly reviewing the decades previous to 1960, the reader can gain a rich understanding and prospective of just what occurred in our history which helped to set the stage for the material you will discover in this volume.

1850-1859

Our very first trees were decorated with edible, perishable ornaments. Pastry, confectionery, red-cheeked apples, and nuts were the most essential Christmas decorations. Decorated on Christmas Eve, the tree was undecorated and consumed on January 1st. Therefore, popcorn and cranberry chains, simple cookies, molded pastry ornaments, and candles attached by placing pins through branches appeared on this tree. Note also the use of lanterns. Many families would place oil in these glass tumblers, place a wick inside, and then light their trees. This practice of using edibles on trees continued until the birth of glass Christmas tree ornament making in the 1830s. The very wealthy continued to decorate with edibles while the poor started to decorate with glass ornaments since they could be recycled year after year and they were extremely affordable. Our very first ornaments emulated edibles: plums, apples, pears, nuts, and candy. Very few documented references to decorated trees are recorded since the Christmas tree was not yet a widely accepted practice in America.

1860-1869

In this period, the majority of trees continued to be small and were placed on tables. In 1861, the *American Agriculturalist* depicted a tabletop tree decorated with flags, fruit, candy containers, and candles. Paper decorations of all sorts were used, including gilt paper folded into various shapes and paper containers for holding edibles. But most popular were flat Dresden ornaments flashed with gold, red, and green lacquers. Heavy glass ornaments were blown since German glass blowers had not yet perfected the art of blowing the thin-walled ornaments with which we are familiar today. Most kugels were blown into round spheres. Kugels are the early, heavy glass ornaments that were the first glass decorations for the Christmas tree. Originally they were used as decorations in glass blowers cottages; eventually, they found their way to the tree, no doubt due to their brightness and color, which so beautifully reflected candles lit on these early trees. Clay ball weighted candleholders patented in 1867 were used to hold the candles that illuminated these early trees. Feather trees, artificial trees made from green dyed turkey and goose feathers and wired around branches and finished off on each branch with a red composition berry or a candleholder, were used as early as 1841, but were not commonplace in Germany until the 1860s.

1870-1879

Lavishly decorated tabletop trees were the order of the day. However, many of the decorations were home-crafted. As early as the mid-1870s, people complained that Christmas was becoming too commercial and we needed to return to creating our own ornaments. Therefore, note the variety of home-crafted paper decorations and cornucopias on this period tree. Most of these were home-crafted by women and children based upon directions found in various magazines of the day. Grape-shaped kugels made their appearance in this decade, along with other very rare fruit shapes. But these heavy ornaments were soon to be replaced with lighter-weight ornaments. In the early 1870s, Germans had perfected the art of blowing thin glass figural ornaments. Some of these

early examples are found on this tree. Very simple in nature, these glass creations were their first attempt in developing the art of glass blowing. Counterweighted candleholders with tin and lead alloy balances created by the toy makers of Nuremberg, Germany, appealed to those who wished to have some decorations with their candles. We also decorated our homes with crepe paper roping, paper decorations, and lots of natural greens and materials.

1880-1889

Thin glass figurals continued to be perfected in this decade and some very elegant examples are seen on these trees. The tradition of using glass beading on the tree becomes somewhat commonplace as families attempted to fill in the large empty spaces with ornamentation. Paper decorations continued to be favorites. Produced by a 24-color plate process, these ornaments took on a three-dimensional effect, especially when embossed by machines. Glass ornaments continued to gain more recognition as tree decorations. Especially favored were those early wire-wrapped ornaments embellished with tinsel, cellophane, cotton, and even crepe paper. Tin and lead candy baskets also made their debut. Often times they were filled with candy . . . other times with tiny gifts. In this period, it was also quite common to hang some of the presents on the tree as decorations. Note the development of candleholders: patented in 1887, clip-on candleholders permitted people to place candles on the far tips of the branches, making it somewhat safer to light the tree. Most of these early holders were lithographed with various designs and were often cut and formed in the shapes of angels, clowns, and even Father Christmas.

1890-1899

During the Victorian period of the late 1800s, lavishly decorated trees were the order of the day. Tabletop trees were now replaced with huge floor-to-ceiling trees in homes with high ceilings. These full-length trees were decorated with huge quantities of ornaments made from many materials: glass, wax, paper, wood, cardboard, and even metal. The more the Victorians could place on their tree, the better it was. Glass figurals continued in popularity, with birds, pinecones, St. Nicholas figures, and other comic figures of the day being produced from glass. Those heavily wire-wrapped ornaments also continued in popularity, especially at the height of the Victorian period. Wax angels, cardboard Dresden ornaments (often candy containers as evidenced on this tree), and even small wooden ornaments were used to decorate trees. Also, it should be noted that the placement of the tinsel roping on the tree was somewhat haphazard. Our Victorian homes reflected this extravagant decorating technique: the more, the better! Note that E-shaped candle holders, patented in the United States, allowed us to more "safely" place lit candles on our trees. Natural greens, dried flowers, paper roping, tinsel sprays, and even plates with Christmas themes were employed.

1900-1909

In reaction to the gaudy and extravagant decorating style of the Victorian period, families sought to return to a more "natural" tree decorating approach. Rather than crowd the tree with loads of edibles and various brightly colored decorations, artists and writers of the time suggested that no color be put on the tree. They recommended only glittering cotton, angel hair, tinsel, clear or silver glass ornaments, imitation snow, pinecones, and only white candles. This style was very popular, as seen by photographs from this period. This "white tree" prevailed up to the start of World War I. Gradually, all the beloved items of earlier days snuck back in, but many times not in their original forms. Santas, bells, birds, and other figural ornaments were used on trees, but they were all white. Many shrewd families saved money by washing the lacquer off the ornaments they had previously purchased. Frugal Americans would strip the needles off their trees and then use them for many years after. Cotton was employed to simulate snow on an evergreen. Thus, an inexpensive artificial tree was quite simple to obtain.

1910-1919

Following the white fashion, trees returned back to brilliant, colorful ornamentation in many forms. Czechoslovakian beaded ornaments in a variety of shapes and paper ornaments added a profusion of color to the tree. Glass figurals continued to be perfected, many of them actually being representations of various comic characters found in newspapers' comic strips. Happy Hooligan, Foxy Grandpa, and Flip appeared on our trees. However, World War I prevented the importation of European ornaments into America. Thus, we had to resort to a few seasons with some very heavy, undesirable ornaments. During this period, Americans, with the aid of German glass blowers brought into New York State, blew glass ornaments. But they were not very successful. We quickly turned to Europe After the war once again for our decorations. Electric lighting began to be employed more and more as Americans sought a new look for their trees. European figural lights were the rage.

1920-1929

This decade marks the start of the "Golden Age of Glass Ornaments," as by now the decorated tree was a now a widely accepted focal point of our American celebration of Christmas. Almost every home now had a tree. Paper, cardboard, wood, and metal ornaments were abandoned and replaced with countless wonderful, brightly colored glass spheres, indents, and figural ornaments of all sorts. Americans especially loved the red, white, and blue painting styles. American society is reflected in ornaments: our love for baseball, our love for transportation, and even our fascination with Indians. Electric lights were the mainstay of the tree. Now more than ever, Americans electrified their trees as the cost of electric lights came ever more within the reach of the "Average American Family." Milk glass lights from Japan became very cheap; thus, we started the trend of adding some variety to our lighting as well. Of course, the end of this decade brought some very impoverished times, but we still sought to decorate our trees as best we could, even if we could purchase only a few glass ornaments or a single string of electric lights. We were not going to have a "sad" Christmas tree.

1930-1939

"The Golden Age of Glass Ornaments" continued in this decade with a profusion of different figural shapes created for the American market. Bells, Santas, fish, pinecones, and horns abounded as we went to Woolworth's and our local "Five and Dime" stores and picked glass ornaments out of the bins to take home. Cotton fruit, waxed angels, and some simple small paper ornaments found their way to our trees, but they were scarce in comparison to glass ornaments. Japanese and Czechoslovakian fashioned decorations also found their way to our trees. Especially popular were the cardboard buildings flocked with tiny glass beads. After the British Blockade in October, 1939, no more ornaments could be imported from Europe. Then Corning Glass Company took over and produced over 400,000 glass ornaments for that 1939 Christmas. However, American began to experiment with lighting creating Mickey Mouse lights in 1938 as well as those marvelous Whirl-Glo shades we placed over our lights to add motion to the tree. We imported fancy metal and glass lights from Japan, manufactured marvelous Matchless Stars with cut glass prisms in the United States, and put plastic covers over our lights. This period, more than any other, started the trend of Americans seeking innovative ways to light our trees.

1940-1949

World War II caused a radical departure from previous decorating customs. No longer were Europeans considered providers of tradition when it came to Christmas. The bitter feelings caused by the war helped to develop a sense of independence in America when it came to buying consumer goods. People turned to American manufacturers for decorations. There was a rush to buy American-made Visca artificial trees. Mass-produced ornaments, especially colored glass spheres, could be inexpensively purchased in boxes of a dozen.

At first American ornaments were clear glass with tinsel inside and had metal caps. Then, as the war intensified, the silver tinsel spray was eliminated. When the Precious Metals Act banned the use of any metal for production of Christmas items, ornaments were capped with cardboard or paper tops so they could be hung on the tree. For a time, no lights were available. Although Americans were forced to use only small quantities of electric lights, a profusion of reflectors helped to give a brighter look to trees otherwise sparsely lit. Immediately after the war, Americans turned to a profusion of plastic ornaments to decorate trees. A second tree exhibited as part of this decade reflects the use of these new, innovative, unbreakable ornaments made from plastic—a material developed during World War II. Reindeers, Santas, spheres, and snowmen were abundant.

1950-1959

Some American families clung to traditional tree decorating, using glass ornaments made in West Germany, Poland, and Italy as well as decorations like those used by their parents and grandparents. However, many Americans refused to use decorations manufactured by a country with whom they had just fought. They preferred American-made, unbreakable ornaments. Thus, plastic perfected during World War II became the medium of choice as countless angels, Santas, reindeer, choir boys, and other shaped ornaments took over the American tree. Completing the tree were the magnificent bubble lights, an American invention of Charles Otis.

Filled with methanol chloride and water, these lighted, bubbling tubes fascinated almost every American youngster who saw them. There was an emergence of plastic ornaments coated with silver and then lacquered. This was the impetus of a new industrial-age creation: the aluminum Christmas tree. Made of aluminum, these trees were decorated with one or two colors of plain glass spheres and then lit by a revolving color wheel floodlight. These trees were the rage of those who dared to be different. Welcome to the new age.

In a sense, aluminum trees reflected the post-war attitude of many Americans: "We are indestructible and we have a new identity in the world." The popularity of the aluminum tree soon waned; while many people found them to be absolutely the greatest, others sought to go back to the natural. This is somewhat reminiscent of the early 1900s when the white tree came along in dramatic contrast to the very gaudy Victorian tree.

Those who clung to tradition continued to hang German ornaments on their trees. The familiar shapes were once again evident, but the paint had changed quite drastically. Yellows, reds, greens, and blues all took on a brownish-tone as many of the paint formulas were lost during the destruction caused by the war. Japan provided some ceramic ornaments as well as some simple glass indents and shapes. Wax ornaments once again appeared on our trees, but they were thin and hollow and depicted soldiers, Santas, boots, and angels.

Christmas through the Decades, the first book I authored on the decade by decade approach to Christmas decorating will give the reader a detailed prospective into these early decades with many historical photos, color pictures of decorations from each of these decades, and a detailed text elaborating on the quick bullets of information contained above. If you have not read this first book, I feel you would enjoy it immensely. *Christmas: 1940-1959* covers the previous two decades in great detail with historical photos, multitudes of color pictures of decorations, a detailed history of these two decades covering Christmas celebrations, decorating trends, electric light company history, and ornament production history. For those of you who are searching for a basic book which covers the different periods of glass Christmas ornament manufacturing; wood, cotton, wax, paper, and metal ornaments; and the lighting of the tree by candles and electricity would find *Christmas Past* of particular interest. Those interested in advertising; crèche scenes, Santa figures; and different glass decorations for the tree including treetops, bead garlands, and Italian ornaments would find *Christmas Revisited* of interest as well.

Regardless of your collecting interests, knowledge through research and reading will help you gain a prospective of what there is to collect as well as information regarding the pricing and reproduction history of such items.

The 1960s—A Return to Simplicity in Our Decorating

Historical Perspective on Our Return to Simplicity

Starting somewhat innocently and quietly, the 1960s found Americans not only at war in Vietnam, but at war with themselves in numerous racial flare-ups throughout our nation as we struggled for equality and peace. But Christmas continued to be a respite from all our difficulties.

The first National Christmas Tree of the decade, in 1960, a 70-foot Douglas fir from Oregon, was lit by President Eisenhower. In 1961, in the absence of President Kennedy, who had to fly to the bedside of his stricken father in Palm Beach, Vice President Johnson lit the tree and gave the Yule Tree Message. It was First Lady Jacqueline Kennedy who began the practice of decorating the Christmas tree in the Blue Room with a special theme. The ornaments that first year were designed to reflect the spirit of Tchaikovsky's *Nutcracker* ballet.

A 72-foot blue spruce from Colorado, decorated with 5,000 multi-colored bulbs and 4,000 ornaments, was lighted in great splendor when President John F. Kennedy threw the switch in his address to the nation. Kennedy said: "This has been a year of peril but a year when the threat of war was faced. Our hopes for peace are a little higher and the Nation can enter the Yuletide season with more than the usual joy in our hearts."

One year later, on December 22, President Lyndon B. Johnson, after the 30-day mourning period for President Kennedy ended, lit our 71-foot red spruce from West Virginia. In 1964, the white spruce from New York State was decorated with 5,000 red and white lights. There were 10,000 other lights on the fifty-three state and territory trees which were set up to form a "Cross of Peace." An arched sign over the entrance to the Cross of Peace carried these words "Peace on Earth to Men of Good Will."

Other lavish displays of Christmas existed beside our national tree and it would be impossible to chronicle all of them; however, it was said that the largest tree in the world appeared in Indianapolis each year. Inaugurated in 1945, after years of war, the city was inspired to pay tribute to peace. Starting in 1962, decorating the Indiana Soldiers and Sailors Monument downtown developed into a giant civic project. The Indiana Soldiers and Sailors Monument was decked out in brilliant light to form a "tree" 246 feet tall and 110 feet at the base. The tree was topped off with four seven-foot stars, one visible from any direction.

In 1965, Tacoma, Washington, claimed they had the largest cut live tree at 98.5 feet. "Planted" in downtown Broadway Square, it was a gift to the city from the soldiers at Fort Lewis. Also known for many years is the lavish Christmas display at Rockefeller Center in New York City. In 1965, a 60-foot evergreen, gaily decorated, served as a backdrop for ice skaters. Thus it was that Americans continued the tradition of the community Christmas tree, a tradition firmly established by their ancestors in the late 1800s.

In 1960, Christmas sales were close to five percent over the year before, which actually disappointed retailers, who had suffered due to the economic slump that year. Chicago Printed String Company, turned out some 900,000 miles of gift-wrapping ribbon that year, for instance. Each American family spent an average of $147 on about thirty gifts. Thin necklace chains were the jewelry present of choice that year. Neiman-Marcus found its biggest sales ever in perfumes ranging between $20 to $30 an ounce.

One of the more interesting trees of the decade was a 74-foot reusable tree for West Erie Plaza in Erie, Pennsylvania. This tree consisted of four diagonally braced structural sections and rings with tinsel and holding lights. Four tow cables suspended the nine rings that ranged in diameter from 25-feet at the bottom to 18-inches at the top. Outdoor wire and sockets supported and supplied power to the colored bulbs. In the evening, its rings of brightly multi-colored lights made a magnificent scene.

Having followed through with their plans to decorate the Soldiers and Sailors Monument downtown with lights, Indianapolis, Indiana, claimed to have the tallest Christmas tree in 1964, being 246-feet high and 110-feet in diameter. The tree was topped off with the aforementioned four stars, one visible from each direction. The draping of the monument with electric lights was successfully executed by professional electrical and illuminating engineers.

Sales of home decorations—not counting lights and live trees—reached $160 million in 1964, a fifteen percent increase over the previous year. Seven percent of that business was captured by drug stores that began to stock large quantities of Christmas decorations. According to Stewart Dougall, who conducted marketing surveys in the mid-1960s, drug stores did five percent of the business on Christmas items.

Through this decade, the Coca-Cola Santa created by Haddon Sundblom continued to be a driving force in our conception of this jolly old man. Born on June 22, 1899, to Swedish immigrant parents, Sundblom began working in Chicago in the early 1920s. What inspired Sundblom's image of Santa is actually quite a mystery. The model for his original renderings was a retired salesman and friend, Lou Prentice. With this start, he created a painting in 1931, and every year thereafter, up to 1964, when Haddon Sundblom submitted his last Santa painting to Coca-Cola, which actually appeared in an advertisement in 1966. The playful moods that Sundblom captured are simply astounding. One year Santa would be playing with a train set he had just delivered, in another he was kicking off his boots and sneaking a bottle of Coke from the refrigerator. Sundblom helped to create a Santa which was everyone's all-American grandpa. After Lou Prentice died, Sundblom commenced using himself as the model. His lucky grandchildren and their friends also appeared in many of his paintings, and subsequent ads. Actually the times helped close the chapter on Sundblom's Santas. As advertisements employed more and more photography, and as television commercials started to dominate, the need for a Coca-Cola Santa dwindled.

Advertising from this decade is intriguing, especially since much of it was particularly important at Christmas when store owners were attempting not only to sell holiday goods, but household items as well.

The Brenners. Christmas 1962. Bob, Dan, Carol, Ginny, and Marilyn. $Priceless.

Laurie Norslien setting up the crèche scene at her home in Mount Horeb, Wisconsin, in 1964. $Priceless.

Alice Thiel setting up the Christmas crèche scene in Sherwood, Wisconsin, in 1965. Note the proliferation of American-blown ornaments. $Priceless.

Marion Thiel finishing decorating the tree on Christmas Eve, 1965 in Sherwood, Wisconsin. Note the plastic NOMA star tree top. $Priceless.

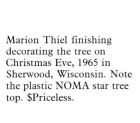

Susan Joy Rettenmund sitting on Santa's lap for Christmas, 1956. $7-10.

Laurie Norslien posing in front of her Christmas decorated fireplace for Christmas, 1964. $Priceless.

Santa with Marion and Alice Thiel in Sherwood, Wisconsin, in the early 1960s. $Priceless.

Christmas in the mid-1960s in the Thiel house in Sherwood, Wisconsin, where they followed the up-to-date trend of heavily flocking their pine tree and adding just one color of painted American ornaments for the tree's decoration. $5-10.

Christmas, 1960 in Mt. Calvary, Wisconsin. Bernard and Jeanette Brenner posing in front of their pine tree. In the 1960s, due to the pressure of their children to have a tree like their friends did, they started to purchase trees off tree lots in Fond du Lac rather than cut down the traditional cedar. $Priceless.

Christmas, 1960 in Mt. Calvary, Wisconsin. Santa has been good to Marilyn, Virginia, and Carol Brenner.

Early 1960s when Al Thiel and his daughter Alice picked out their tree from a tree lot in Appleton, Wisconsin. $Priceless.

Christmas, 1963 illustrating the large Italian crèche figures so popular in this decade. $10-15.

Christmas, 1962 in the Brenner's home. Note the pine tree and the NOMA tree top so very popular in the 1950s and continued in use through this entire decade. Left to right, Carol, Marilyn, and Ginny. $Priceless.

Christmas, 1960. Fred Studach in Gresham, Wisconsin, at Christmas on his new bike. $10-15.

Santa advertising piece from the early 1960s. $25-35.

Heavily sheared pine tree in a decade where the shape of the tree and number of branches was more important than how you decorated the tree. Christmas, 1968, tree of Al and Carmen Thiel. $5-10.

Sunbeam Santa stand-up from the early 1960s. $45-55.

Advertising matches used by stores and businesses as a give-a-way at the holiday season to help promote stores and products. $7-10 each.

Advertising match holders from the late 1940s into the early 1950s. $5-10 each.

Family Christmas setting advertising Zenith television sets. Early 1960s. $65-75.

Large elaborate Santa and sleigh advertising piece for Zenith television sets. Note marketing of "static free" which was not very possible in remote areas nor in a home without an antenna. $95-100.

Unusual advertising piece in that the promoted product was placed on the sleigh to the right of Santa Claus. Early 1960s. $85-95.

Zenith Advertising for television sets in a decade where every American either owned one or dreamed of owning one. $55-65.

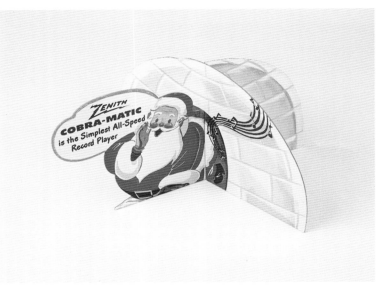

Wonderful advertising piece meant to go on turntable of a Zenith record player to promote its sale at Christmas. $100-120.

Advertising for the Zenith portable super transoceanic radio. Early 1960s. $85-95.

Various advertising pieces for the promotion of electrical gifts at Christmas. $30-35 each.

General advertising for various Zenith models of transistor, portable radios. $75-85.

Advertising give-away Santa. Given to store patrons, it was a flat sheet of printed paper. Through a series of directions and folds, this marvelous Santa decoration was a premium given for purchasing a Zenith product. Early 1960s. $25-35.

Our Cards and Books

Cards underwent radical changes in the mid-1960s. The Kennedy brothers, Martin Luther King, the unbelievable turmoil of the 1960s, contiguous with the Vietnam War, caused Americans to turn to many religious-themed designs on their cards. At this time, our cards reflected the fact that we were groping for a sense of who we were, where we were coming from, and "How are we all going to live through this?"

Our cards continued to look much like those of the previous decade, but designs tended to be more simplistic and more white than usual. This seemed to reflect the "white flocked look" of our Christmas trees and house decorations. Many of the same Santa Claus and bell designs were used, but merely placed on a simple white backdrop.

Due to fierce competition and the throw-away mentality of our populace, Christmas cards were printed on very thin cardboard stock. Today's families were on the move more than ever and found it unnecessary to save anything from the past. Therefore, cards were almost immediately discarded after they were received. Since so little was saved, card manufacturers quickly picked up on this trend and produced cards in smaller sizes as well as cards with simplistic designs. In 1966, it was estimated that 3.5 billion cards were purchased—400 million more than in the previous year. Over 50,000 different designs were available to Americans in 1966.

Some of the giants in the card industry continued to produce both sets of Christmas cards (usually 25 to a box) and individual cards (most often sold in card and other specialty shops). Cleveland based American Greetings continued to prosper and grow. In 1960, Irving Stone (all three sons of the Sapirstein family had changed their last name to Stone) was named president and J. S. became chairman. The next year the company opened a plant in Arkansas. Employment grew to over 6,000 in 1966, and plants were opened in Kentucky in 1967 and 1969. In 1967, Holly Hobbie made her first appearance on valentines and Christmas cards. In 1968, their sales exceeded $100 million, and the next year the company opened a manufacturing subsidiary in Mexico City.

Hallmark also continued its tradition of providing many artistic and creative cards in this decade. In 1967, Hallmark bought Springbook Editions, a company that manufactured quality jigsaw puzzles, mainly reproductions of fine paintings by such artists as Jackson Pollack, Miro, and Picasso. Therefore, their artistic line greatly expanded with this addition. Joyce C. Hall relinquished his chief executive responsibilities to his son, Donald J. Hall, in 1966.

Other companies continued to produce Christmas cards in a market which became more competitive with each passing year. It should also be noted that the tradition of sending Christmas cards also declined toward the end of the 1960s in an era which was marred by the Vietnam Conflict and a hippie population that shunned past traditions. Improved communications, including the telephone, also took its toll on card sending. It was much easier to call someone on Valentine's Day than to take the time to choose, address, and send a card.

While most Americans continued to send the traditional commercially-designed greeting cards, there were many who quickly adopted the custom of sending photograph greet cards, which contained a photo of their tree, family, children, or pets at Christmas. Kodak avidly promoted this trend, resulting in multitudes of Americans turning to their Kodak Instamatic cameras to record scenes for cards.

Salesman's sample folder illustrating some of the designs typical of the mid-1960s. $15-20 for sample folder. $.50-1 for richly designed cards and those with Santa Claus illustrated.

Sampling of late 1960s cards. Note colors and themes which mostly reflected a simpler time. $.50-1 for large examples and those illustrating Santa Claus.

Children's cards from the early 1960s. All with whimsical verses inside. $1-2 each.

Array of gift tags, gift cards, greeting cards, seals, and card boxes from this decade. $3-5 for complete boxed sets of cards. $2-3 for sets of complete seals, gift tags, and gift cards.

Gift boxes given by department stores for advertising purposes as well as gift boxes sold so that they may be used over and over. $5-10 for boxes depending upon design and size.

Wrapping paper, seals, and box of cards illustrating typical wrapping of the decade. Note the Christmas designs upon white paper. $3-5 for boxed set of wrapping paper.

Kodak advertisement from late 1960s promoting the use of photo cards at Christmas. $75-85.

Ribbon employed during this decade to finish off Christmas packages. Most of the satin ribbon was wide. $2-3 for complete rolls of ribbon.

Advertisement from late 1960s heralding the promptness of developing for those who wished to used photos as part of their greeting cards. $45-55.

Whitman Publishing and Western Publishing puzzles from 1960s. $20-25 each.

Advertisement from late 1960s enticing consumers to send photo greeting cards with a fold-out flap into which sample cards were placed. $85-95.

Assortment of 1960s children's Christmas books. All American. $5-7 each.

Advertisement from late 1960s with sizes and prices of cards on stand-up poster from store. $45-55.

Late 1950s into early 1960s children's books. All American. $6-8 each.

Viewmaster slides from Santa's Village—set of three. $10-15.

Our Trees

The most popular trees of this decade were the balsam firs. While spruce was considered quite attractive, Americans were concerned about their rapid shedding of needles after a few days indoors. Starting in 1965, Yule trees began to be "net wrapped." The "vexar" plastic netting manufactured by Dupont was neutral in color. Mechanized funnels drew trees through the funnel, securing the trees with netting, at the speed of 100-200 trees an hour, allowing for easier shipping to different parts of the country. G. R. Kirk of Puyallup, Washington, and Wautoma, Wisconsin, distributed this netting.

In 1967, the Great Lakes Nursery Corporation of Waukesha, Wisconsin, nationally marketed its live trees. Its twenty-three-man sales force oversaw nurseries from coast to coast and decided that a national marketing campaign would help to increase their sales. The campaign included radio spots, newspaper ads, and even large magazine ads in consumer markets.

The aluminum tree continued to enjoy some popularity into the early to mid-1960s. Americans still found this technological, industrial-type artificial tree to be trendy. In fact, many manufacturers scrambled to produce blue, green, purple, and even bright pink aluminum trees which in turn rekindled interest in this 1950s fashion. However, live trees enjoyed increased popularity in a back-to-nature trend that promoted the use of long needled trees, flocked, decorated with a few monochromatic ornaments, and then floodlit by a clear or blue spotlight. Appearing in picture windows across this country, these natural trees were a sharp contrast to the aluminum tree craze. Scots pine, stone pine, white pine, and pinion pine were considered the best for flocking. In 1964 Scots pine accounted for twenty-seven percent of the total trees sold Thus balsam firs, once considered the only tree to have in one's home, fell out of favor.

While flocking kits were available for home use, the mess more than the process dictated that flocking be commercially done. The commercial operation was simple. Sodium silicate, a clear syrupy liquid diluted with water to spraying consistency (but not more than fifty percent) was used as the adhesive. Flock fibers and metallic glitter were the coating materials. Sodium silicate is odorless, free of fumes and completely fireproof. Two spray guns were required. The adhesive was sprayed from one pressure tank at about 40-lbs air pressure. Flock fibers were sprayed from a separate container at much less pressure—in fact, at only enough pressure to project the fibers onto the adhesive spray.

With the tree placed on a turn-table, the operator stood back about three feet to spray a wet coat of adhesive over the entire tree. This was done to wet the surface before any flock fibers were applied. Immediately following this, the operator sprayed adhesive with one hand, and at the same time sprayed the flock with the other hand. The flock gun was held so the stream of flock was directed into the silicate solution spray, at anywhere from a 45 to 90 degree angle. If further decoration was desired, small bits of cellophane or glitter were sprayed, following the final silicate coating. If glitter was used, it was usually white or clear to imitate glistening snow. After decorating, the trees were hung upside down from wires to air dry. Forced drying was not recommended unless very low heat was used.

Evergreen ropings were popular in the home and outside as well; however, they were difficult for florists and nurseries to create. Yet, in the 1960s, the House of Evergreens in Pontiac, Michigan, developed an Evergreen Roping Machine. It helped overcome the high price of labor and produced a higher quality roping than that of the old-fashioned hand method. The machine was designed to use single or mixed greens—cedar, pine, spruce, lycopodium, laurel, and holly—of any size or thickness. It produced thick, bushy, uniform roping at rates from 80 to 360 feet per hour with one operator.

Dow Chemical of Midland, Michigan, reported that over 1.5 million artificial trees were sold in 1960, accounting for the use of 750,000 pounds of vinyl reins. In 1960, a polyethylene tree at the cost of $21 was used by many elegant homeowners who tried to stay with decorating fads of the day.

In 1966, the Carey-McFall Company introduced its new Woods-Sprite flameproof Christmas tree nationally with two-color, half-page inserts in the November and December issues of *Good Housekeeping* magazine. A key feature of their advertisement was the tag attached to each plastic tree, illustrating that the product had earned the "Good Housekeeping" seal of approval and emphasized its 100% flameproof branches. Coming with its own base, the tree ranged in size from tabletop up to 10-feet. The trees were sold through variety, department, hardware, and flower stores. They retailed from $8.95 to $39.95.

The American Technical Machinery Corporation was a huge producer of artificial trees in this decade. Once chiefly a manufacturer of twisted wire brush machinery, it gained a great deal of the holiday tree and wreath line, generating almost forty percent of business volume. Formed in 1961, the American Tree & Wreath division's volume of Christmas business increased dramatically almost every year. Artificial trees were increasing in popularity because of more stringent fire regulations, their greater cleanliness, and improved designs which more closely matched those grown by Mother Nature outside. As a result of their increased business, American Technical Machinery Corporation expanded their national sales organizations, appointed new sales representatives for the Northeastern and Middle Atlantic states, and opened a new showroom and national sales office in New York City.

Their largest customers were J. C. Penney, Montgomery Ward, and J. J. Newberry. Thirty different trees were in their line including Scotch pine, blue spruce, and snow pine. Sizes ranged from two to eighteen-feet, and sold for as little as $4 and as high as $250-400 for the largest sizes.

More and more, artificial trees gained in popularity, accounting for a twenty-five percent increase from 1968 to 1969. Paul Frank, of the American Tree and Wreath Division of ATI, felt that the current growth would be sustained over the next five years. "In fact, even if we have a depression, people will buy trees," he stated. Most U.S. trees were made with polyvinyl chloride, some flame-retardant polypropylene was also employed, and a few Hong Kong imports were made from molded polyethylene. Part of their increased youth was due to the fact that the public building market—schools, hospitals, stores, etc. were prohibited from using live trees by fire safety laws in most major cities.

The synthetic tree makers started out with a rigid PVC—an estimated 30-million pounds in 1969—and then extruded this material into round needles or calendered as 6-9.5-mil. sheeting. The extruded needles were made by Polymers, Inc. of Middlebury, Vermont, the only U.S. producer, and by companies in Italy and Taiwan. In Polymers's patented process, the PVC is extruded from multiple-orifice dies. The plastic was then cut into needles, usually about 3.5-inches long, and bundled into packages for tree makers. Needles made in Italy and the U.S. were about 40-cents a pound; Taiwan needles, about 30-cents a pound. Alfred Drewes, vice-president of Polymers, noted that the Italian imports were the more serious competition, with Far Eastern imports inconsequential due to their inferior quality.

The tree makers, who fringed the plastic into needles, on the other hand, purchased the calendered PVC sheeting, in roll form. The needles—single or fringed—were inserted into twisted wire branches. The branches then were inserted into center poles, which were color coded for simple assembly.

Two production processes made the needles. The first needle type, the so-called round needle, which is really X-shaped when viewed in cross section, was extruded from multiple-orifice dies, chopped off in lengths of about 3-1/2", and packaged for shipment with all the needles facing the same way. The second needle type involved a different basic approach using calendered rigid PVC sheets, usually between 6 and 9.5 mils thick, produced by a conventional calender process. The tree makers bought the vinyl material in row form, fringed it to make "needles," and twisted the fringed material between two wires to make a branch.

ATI (American Technical Industries) used patented equipment that was originally developed for household brushes. The process for making trees was much the same as for making brushes. The branches are inserted in center poles, which have been color-coded or lettered for simple assembly. Of course, Americans complained about the lack of pine scent. Several tree makers offered aerosol pine sprays as a solution; but, needless to say, the "real scent" was the best.

American Technical Machinery Corporation, formerly a big producer of wire brush machinery, became a major producer of brush artificial trees in the 1960s. Sales in 1966 were $6.5 million dollars. Formed in 1961, the American Tree & Wreath division's volume increased its Christmas tree and wreath production each year in this decade. Americans held nineteen U.S. and thirteen foreign patent with another thirteen patents pending in 1967, principally on twisted brush and related machinery. The trees had limbs that looked like bottlebrushes.

ATMC's largest tree customers in this decade were Montgomery Ward, J. J. Newberry, and J. C. Penney. Thirty different trees were in their line, including Scotch Pine, Blue Spruce, and Snow Pine. Other types marketed at this time included mountain firs, Canadian firs, Princess Pine, Downswept Pine, and "White Elegance" (flocked). Sizes ranged from two to twelve feet.

As previously mentioned, one of the largest complaints of these trees was the absence of a natural scent. Therefore, pine-scented compounds were infused into the branches, but that did not work very well. As a result, manufacturers offered aerosol pine sprays to give some hint of a pine scent to the trees.

Even General Electric entered this market in 1966 with a six-foot tall artificial tree, complete with a musical rotating stand, handmade Bavarian ornaments, and four sets of "Merry Midget" lights. The package retailed for $150. GE's name for the new venture was "Carousel," a reference to the rotating bases equipped with Swiss music boxes that played "Silent Night" and "O Come All Ye Faithful." The base was marketed separately at a price of $39.95. The rotator stand was finished in a semi-gloss white with gold-colored snowflake pattern. A remote control box extended from the stand; the box contained three individual switches to permit operation of the lights, music, or rotation in any combination. An electrical lead from the top of the rotator extended into the Christmas tree, designed to hide the string set light plugs.

While aluminum Christmas trees appeared in the late 1950s, it was not until this decade that they achieved some status. Americans, somewhat tired of both the flocked tree and the live decorated tree, decided that the time was right to begin a radical new tradition. The fascination with the aluminum tree was born! Aluminum trees, complete with color wheel lights in a self-standing base, were a popular choice of many as early as 1962. Selling for $17.98, the stand was a perfect accompaniment for a 7 1/2-foot tree. In the 1960s, the trees were available in silver, gold, blue, and pink. Different styles were made, with some of the most unusual having silver branches with green or red pom-poms at the tips. Pom-pom ends appeared in 1962 as manufacturers experimented with creating fuller branches and tips that would reflect more light when lit by floodlights. In an attempt to capture new consumers, some trees were made with blue and green needles. These trees were popularly decorated with ornaments of the same shape and color. Consumer advocates continued to warn of the danger of using lights with metal foil trees because one small frayed spot on the wire of a light touching a branch could cause either part of the tree or the entire tree to be electrically live and a dangerous item in the home.

Reynolds Metals Company of Richmond, Virginia, was the largest producer of this man-made tree. Most other manufacturers of aluminum trees were in the Chicago area. They included Modern Coating, Tomar Industries, Metal Christmas Tree Manufacturing, and Superior Manufacturing. Other firms included Aluminum Specialty of Manitowoc, Wisconsin, and Star Band of Portsmouth, Pennsylvania. These manufacturers, and Reynolds Aluminum, promoted the trees through toy, gift, and novelty shows. Tree producers also advertised prominently in trade publications and bought inserts in wholesale toy and general mail-order catalogs. Reynolds began advertising these trees in 1959 on its network TV programs, "All-Star Golf" and "Adventures in Paradise." Their TV commercials were of two types. The first televised commercial promoted the trees; the second commercial advertised them together with other aluminum products. In 1959, almost one million trees were sold. In 1960, sales numbered around three million trees, with close to five million pounds of aluminum used in their production.

These trees came in a compact cardboard carton, and were available in sizes ranging from two feet to eight feet. Aluminum Specialty of Manitowoc, Wisconsin, made trees in pink, green and gold, as well as in natural silver. Set-up was easy. Two sections of trunk were first assembled and fitted into the stand provided. Individual branches were taken from paper sleeves, fitted in holes pre-drilled in the trunk, and the sleeves were then put aside for use later when disassembling the tree. Assembly went from the top down, with disassembly being just the opposite.

Aluminum trees continued to improve. The first tree trunks were painted; the first improvement was to spirally-wrap the trunk with "foil-kraft" so that the foil matched the rest of the tree. Also, most trees came with more rigid, straighter branches with more resilient needles. Branches were wrapped in paper sleeves to compress the needles, so that when the paper was removed, the needles sprang into position.

By the late 1960s, aluminum trees fell out of favor as Americans rushed to purchase realistic green artificial trees, many complete with pinecones. Even outdoor trees meant to be decorated at the holiday season and then left to be part of the permanent landscape were advertised and promoted. However, even though Americans were willing to have an artificial Christmas tree, they quickly resisted the idea of a "fake" year-around landscape.

There was some experimentation with metallic vinyl trees which could be safely strung with lights, but manufacturers recommended small or midget lights because the heat from larger lights could possibly wilt the needles. These trees were available in gold, blue, pink, and green.

Viscose trees (Visca) continued to be made of a rayon material treated to make it fire-retardant. Their main fault was that they easily crushed in handling and were sparse in appearance in an age that began to count "fullness" and "perfection of form" as requisites of a Christmas tree. These trees were manufactured in green, blue, pink, and white.

Artificial flocked trees had viscose, aluminum, vinyl, or heavier plastic needles coated with a white plastic or cotton material meant to resemble snow. Most of these were of the tabletop size.

"North Woods" real pine scent continued to be marketed in the 1960s in an attempt to help those who missed the fragrance of real pine. For about one dollar, Christmas enthusiasts could have plastic and some sense of the outdoors with this spray.

How We Decorated Our Homes and Trees

In December 1960, *Better Homes and Gardens* suggested "fantasy ornaments of your own making." Their decorators suggested gilding a Styrofoam ball, covering it with silk thread, and then adding pearls, colored plastic jewels, and gold lace decal. Suggestions included recycling old jewelry by placing it with pins into Styrofoam balls. *House and Garden* in that same year suggested that Americans concentrate on a theme each year—perhaps a traditional tree decked only with old-fashioned ornaments; or a special color scheme of one or two hues; or a national flavor carried out with decorations picked up on a trip abroad. This could provide a three-year cycle of novel trees. The first year, ornaments should be picked with the year's theme in mind. The next year, repeat some of the trimmings of the year before, add a supply of new ones to carry out the new theme, and top them off with another creation of your own. New contemporary additions might be snowflake lights, white Styrofoam balls, and notary seal chains. The following year ethnic decorations such as Swedish wreaths, Italian ricotta baskets, and toothpick stars were suggested.

Trim-a-Home departments across the country recorded this decade as a theme decade. Among themes of this decade were teddy bears; crystal ornaments; Old World/Victorian; Santa/whimsical; painted wood; gold, silver, and brass; plaid; and the traditional holiday colors, red, white, and green. While ornaments were hung on the trees, retailers found that people resisted taking them off the tree. Baskets under the trees led to great breakage. Therefore, special displays near the theme-decorated trees were employed and worked very well.

One of the more intriguing suggestions was a tree without a tree: a three by three piece of hardboard with perforation about an inch apart. About 85 ornaments were suggested. Concentric circles were drawn on the board. Then the solid color ornaments were threaded, allowing some length to hang in position and some additional to anchor to the paper clip on the top side of the board. Threads were poked through the holes from beneath. Instructions from *Sunset* magazine continued, "level the ornaments with the others in its circle, then wind enough thread on the clip to anchor it; tape it later when you've checked it for overall positioning. Start with the center with the ornament you've chosen to top the tree and suspend it 12-inches from the board. Space consequent circles as desired and hang ornaments accordingly." The final step included anchoring the tree to the ceiling or overhead beams with eight large-headed nails or screws. The effect was dazzling: a perfect tree with shining ornaments but no green tree—just eighty-five bright and reflective ornaments in a tree shape.

In the early 1960s, Holt-Howard continued to import thousands upon thousands of ceramic items for holiday decorating. Santa mugs and pitchers were among the most favorite, quickly followed by candleholders. All of the items bore a rectangular silver and gold foil label on the underside. Holt-Howard was purchased by the General Housewares Corporation in June 1968, and became part of the firm's Giftware Group, along with the Colonial Candle Company. The focus of the new owners changed, and declining sales resulted. Finally, in 1990, what remained of Holt-Howard was sold to Kay Dee Designs of Rhode Island, ending the Holt-Howard brand name.

In 1966, Kimberly-Clark Corporation of Wisconsin heavily promoted its Marvalon adhesive coverings as the makings for various Christmas ornaments, gifts wrappings, and decorations. Marvalon came in twelve colors and twenty assorted patterns. Kimberly-Clark promoted tracing designs on the back of Marvalon, cutting it out, and then sticking it onto paper and cardboard to create fanciful, homemade house decorations.

In 1966, Chicago's CPS Industries, a leading manufacturer of gift wrappings and ribbons, sold over 1.4 billion yards of ribbon, enough to tie up the moon 385,000 times. The average American family used 70-feet of Christmas paper and 53-yards of ribbon to wrap thirty-two gifts. Now, more than ever, Americans wrapped their Christmas presents lavishly, consuming vast amounts of Christmas finery.

Assortment of Holt-Howard coffee mugs from 1960s decade. This was their most popular item, selling thousands upon thousands of mugs. $3-6 each.

Variety of ceramic items from this decade, most of which are Holt-Howard creations. $3-5 each.

Holt-Howard sugar bowl. Santa's head lifts off and sugar was placed inside. Meant to be part of a creamer, sugar, pitcher, and mug set. $10-14.

Holt-Howard NOEL angel grouping, all of which were candle holders. Holt-Howard prided itself in producing ceramic decorations which would double as candle holders. $10-15 for set.

NAPCO salt and pepper shakers. Santa with greens and the other ringing a bell. $10-15 for set.

Holt-Howard Santa and sleigh with four reindeer. Such sets were popular decorations during this decade and Holt-Howard sought to bring a variety of different such sleighs and Santa planters and figures to the market each year. $30-40.

NAPCO salt and pepper shakers. Santa shakers holding holiday greeting signs. $10-15 for set.

Late 1940s into early 1950s Lefton Christmas china. Very translucent with marking on back. Plate and accompanying cup, $20-25.

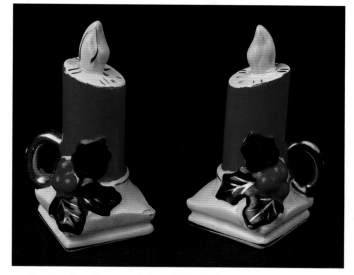

Candle salt and pepper shakers. NAPCO. $10-15 for set.

Late 1950s into 1960s Lefton China. Holly Berry pattern. Creamer and cover, $20-25; candy dish, $35-45; creamer, $15-20.

Late 1950s into 1960s Lefton China. Holly Berry pattern. Candle holders, $45-55 for set; leaf candy dish, $20-25.

American Influences on Glass Ornaments

Corning Glass commenced manufacturing glass ornaments under their own name during the 1960s. Of great demand, due to aluminum trees and flocked trees, were solid color spheres in many different sizes. Corning Glass and other American companies produced millions of these solid glass ornaments in bright blues, greens, golds, and even decorator colors such as pink, lavender, and mauve.

Max Eckardt & Sons tested its Shiny Brite line of ornaments via Sunday supplements in Columbus and Indianapolis. Larry Pesin, director of marketing for Eckardt and a former account man at Compton Advertising on Alberto-Culver, said that the company considered selling ornaments a "fashion business," an approach that nobody had ever taken. For the first time, national advertising was used to gain a larger portion of the Christmas tree ornament market. President of the Eckardt division was Elliott Goldwag, formerly director of merchandising for Helene Curtis Industries. Daniel & Charles of New York handled the Shiny Brite campaign.

Shiny-Brite boxed sets of miniature ornaments. American. 1950s. $3-5 for boxed set.

European Influences on Glass Ornaments

In the 1960s there was renewed interest in tradition and this was evidenced by the number of West German and other European glass ornaments being imported once again into the United States. *House and Garden* in 1960 reminded us of the fact that unwrapping the tree trimmings packed the year before is a special delight. "The sight of each forgotten treasure conjures up magical memories of Christmases past to enhance the glow of Christmas present. When all your lights and baubles are on the tree, you may find that the total effect is somewhat less magical." Americans were losing this joy because entire collections of ornaments, lights, and decorations were purchased in one year unlike the past generation which gradually built a collection by adding a few items to the tree each year. *Good Housekeeping* suggested each year a family should concentrate on a theme—perhaps a traditional tree to be decorated only with old-fashioned ornaments. Ornaments should be chosen to carry out this theme. The second year, a new theme should be chosen, ornaments to complete this theme should be home-crafted, and a few store-purchased items mixed with the ornaments of last year. If a few store items were added each year, soon memories would flood back each holiday season as the decorations are pulled from their boxes and placed on the tree.

Extensive magazine advertising was employed by numerous companies in an attempt to reach new markets. U.S. imports of glass ornaments for the first eight months of 1961 increased 127% in quality and 50% in value over the comparable 1960 period. Imports totaled 867,801 gross valued at $1,394,396 in the January to August 1961 period compared to 382,125 gross valued at $929,273 for the 1960 period. Glass ornament imports were divided into groups by value—less than $7.50 a gross and over $7.50 a gross. About 95% of the total value of imported glass ornaments were valued at less than $7.50 a gross. Japan supplied the majority imported in the 1961 period. The average price per gross declined from 83-cents per gross in 1960 to 67-cents per gross in 1961. West Germany was the second principal supplier. The average price per gross of ornaments imported from Germany in this category increased from $4.61 to $5.14 in 1961 and total imports were only two percent of those foreign goods imported for Christmas decorating. Japan definitely was able to supply extremely inexpensive ornaments which quickly caught the attention of thrifty American consumers.

Polish ornaments typical of the 1960s decade during which the colors were more bright and intense than previous decades. Hand-painted, heavily designed ornaments somewhat disappeared and were replaced by more simple geometric striped ornaments. $1-1.50 each.

Polish ornaments with a bit more detail, but note the absence of very fine detail. Most hand-painted, detailed ornaments were of a smaller size. $.50-1 each.

Italian ornaments from 1960s. Top to bottom. Left to right: Elf, $75-85; Clown with paper collar, $100-110; bird, $45-55; sitting clown, $65-75; clown head with ribbon bottom, $75-85; elf with red cap, $65-75.

More unusual Italian ornaments from 1960s. Top to bottom. Left to right: Party figure with hat off to left side, $110-120; one of the Beatles, $200-240; boy with cloth sack over his shoulder, $100-110; Oriental man, $135-145; comic strip figure, $145-155; man with derby and tie, $150-160.

Germany Continues to Provide Ornaments

Hand-decorated German ornaments appeared in this decade. A distinguishing characteristic of these are gold twisted, crinkly wire and pearls woven in the gold wire around glass indents, balls, and even clear colored ornaments inside which plastic and paper figures were placed. White cardboard bottoms finished these ornaments.

During this decade, it was common practice for communist government export agencies to permit domestically produced merchandise to be labeled with the European exporter's country of origin. In this manner, the Communist agencies increased their sales, and the exporter could avoid high duties levied by the United States against such Communist agencies. Therefore, many times items made in Poland and East Germany were marked with "Made in West Germany." If a West German factory had a part of their production work done in East Germany, they were also allowed to use the "Made in West Germany" stamping.

"Christborn" became a leading producer of glass ornaments in West Germany after World War II. In 1968, Horst Wegner joined his father's company, producing glass ornaments in Coburg, Germany. At this time, much of the production line of "Christborn," their ornament company, was in laboratory flasks and scientific glass supplies. However, when Horst met and married Waltraud, Waltraud's love of traditional ornaments influenced the return to the factory's roots. Thus they commenced the earnest manufacturing of glass figurals and spheres in traditional shapes reminiscent of those produced by Germany prior to World War II.

Since flocked trees were very popular, many old-fashioned European ornaments did not look so attractive on these trees. But some European-crafted ornaments did look attractive on these later flocked trees. Making their appearance in the 1960s were clear glass ornaments, most often frosted or clear, inside of which one could find a tiny animal, Santa, angel, or other human figure.

These and other West German ornaments were a direct result of the efforts of Max Eckardt. In order to help build up the postwar economy, the U. S. Government sent Max Eckardt, of Shiny Brite fame, and his son Harold to West Germany to revitalize the defunct ornament business with American dollars. Eckardt closed his plant in East Germany, removing it to Wallenfeils in the Western Zone. He renamed it "Lanissa" for his three granddaughters, Lynne, Anne, and Allison (L=Lynne, An=Anne, and issa=Ussa, Allison's name as a small child). When "Shiny Brite" was sold in America, Lanissa, the largest company, closed its doors. This left Oberfrankishe Glas, Heinz Matthai K. G., and Suddeutsche Benda of Barnsdorf, the three giants in the industry known to American collectors who seek out ornaments made in this decade.

It was still basically a cottage industry, however, often with just a family as the entire work force. The output in 1966 was $250,000. Our love of detail and low labor costs with high quality was what more and more American customers liked. "The U.S. has neither the mentality or the skill to do the kind of work that's involved in a hand-blown glass Christmas ball," said Kurt S. Adler in 1966. Adler, a native of Germany, bought two-thirds of his line on the continent. (As a rule, importers bought far more from the Orient than from Europe.) In 1966, he imported light sets, glass balls, and hand-painted crèches from Italy. From Germany and Czechoslovakia, he imported glass and tinsel decorations. He had an exclusive distribution arrangement with the Czechoslovakian government, with all sorts of impressive credentials to make it legal. Even so, the John Birch Society attempted to ruin his business when it agitated against bringing in Christmas wares from behind the Iron Curtain.

In the 1960s, there were many ornament companies in the Lauscha area. Most were state owned cooperatives. Families owned a scant few companies. The cooperatives included divisions dedicated to the production of Christmas ornaments, silvered glass (vases, etc.), glass processing (creation of the glass itself and glass rods), mechanics workshops, carton-producing division, and decorative fruit production. There were more than forty different villages involved in the manufacturing and warehousing of Christmas ornaments and other handicrafts. Unfortunately many of the warehouse employees possessed no technical skills and all the goods were handled by hand. Another problem was the fact that there was a sixty percent duty on all export items at this time, so these Christmas cooperatives suffered greatly. Added to this problem was the fact that the Leipzig (in East Germany) Christmas Show was the only place to display and promote their wares at this time.

Government control was another factor. In 1961, the government took over the training workshops for glass blowers and turned this control over to the VEB. In 1964, the government changed the profile of the business somewhat by adding a NEON division to the then only Christmas ornament business. Thus neon lights were produced employing many of the same techniques used in producing glass Christmas ornaments. The year 1968 marked the formation of an export office for glass Christmas ornaments known as eGmbH (eingetragene Gesellschafdt mit bechrankter Haftung). This state owned sales department joined the production and warehouse cooperatives to provide manpower and other basic promotional campaigns and strategies to improve the then poor exportation rate of glass ornaments to the United States. In 1969, glass started to be produced in Ernstthal just over the hill from Lauscha.

The development of the Christmas tree decorations made of glass brought growing possibilities for other parts of the economy, too. Little metal caps were needed to cover the place where the spear was cut off and a spring wire was inserted to hang the ornament up on the Christmas tree. For the same purpose clamps were needed for the birds, mushrooms, and other special articles. Craftsmen managed metal workshops where they designed and constructed such metal clamps and ornament caps. At the same time they made other Christmas articles, such as light holders, chimes, and other Christmas decorations fabricated from metal.

By the time the production of Christmas tree decorations made of glass started again after the Second World War, one of those small companies with eight employees was affiliated to the VEB Glaswerk *(glass works)* Lauscha. The history of the VEB Lauschaer Baumschmuck *(Lauscha Tree Decorations)* is quite involved, yet essential to understanding how the glass ornament industry survived in some very harsh times. On September 26, 1959, Lauschan glass blowers formed a production cooperative of Christmas decoration producing craftsmen and named it the "10th Anniversary of the GDR Foundation."

There were 55 master craftsmen and employees on the foundation day that decided to go a new way in the production of Christmas tree decorations. Today there are 120 members of the cooperative. These were the chairman's words to the "Freies Wort" newspaper in the first days of January 1960.

Still, in the end of 1959, as a first step of mechanization, a redesigned automatic machine for ampule production started its work for making the so-called "little pieces;" further machines followed in 1960. Extensive building measures at the company building took place at the beginning of the 1960s to install central production places and to keep to the health, industrial safety, and fire safety rules. A machine hall for automatic machines and rooms for processing were equipped. The sanitary rooms were renewed, a canteen with dining hall for the workers was equipped, and for the management, new centrally heated offices were available. The imported flask blowing machines for making balls up to a diameter of 4.5 cm (1.77 inches), that temporarily had worked in the building in 46 Kirchstraße *(Church Street)*, were taken there and in 1964/65 new machines for pulling "little pieces" (glass beaded ornaments for use in garlands) and automatic flask blowing machines were purchased and brought into production. For the processing of the machine-made raw products, a self-developed silver-plating and varnishing method was introduced and used.

After finishing the reconstruction works, more and more processing workers were concentrated and a strong department for making manual products, including "grape clusters," developed. The needed processing technology, like drawing and drying assembly lines, were built by the company itself.

At this time, the breakup of cardboard producing companies had a great effect on the glass manufacturing of ornaments, leading to a sharp shortage of cardboard containers to hold the ornaments VEB had been producing. The leading company instructed the firm to enlarge the boxing department that had existed since 1960 to meet the demand on wrapping material. The introduction of cellophane covers became of special importance because the export customers wished the goods to be seen by their customers. In addition a stamp and glue department was built up to make the needed window cartons in cooperation with print companies.

Employees of the cooperative devised a new process that allowed for the introduction of the silver saving "Ermax silverplating technology" in the company and in the central production places of the product group to reduce the consumption of materials. In agreement with the responsible state departments in 1963, the cooperative made a contract with the VEB Bergbau- und Hüttenkombinat *(Mining and plant combined collective)* in Freiberg to acquire so-called "silver kings" from the people. This way tons of "second hand" silver could be made available by the recovery of the precious metal from individuals. This practice stayed in effect until 1981.

In 1972 the cooperative was changed into VEB Lauschaer Baumschmuck *(Lauscha tree decorations)*. The existing production and store possibilities weren't enough to cope with all the tasks. The former sawmill, Steiner at 106 Straße des Friedens *(Peace Road)*, and the works were purchased to build a central material storehouse. These works went on after the company had been affiliated with the VEB Thüringer Glasschmuck *(Thuringian glass decorations)* by January 1st, 1976 and the building has been used this way since its completion.

Due to the growing demands of the tree decorations industry, the number of employees of the department increased to eighty persons. These new workers were involved mainly in home work. These home craftsmen worked on the completion of "hats" and clamps.

At the beginning of the sixties, the production of candlesticks was brought to Lauscha from Doberlug-Kirchheim for production centralization purposes. The available workers had to do the additional work of the planned economy. Soon there were first ideas to rationalize work and the realization of lots of innovators' suggestions became a base for an improvement of the productivity of work.

The design and construction of an automatic machine, after an innovator's suggestion that was able to produce completely wired caps, was a crucial step toward eliminating redundant labor. Home workers that weren't needed for producing caps after this machine had been put into operation, and additional machines of the same sort had been constructed, worked in the increased production of candlesticks and light holders or got a job in central production places of the Christmas decoration industry.

In the middle of the sixties, the developing mechanization in the leading department Baumschmuck *(tree decorations)*, especially the factory production of "blown from the tube" (mechanically blown in ovens) Olivotto balls, brought new challenges to the metal department. Within the shortest possible time, new caps were designed for bigger neck diameters. The production began as a half automatic process, with wire inserted by hand; however, the rapidly increasing demand for these new parts could only be met by a fully automated production. Therefore, new automatic machines were built or existing machines were changed over to meet the new dimensions and demands.

Through the specialization of the production, the metal department was eliminated from the VEB Glaswerk *(glass works)* and affiliated to the VEB Thueringer Glasschmuck *(Thuringian glass decorations)* Lauscha in 1970. For years the "Collective of socialist work" positively influenced the use of modern methods within the socialist competition. Therefore, the brigade "Valentina Tereshkova" (the name of Lenin's wife) was awarded with the medal, the "Banner der Arbeit Stufe III" (Banner of work level III).

In West Germany, ornament production was in full swing, especially in an effort to provide Christmas decorations for Germany and other West European countries. One company was instrumental in this early pioneering merchandising of Christmas decorations in Germany. The Käthe Wohlfahrt Company had its early beginnings in this decade.

Wilhelm Wohlfahrt, Harald's father, founded the Käthe Wohlfahrt Company in Böblingen in 1964. Wilhelm's and his wife Käthe's first venture was setting up shop at weekend bazaars on U.S. Army bases where they sold Erzgebirge items. The business was a family affair from the start, which involved Wilhelm and Käthe's children, Harald and Birgitt, and grandparents, Willi and Johanne. The business may have been small at the outset, but the history of its beginnings holds fascination for those who have become acquainted with Käthe Wohlfahrt.

Wilhelm Wohlfahrt, founder of the Käthe Wohlfahrt Company, was born in 1928 as the son of a farmer in the German Vogtland. The family farmed under the communist regime, which proved to be a disadvantageous and dissatisfying enterprise. Unwilling to tolerate the situation, Wilhelm fled from the former East Germany to Böblingen in southern West Germany in 1956 with his wife, his two children, and his parents. With the help of a friend, Wilhelm found a job at the IBM Company located in this area. While employed at IBM, Wilhelm and Käthe developed a friendship with the Lanier family from the U.S., stationed in Böblingen. In 1963 they celebrated Christmas together at the Wohlfahrt home. The new American friends were fascinated with a wooden Christmas music box, a small keepsake from the Erzgebirge, in the home of the Wohlfahrt's. Taking note of his friends' interest, Mr. Wohlfahrt was eager to give a belated Christmas present to the Laniers. However, because it was after Christmas, all Christmas items were either sold out or stored away for the next season. Wilhelm racked his brain to come up with some way to find a music box for his friends, and finally he approached a wholesaler.

To please his American friends, he was willing to take the financial risk of purchasing the minimum quantity of ten music boxes from the wholesaler. The Laniers were thrilled with the belated Christmas gift. Wilhelm Wohlfahrt took the suggestion of his friends to sell the nine remaining music boxes in a door-to-door effort at the American military housing complex. Their clever plan was thwarted, however, when the Military Police arrived, informing Wilhelm that door-to-door solicitations were illegal. Wilhelm charmed the police with his German stories and the finely crafted items he was peddling. Willing to help his cause, the police suggested that Wilhelm participate in the weekend shopping bazaars held by the officers' wives on the U.S. army base.

The love for retail business was like a seed now planted in Wilhelm's blood. He expanded his inventory to include several traditional Erzgebirge Christmas products: nutcrackers, pyramids, smokers, and music boxes that drew raves from visitors to the bazaars. He founded the Käthe Wohlfahrt Company in 1964, and started the year-round sale of Christmas items.

A few years later, the family moved to Herrenberg and opened a year-round show room and retail store. Harald's vision of a store where Christmas could be experienced through all the senses in every inch of space became the model for the Käthe Wohlfahrt "look." Mobile booths were created, decorated with this same Christmas ambience, and set up for business at the numerous weekend bazaars. The company name was then changed to Käthe Wohlfahrt's Christkindlmarkt.

Lauscha in 1964 illustrating the VEB Glaswerk *(glass works)* factory in the center of the town.

Woman decorator in East German factory applying lacquer to the ornament previously blown in a machine, not by hand. Hand blown items were still manufactured in the homes of individual glass blowers.

Two women in East German factory doing the hand painting and decorating of glass ornaments.

Woman decorator in East German factory applying tiny lines of decorative paint, to which glitter was many times attached.

A 1960s catalog page from East Germany illustrating typical shapes of the early 1960s.

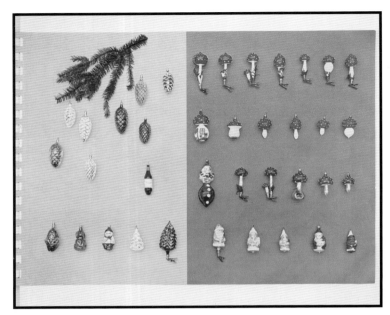

A 1960s catalog page illustrating mushrooms, Santa Claus, pine cones, and trees which are the most popular shapes of this decade.

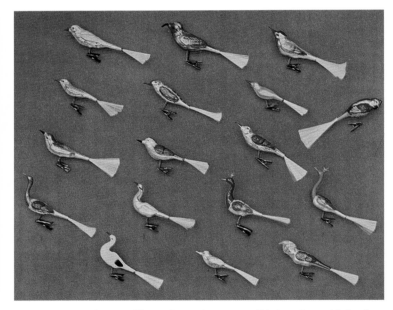

A 1960s catalog page illustrating various types of birds and song birds, all with spun glass tails.

Ornaments with heavily flocked and glittered trim. All from West Germany. Left to right, top to bottom: Bird on clip, $5-8; tiny mandolin, $4-6; swan on clip, $45-55; three sizes of icicles, $5-8 each; peacock on ball, $55-65; church, $7-9; berry, $3-4; apple, $7-9; pear, $7-10; pelican, $60-70.

Elaborate mid-1960s shapes including house, train, frog, fish, windmill, church, car, and lantern.

Representative samples of the white period of this decade where ornaments took on a soft appearance with white as its predominant color. All West Germany. Left to right and top to bottom. Clown, $35-45; ball with bird molding, $20-25; horn, $5-10; lamp, 15-20; mandolin, 15-20; clock, $18-22; icicle, $4-5; face in quarter moon, $65-75; heart, $5-7; star-shaped ornament, $3-4; pelican, $65-75; lantern, $3-5; bugle, $4-5; and church indent, $7-10.

Some typical West German ornaments illustrating early 1960s look with an abundant amount of silver evident as trim. Left to right, top to bottom: Santa, $10-15; silver fish, $10-15; cottage, $5-7; church, $7-9; fish with blue air-brush effect, $20-25; fish with pink air brush effect, $20-25; pine cones, $2-3 each.

Mid- to late 1960s West German wire-wrapped ornaments decorated with tiny glass beads. Usually sold in boxed sets. $5-7 each.

West Germany developed a clear glass ball to which a cardboard base was attached. Inside could be found silver and foil figures including angels, Santa Claus, snowmen, and even flowers. Mid- to late 1960s into early 1970s. $20-30 each.

Mid-1960s West German ornaments which accented faces through the use of flesh colored paint reminiscent of those before World War II. But this paint is shiny rather than flat. Left to right, top to bottom: Miniature frog, $35-45; fat clown, $40-50; Punch, $35-45; clown on ball, $75-85; clown with hands on stomach, $55-65; miniature full figured clown, $45-55; large red clown, $75-85; clown head, $55-65.

Austria Becomes a Viable Partner in Exporting Ornaments to the United States

Under the control of the banking house of Schoeller and Co., Wiener Christbaumschmuck continued to produce beautiful figurals for the American market. Especially beautiful were birds on spring clips always identified by "Austria" embossed on the pinecone clips. They were extremely active in the market during the 1960s, producing many glass ornaments for America.

In the early 1960s, the family left the business which had been reorganized by the former plant manager, Wolfgang Zipser, and relocated forty miles north of Vienna in the old Roman built town of Traismauer under the new name of "Advent undChristbaum Decor."

A Closer Look at Our Tree Decorations

Tree Toppers

West Germany continued to produce some of the most elegant treetops in the 1960s. Many of them were quite large and were copies of ornaments produced before World War II. Among the most elegant treetops was a 16-inch top totally wrapped with crinkly wire, decorated with spangles, four tiny glass wire-wrapped balls, and a plum of six-inch silver tinsel at the top. Other smaller varieties almost invariably had indented, painted circles and designs embedded in one of the blown bubbles characteristic of such a top.

American glass manufacturers also produced tree tops, but those made by Shiny Brite and other such companies were very simple, painted one or two colors, and contained no indents whatsoever.

Plastic also continued in popularity with stars, Santas, and angels in an infinite variety of sizes produced over these years, some of which lit up and others which merely perched at the top of the tree.

But most important is the fact that tree tops gradually declined in popularity as Americans turned to miniature lights. It seemed that the tops looked somewhat out of fashion and out of place in these modern times.

Tinsel West German tree top. Early 1960s. $4-6.

West German tree tops with paper labels identifying them as such. Mid-1960s. Smaller, $3-5; larger, $5-7.

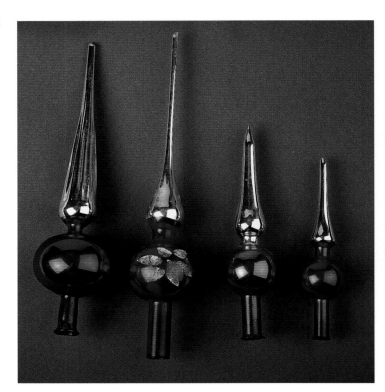

American-blown tree tops representative of glass toppers made during this decade. All were simple without any indents. $5-8 depending upon size.

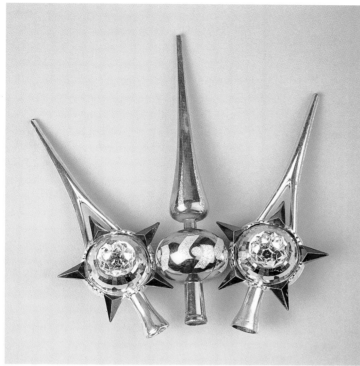

Plastic tree tops so popular during the aluminum tree craze and when people used such metallic coated plastic ornaments on their trees. American. $3-5 each.

Tinsel star top from Japan. $7-9 complete with box.

One of the last simple heavy foil perforated electrified tree tops employing a candelabra-based lamp. American. Early 1960s. $3-5.

Elf tree top which accompanied midget elf lights and other such felt cloth tree decorations. Early 1960s. Japan. $35-40 complete with box.

Halo tree top with plastic fibers. Japan. $5-7 complete with box.

Candy Containers

In this decade, Americans no longer purchased large numbers of candy containers which held miniscule amounts of confections. Rather, they sought box assortments of chocolates sold in boxes ranging from one to ten pounds. While malted milk balls, chocolate covered peanuts and raisins, chocolate marshmallows, and coconut haystacks continued in individual popularity, they were also sold in large paper-boxed assortments. Candy canes gained in popularity as the simple white and red colors seemed natural in a period of decorating simplicity and white trees. The most popular novelty containers of this decade included a Santa and Snowman duet which were glass containers with removable plastic heads. However, one container remained a constant: the Christmas stocking. Sold in sizes of 12-inch to 44-inch, these stockings included not only candy, but also popcorn balls, and assorted toys.

For those who were willing to part with more dollars, West Germany produced some very wonderful "Big Chubby Santa" papier-mâché containers that separated at the belly. Made by the Schaller family, these containers were covered with a plush-like red coating, had a bobbing head on a spring, and furry whiskers (made of rabbit's fir). About 13-1/2-inches in height, each container sold for $1.98. In the mid-1960s, Sears Roebuck sold some inexpensive two-tone plastic toy trucks (full of candy produce) and plastic Dachshunds (the clear-view body tube was filled with rainbow-colored Bubble Gum Balls).

Also intriguing were storybook puppets in shapes of Santa, reindeer, and snowmen with vinyl heads, all three of which contained two ounces of hard candy.

Cardboard rectangular shaped candy boxes with string handles continued to be sold to schools and churches for distribution at Christmas programs and school performances. They were usually sold in sets of 36 or 100.

Santa tree top which accompanied midget Santa lights and other such felt cloth tree decorations. Early 1960s. Japan. $35-40 complete with box

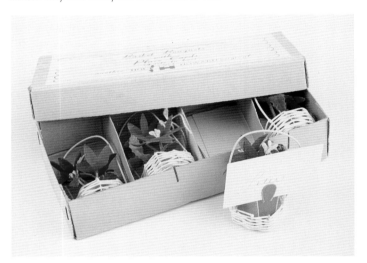

Late 1950s into early 1960s set of candy baskets meant to be used at the dinner table. Many of these later appeared as tree decorations on the branches filled with tiny bits of candy. Japan. $20-25 for complete set.

Plastic poinsettia tree top which accompanied midget poinsettia lights and other such plastic tree decorations. Early 1960s. Japan. $35-40 complete with box.

Early 1960s snowman, the bottom of which contained a cardboard disk which, when removed, reveals a cavity filled to the brim with hard candy and vanilla chocolate drops. $65-75.

The ever popular Santa boot made from egg carton-type papier-mâché and made by various manufacturers, most of which existed in the Midwest: Milwaukee and Chicago. 16" to 3". $5-55 depending on size.

West German candy containers made from mid-1950s into the 1960s before factories ceased the production of papier-mâché items. All of them opened at their stomachs to reveal a cavity in which candy once rested. Left to right: Santa with sack over shoulder, $95-105; Santa with rabbit fur beard and unusual round hat, $145-165; and Santa with rabbit fir beard carrying tiny green tree, $75-85.

Large 12" West German Santa with rabbit fur beard. Separates at middle. Made from mid-1950s into early 1960s. $120-130.

Heavily flocked thin cardboard snowmen marked "Made in West Germany." Made from early 1950s and marked with "Made in Germany U.S. Zone." These snowmen are from mid-1950s to early 1960s. $65-75 each.

Representative snowmen from West Germany. All range from mid-1950s into mid-1960s when such production of papier-mâché items ceased in favor of producing plastic containers. Left to right: Snowman with flocked cellophane branch, $55-65; snowman with hat and umbrella, $65-75; snowman with pipe, $50-60.

Late 1950s into 1963 type candy boxes with cloth handles so popular with churches and schools for filling at Christmas with peanuts, hard candy, and usually one piece of chocolate. $15-20 each.

Japanese manufactured candy containers. From mid-1950s into mid-1960s. Heads were removed and filled with tiny bits of candy. Heavy flocked and glittered cardboard. $5-8 each.

Felt Christmas stockings from the 1960s. American printed and manufactured. $25-30 each.

Tinsel Icicles and Foil Ornaments

Foil decorations enjoyed immense popularity because, not only were they unbreakable, they sparkled like the glass ones. In addition, while many felt they could not be so radical as to have an aluminum tree, "aluminum-appearing" decorations on a live tree were a means by which less adventurous Americans could mimic this "metallic" look. Cornucopias made of heavy aluminum held hard candy, candy canes, and small presents for children like those old-fashion paper models of years past. Fold-out trees, stars, bells, and snowflakes in multitudes of colors twirled from thread on almost every tree during this particular time period. Aluminum foil, readily available, was a popular choice of material for home-crafted decorations as well. Patterns for aluminum foil decorations appeared in almost every women's magazine of the decade.

Plastic icicles after the lead variety were banned for use in the United States. While these sparkled the same, they were light and often would sway and refuse to hang straight in drafts and when there was movement by tree. $2-3 for boxed set.

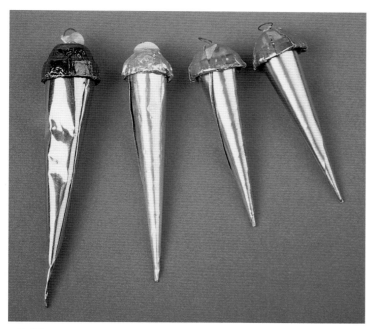

Foil ice cream cones made in U.S.A. and very popular as tree decorations in the early 1960s. $3-4 each.

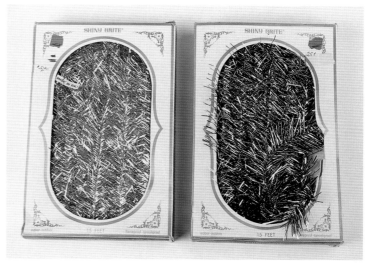

Silver and green tinsel roping from the 1960s. U.S.A. Roping was a bit thicker in diameter and was released in multitudes of different color combinations. $2-5 for boxed set.

Fold-out ornaments which came in shapes of trees, stars, circles, bells, butterflies, birds, and even Santa Claus. U.S.A. $.50-2 each.

Late 1960s tinsel roping. Blue and silver. $10-15 for a fifteen foot piece.

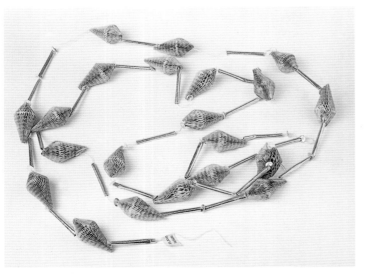

Japanese paper and gold cardboard tubing which form 10 ft. garland for tree. Late 1960s. $12-15.

Simple monochromatic glass beading from Japan. 5 ft. strands. $5-8 per garland.

Plastic and Styrofoam Decorations

While the look remained traditional, Americans turned to plastic. Dow Chemical Company reported that "Saran" icicles had a consumer market value of between twelve to thirteen million dollars in 1960. Styrene's use in Christmas decorations was estimated at four to five million pounds annually. Polyethylene use in plastic balls was just a bit less than one million pounds a year.

Plastics continued to play an important role in Christmas manufacturing. Five million dollars worth of vinyl resin was used for the needles of artificial trees in 1964. Also part of this 100-million market were Saran icicles, fine glass fiber, foam for cut-out decorations and tree stands, thermoplastic floral wreaths, and fruit arrangements. Additionally, Christmas light sets often times were used inside molded religious or holiday plastic figures for both inside and outside decorations. Gift wrappings—ribbons, dangles, foil-coated paper, etc.—were further uses for plastic materials.

Not all ornaments were commercially produced. One of the more interesting developments of this period were the ornaments made from Styrofoam balls and other decorative materials. In fact, many magazines referred to them as "Faberge" like. Detailed directions were given for wrapping the sphere with ribbons of three widths (1-inch and narrower). Wrapped carefully around the Styrofoam and secured with a "jewel"-headed pin for a finial and one long "jeweled" hatpin, these ornaments were extremely colorful and of special interest to those who desired to make their own rather than rely on commercially purchased decorations. Thousands of kits were sold by many craft houses, with some of the most elaborate sold by Lee Wards. Snowflake Pinbursts, jeweled spheres of crystal pearls you could make yourself, were sold in kits for $9.00. Each kit created five large 5-inch ornaments.

One interesting decoration type evolved in the late 1960s. Styrofoam forms were covered with a deep, heavy velvet flocking in rich dark colors, and trimmed with bits of velvet and gold braiding. These imported sets from Taiwan included locomotives, snowflakes, birds, cadets, and various musical instruments.

Rather than glass fruit for the tree, plastic multi-color fruit and vegetables were marketed. A 9-foot garland of pinecones, grapes, and apples was sold for $12.00 in 1962. Rayon thread-wrapped ornaments made their appearance in solid colors of gold, green, blue, and red. They were used as was or decorated with sequins, beads, pearls, bits of lace, and fancy foil. Sold in packages of twelve, they ranged in price from $1.17 to $2.15. Even rayon-covered fruit in strawberries, bananas, grapes, oranges, and lemons were made for table and tree decorations. However, the market leveled as Americans found plastic items just what they had in mind for Christmas decorating.

Styrofoam balls into which sequins, ribbons, and other decorative trim was pushed and applied to create ornaments. Began this new trend in late 1960s. $1-2 each.

Silver coated and painted plastic ornaments continued their popularity into the early 1960s. $1-2 each.

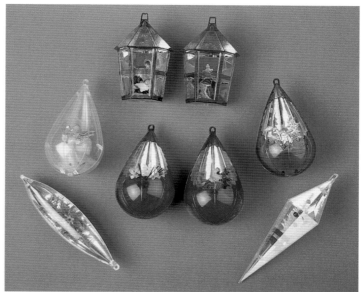

Early 1960s silver coated ornaments which reflected experimentation to market these types since they were declining in popularity. Angel hair and other hanging, movable inserts helped to sell them for a few more years. $1-2 each.

Assortment of such see-through ornaments including pear shaped ornaments, lanterns, and geometric shapes. $1-3 each.

Assortment of geometric shaped ornaments with an infinite variety of plastic inserts including angels, snowmen, Santa Claus, and even flowers. $1-2 each.

New trend of the decade was to take plastic ornament, mold it into two parts: one silver backed and the other clear. Then different decorative items were placed inside creating a little plastic window through which this scene could be viewed by those looking at the Christmas tree. Boxed set with elaborate bell interiors. $15-20 for boxed set.

Set of four lanterns with bells inside. $20-25 for complete boxed set.

Mid-1950s to mid-1960s plastic snowflake ornaments. They were sold in flat sheets for the decorator to separate. Then the two flat pieces were inserted into each other and a three-dimensional ornament was created. While clear was the most popular, other colors included green, blue, and red. $2-3 each.

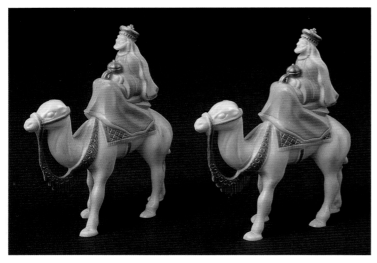

1960s plastic wise men made from 1950s mold but made from a soft plastic and merely airbrushed with pastel colors to reflect decorating trends. $3-5 each.

Japanese-manufactured plastic angels from early 1960s. $5-8 for boxed set.

Under Our Trees

Nativity Scenes

German nativity crèche scenes continued to be imported and sold, but not in any ample quantities. The German-produced sets were of good quality, but their prices were quite high in comparison to the Italian-produced sets. The Italians had captured the market in the late 1950s and continue to dominate by providing some very well painted and detailed figures. Most importantly, Kreske's, Woolworths, and other such variety stores often sold individual pieces at some very affordable prices, so even those on a low budget could start one year with the basic figures, and then add every year a few more. These figures came in a variety of sizes ranging from three-inches up to sixteen-inches. The detail and molding was of very high quality, especially considering the inexpensive prices. Sears Roebuck and Montgomery Wards marketed many Italian-produced sets through their mail order catalogs.

However, most intriguing were Santon figures being rediscovered in France by tourists and some high-end gift shops. Intrigued by the customs of the Santon in Provence, these soon were destined to interest collectors in the United States. Not widely known or available, these figures were to become increasing popular in decades to come.

Santons, or "little saints," are the French equivalent of the German Krippe. The setting is always a Provincial scene. The stable in a cave holds center stage, around which are set buildings, a farmhouse, sometimes an entire village, the mill (usually a reproduction of the mill at Fontvieille), the well, the bridge, and, of course, the river. The Santons of various sizes are dotted over the landscape to maintain the sense of perspective. These are simple folk, of all ages, taken from all ranks of society, some simply devoted but all going in the same direction carrying their offerings for the infant king.

Most characters are from rural society, with farmers and shepherds forming the majority. Craftsmen such as the odd-job man, the knife grinder, the basket maker, the huntsman, the beggar, the old lady laden with baskets, the fisherman with his red beret, the fishwife, the greengrocer or the flower seller, and the water carrier all are represented.

They are familiar characters. Each has his own personality, his qualities, and his faults; some are cowards, some jokers, and some are shy. Illustrious men and women are repaid by becoming Santons in period costumes. Blondel, an actor in nativity plays, was the first to be honored this way. He is the character of the play or of the village, wearing nineteen waistcoats one on top of the other, one of the actor's famous stage tricks. Frederic Mistral has also figured in cribs in the last forty years, usually as a hunter. The famous entomologist from Serignan, Henri Fabre, is also recognizable as a shepherd lying in the grass. Marquis de Baroncelli, the legendary guardian, may be present bearing his trident.

All are costumed in dress of Provincial and Marseilles society at the time of the Revolution. Only the holy characters, Mary, Joseph, the Three Kings, and their entourage wear long flowing robes and cloaks. The Mayor is the only person of authority allowed in the crib. He is usually represented in official dress with his red, white, and blue sash. Although he symbolizes authority, he is overcome by the event. The constable is always close at hand. The spinster is spinning a woolen thread that, unbeknownst to her, will become the Infant's eventual shroud. The washerwoman is usually represented as a strapping, capable woman. The knife grinder wears a leather hat and apron and travels from village to village to sharpen knives and scissors. The miller, white with flour, alert and good-natured, leads the dance while playing the whistle and is always happy. The blind man and his son are a desolate pair walking along the path of hope. The Gypsy, tanned face and eyes of fire, hides a dagger under his red-joined black cape and represents the traveling people. He gives dramatic contrast to the naïve honest characters of the crib. The hunter, teller of tall tales, carries his gun across his chest, his head turned in the opposite direction. This is one of anachronisms of the crib because firearms obviously had not been invented at the time Christ was born, but he has managed to creep into the crib. The "entranced one" is one of the first to be represented in the crib. Clothed in tatters, he lifts his arms to heaven in an act of enthrallment and joy. His childish posture, beyond the normal bounds of behavior, reminds us of the deeper mysteries of life. Pistachie is the Village idiot, a mysterious man held almost sacred in Provence because he is thought by the peasants to be a sort of visionary, and a medium between heaven and earth. Receiving respect and hospitality from all, he is innocence personified. Angel Boufareu, the Infant Jesus' troubadour, knows that a momentous destiny awaits his babe and sings for the message to the hills. People in Provence often say of bonny children that they look like the Angel Boufareu.

Two sorts of clay (gray or red) that occur abundantly at Aubagne, Aix, and Marseilles are used to create Santons. Formerly, this clay was bought in its raw state and needed to undergo several processes to make it workable. It was then kept cool by damp cloths or stored in huge earthenware vessels. By the 1960s, Santon makers bought their clay already processed and ready to use. First, the artist makes a rough outline from a ball of clay, which he copies from a larger outline in wood. This clay figure is expertly finished with intricate detail and then left to cure. Second, he makes a plaster mold of this clay figure. The clay is coated in oil or soapy water and pressed all around the object up to the half-way mark. Next a wooden, metal, or glass frame is set around the object and liquid plaster is poured in to the half way level. Notch marks are made around the imprint of the Santon and the other half of the mold is made in the same way. The first mold is never used, but dated, signed, and carefully stored as an original example. Other molds are used for producing the figure. The next operation is to take a ball of clay slightly larger than the volume of the figure and press it into each half of the mold with the thumb and forefinger so as to completely fill the shape. The two parts are then pressed tightly together and held for several minutes, until fused. The Santon can then be taken out of the mold, still damp. It is trimmed and sometimes carefully washed with a paintbrush to remove any irregularities. Then it is dried in the air before being fired in a furnace at 900 degrees centigrade. Up until 1945, most Santons were made of coarse clay left to dry in the open air. Later, the clay was fired to make it stronger.

The Santon maker then chooses and prepares the paints. The Santons are painted in series. All the faces, then the hair, then the clothes, starting from the top and going down to the traditional green base. Some Santon makers fire the figures in one piece before dressing them, others mold the body, head and limbs separately and wire them together. Costumes are then very painstakingly cut out, sown together, and fitted to each Santon with taste and delicacy. Then accessories are added—hats, weighing scales, baskets, etc.

In 1960, Hartland Plastics, Inc. of Hartland, Wisconsin, produced a seventeen piece Christmas set, made of unbreakable acetate plastics. This company specialized in hard plastic items, and these nativity sets were a good seller at Christmas. While they were simply painted, they were unbreakable and families didn't have to worry about their children destroying family heirlooms. While many older American families continued to purchase European-manufactured nativity sets, younger families quickly turned to these new plastic sets, thinking that these sets were indestructible and would last forever. However, their appeal largely disappeared toward the end of the decade.

Under the tree, many children found board games. The best-sellers appearing under the tree included Candyland, Clue, Go to the Head of the Class, Jeopardy, Operation!, and Yahtzee. Popular toys included Barbies, Creepy Crawlers, Chrissy Dolls, Hot Wheels, GI Joes, Easy-Bake Ovens, and Rock'em Sock'em Robots.

Santons used under the tree as part of the Christmas crèche scene underneath the tree.

Busy market scene illustrating peddlers, women buying their food and fancy goods, and other townspeople as part of a Santon village in southern France.

Chez Boulangerie (At the Bakery). One characteristic of such scenes is that most often this under the tree or Christmas scene contains buildings and people from the town in which this scene is created.

Left:
Santons of the type so popular with Americans. Most often purchased on trips to Europe or brought to the United States by French immigrants. 1950s vintage.

French Santon close-up illustrating the intricate detail in buildings and accessories so common of this Christmas tradition.

Boule, a popular French lawn game, is enjoyed by those in southern France and this traditional game is illustrated through this Christmas scene.

Fences

Plastic fencing sets replaced the wooden varieties. Most were simple and inexpensive, for this decade found Americans abandoning elaborate village scenes under the tree in favor of just a few houses and brush trees placed upon cotton batting sheeting.

Village Houses

In the earlier years of this decade, many detailed and elaborately painted village sets were imported from Japan. Details included scalloped roof edges, balconies, sponge trees placed in front of the houses, and detailed cellophane windows. By the middle of the decade, Japan began producing a more inexpensive line which appealed more to thrift-conscious Americans. By the late 1960s, they were fashioned from a thin cardboard and the decorative details were very sparse. These late houses were merely painted in basic colors and were given white roofs. Tiny, simple sponge trees were placed off to the side of the houses. These sets were arranged on tree skirts made of white or colored cotton batting, usually 32 to 36-inches in diameter, with a side opening and a hole in the middle for the tree trunk.

American houses manufactured by the Dolly Toy Co. of Tipp City, Ohio. $7-10 each in original box.

American thin cardboard stock village house for under tree and on mantles. $3-4 each

Larger style and more elaborately detailed village house. American. $4-6 each.

Original set of American-manufactured houses complete with electric cords and miniature-based lights for use underneath the tree. Mid-1950s to early 1960s. $35-45 for boxed set.

Two types of artificial snow used at Christmas. Styrofoam chips on left, $2-3 for package. Mica on the right, $4-5 for package.

Early 1960s stencils and aerosol can of artificial snow. $10-12 for stencil set. $4-6 for can of snow.

Brush Trees

While brush trees continued to be made in Japan, most were manufactured in the United States by the same companies producing the artificial trees. In this period of the white-tree, the snow-flocked trees gained somewhat in popularity. But their quality continued to decline as manufacturers sought to increase the profit margin on such items. The trees were more sparse, snow more "sloppily attached," and the bases were very light. Thus, it was difficult to keep the trees upright on cotton-sheeting placed under the tree.

Angel hair for use under the tree on cotton batting sheets, on trees (for that popular white look), and for other house decorations. $3-5 for boxed spun glass.

Brush trees, but of a heavier rayon fiber type, typical of those manufactured during this period. Note the flat red cylinder bases. $7-9 each.

Assorted light-up trees for use underneath tree or on mantles. All of which held a battery in the base which lit the tiny flashlight-sized bulb underneath the tree. Different colored glass ornaments and miniature candles then glowed as the tree was lit. $15-25 each.

Plastic tree assembled from pieces all placed in box with directions. Tiny Japanese-blown bulbs appear at the tips of each branch. American-manufactured. $20-25 complete with box.

Animals and Figures

In 1967, Barclay produced thirteen hand-cast, hand-painted little lead figures with a foil pond and cotton batting for placement in village scenes under the tree. This set was marketed by Sears Roebuck and Kresge's. Selling for $2.64 a set, each figure was about three-inches high and hand painted for realism. There were skiers, people on sleds, Santa sitting on a sled, skaters, and even Santa on ice skates. However, most figures made for these village scenes were manufactured in Japan and the Japanese still dominated this part of the Christmas market. Celluloid animals, both exotic and domestic, continued to be marketed by the Japanese at very affordable prices. Also available were countless varieties of domestic farm animals made by American plastic manufacturers.

Soft plastic deer employed in scenes underneath tree. Japanese-manufactured. Late 1960s. $1-2 each.

Soft plastic deer from the late 1960s. Japanese-manufactured. $2-3 each.

Felt and cardboard Santa figures from Japan. Note use of plastic for faces, typical of mid- to late 1960s. $10-15 each.

Large 12" Santa cardboard and felt pictures. Unusual in that the set creates a musical trio. $45-55 for set.

Santa doll from Japan used underneath trees, but most often as centerpiece table decoration. $15-20 with original box.

Celluloid Santa and sleigh which continued to be produced and sold through the early to mid-1960s. Japan. $15-20.

Large 12" to 18" Santa dolls, all with cotton beards and plastic boots. $15-25 each.

Large 9" plaster Santa. Where he clasps his hands, an indentation is found into which a candle was inserted. American. $10-15.

Plastic wind-up toy from Japan. When wound, the Santa jiggles his head and his top moves from Left to right: $55-65 with original box.

Wax candles used as decorative pieces under tree or on mantles. Mid-1960s. $6-10 each.

Plastic wind-up toy from Japan. When wound, the Santa vibrates and rings his bell. $65-75.

Assorted novelty candles from Gurley Company. Mid-1960s. $4-5 each.

Santa candles from mid- to late 1960s. $6-8 each.

Indoor Electric Lighting of Our Trees and Homes

In 1960, over 374 million tree lights were sold, accounting for over $15 million dollars expended. In 1961, Americans rushed out to buy over 250 million "twinkly" bulbs in the six days prior to Christmas Eve. That amounted to about half of their yearly purchases of tree lamps; they had purchased the other 250 millions worth in the previous three to four weeks preceding Christmas. Two-thirds of those lamps came from Japan. In 1954, domestic producers, primarily GE and Westinghouse Electric Corporation, shared virtually the whole 320 million Christmas lamp market. In 1961, GE shut down one of its Christmas lamp plants in East Boston. The Japanese exported 200 million bulbs under their own quota system, and another 150 million midget lamps, along with other assorted odd sizes. Italy held only a minute portion of the market.

Americans quickly turned to foreign lights in this decade as the lights of traditional sizes and shapes from Japan were far less expensive than those sold under the General Electric or Westinghouse trademarks. However, a study conducted by *Consumer Reports* in 1963 found that imported bulbs showed a higher rate of failure in the first few hours of use than did the domestics, but those that survived lasted as long as the latter. The researchers felt that the early failures probably resulted from mishandling in shipment rather than from poor design or construction. In the early 1960s, the new GE indoor and outdoor sets were wired in parallel, allowing for independently burning bulbs. Outdoor strings took intermediate-base bulbs (designated C9 1/2), indoor sets took candelabra-base bulbs (C7 1/2 or C7 1/4), and the old series-type indoor sets took miniature-base bulbs (C6).

Americans were again warned never to put lights on trees made of metal foil. There was a great fear that a loose, exposed wire could shock and harm a Christmas celebrant—a merrymaker who would receive an unwanted surprise during the Christmas season. Also, a great fear of fire existed when metal foil met tree lights.

NOMA continued its dominance in the electric Christmas tree lighting in this decade. They advertised their expertise by stating that they were the first with the safety fuse plug, the first with an add-on plug for attaching outfits, and the first with adjustable berry bead fasteners for securing lamps to branches. They were also the first with intermediate base outfits for outdoor lighting, the first with pin-type sockets, and the first to introduce flame-resistant plastic novelty Christmas sets.

Midget lights from Italy were the novelty of this decade, as Americans were faced with deciding whether they would go with the traditional larger lights or use the new "miniature" midget lights. Some of the early midget lights had permanent lamps which could not be replaced. Most of these early lights were not used on the tree itself. They were incorporated into centerpieces and other small arrangements and appeared inside plastic angels, Santas, birds, or in the center of plastic stars or flowers, and were used in strings around mantles, windows, and even between living areas such as the living room and the dining room. One of the first midget sets marketed by NOMA was the Poinsettia, with replaceable red lamps. With red plastic flowers and green foliage and wire, they were the perfect choice for a tree or table decoration.

These sets were wired in series because of their low voltage, but often were designed to have each bulb burn independently. Each bulb is so wired that when the filament burns out, electricity is shunted through the bulb base, and its flow to the rest of the string is not interrupted. (However, if a bulb loosens and loses contact with its socket, all the other bulbs will go out.) *Consumer Reports*, in an article in November 1963, suggested that people choose midget light sets with shunt-type bases or bulbs which screwed-in, as these bulbs were less likely to give trouble because of poor contacts.

Icicle Lights, of clear plastic, cupped in a frost-white covering, were lit by clear miniature bulbs inside to give a snow-palace gleam to trees. Sold in strings of ten lights, with each light being 4 1/2-inches in length, this set came in a 13-foot string and marketed for $6.00. The majority of screw-in bulb midget light sets were manufactured in Japan. In the 1960s, all midget bulbs and light strings were imported. Noma Lite, Inc., the most important U.S. supplier of Christmas light sets, featured foreign sets in its entire line. Noma also made its own strings, only in the traditional size, employing GE, Westinghouse, or Japanese bulbs. One set sold in 1961, "Holiday Lites" on a 10-yard string, contained twenty-five 1-inch pin-point lights with metal clip fasteners, and were marketed in crystal or assorted colors (amber, red, green, blue, cerise) for about $11.

A wonderful Jewel Light string was a garland of midget lights encased in a plastic cube which glowed in six precious-stone colors. The ten-light set marketed for $10.00 in 1963. Guilden Development Company pioneered the "Merry Glow tree ornament" in 1968. A graceful, colored plastic star burst shape fit over an ordinary tree light bulb. Bubble lights all but disappeared at the end of this decade. Raylite was one of the very few manufacturers who displayed bubble lights at the Toy Fair display in New York City in 1968.

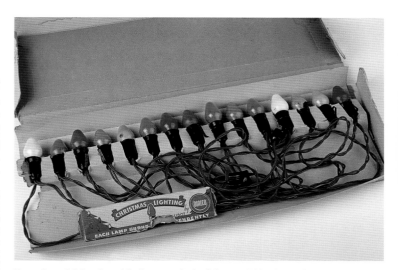

Box of candelabra-based bulb set typical of those sold in the early 1960s along side the midget lights from Italy. Their popularity waned as Italian lights caught the fancy of tree decorators. Pearlized colored bulbs were popular choices and helped to market these lights. $15-20 for boxed set. Replacement lights, $2-3 for box.

Original box of foil reflectors used behind lights. Their popularity waned somewhat in this decade, but continued to be used by traditionalists who remembered their popularity in the 1940s and early 1950s. $3-5 for boxed set.

Variety of foil reflectors for use behind bulbs in some of the larger sizes available in this decade. They were destined to disappear as midget lights appeared on the market. $.50-1 each.

Replacement Royal-lite bubble light, $15-18 each. Bell replacement lights, $12-15 for set of two in box. Flame shaped replacement bulbs, $5-7 for set in box.

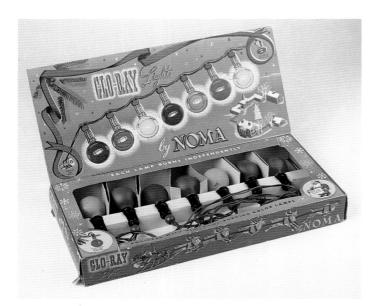

Glo-Ray lights produced into the 1960s with round candelabra-base bulbs. Were marketed by NOMA for use at different times of the year, especially for birthday parties. $20-25 for boxed set.

Candelabra-base bubble replacement lights from NOMA. $3-5 each.

Original boxed set of replacement lights for GE "Lighted Ice" candelabra-base bulbs. Glass was dipped in paint, the covered with plastic bits, which gave a wonderful effect when lit. Styrofoam-covered bulbs were also similar items sold. $2-3 for individual lights.

Italian Midget lights in plastic poinsettia shapes. Bulbs pushed into the sockets in this decade. $35-45 for boxed set.

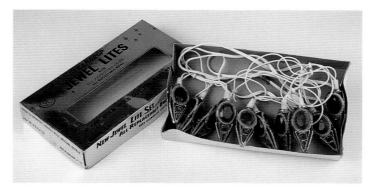

Midget lights in teardrop geometric shapes. $25-35 for boxed set.

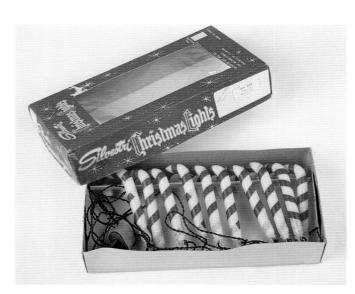

Set of Italian midget lights in candy cane shapes. $65-75.

Italian midget lights with foil lanterns into which the bulbs were inserted. $30-40 for boxed set.

Set of oil lantern Italian midget lights with silverized colored covers. $85-95.

Set of oil lamp Italian midget lights with plastic, flower-decorated shades. $100-110.

Italian midget lights in bell shapes. Light plastic snow-flocked bell into which colored midget lamps were inserted. $30-40 for boxed set.

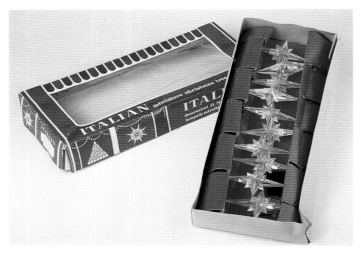

Plastic clear star Italian midget lights. $40-50 for boxed set.

Unusual Italian lights in large cluster of yellow beads (to simulate pine cones) $35-45 for string and lights.

Soft plastic elves into which tiny midget lights were inserted. Italian. $40-50 for boxed set.

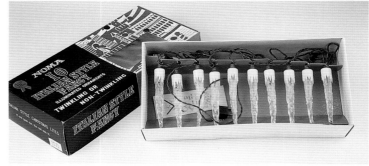

NOMA Italian-style lights. Made in Japan. Icicle-drop plastic shapes. $25-35 for boxed set.

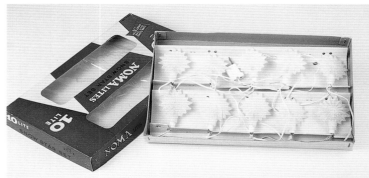

Japanese midget lights in snowflake design. $15-25 for boxed set.

Italian midget lights reminiscent of the plastic star lights made in Japan in the miniature-base bulb size. Believed to be Italian. $20-30 for string and lights.

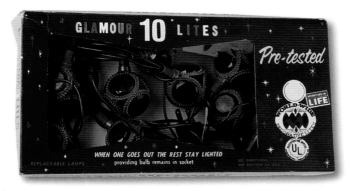

Geometric Japanese midget lights. Late 1960s. $30-40 for boxed set.

Clip-on candle shaped midget light set. Japan. $20-25 for lights and string.

Outdoor Electric Lighting

Outdoor lighting set our shopping districts ablaze at Christmas time. Most of the bulbs used were large lamps produced in the United States for such use. The market for outdoor lighting was growing about five percent a year, according to Joseph H. Ward, president of Noma Lites, Inc. U.S. producers also held the market for single-lamp floodlights, so popular with aluminum trees. The ever-popular four-color wheel floodlights used indoors began to be manufactured in sturdier models for outdoor use. Aluminum trees accounted for some fourteen percent of artificial trees used in homes in 1961. Even outdoor lighting domestic production was in jeopardy as ten to fifteen percent of midget lamps ,which went outdoors for decorating, were foreign-produced. Silvestri Art Mfg. Company imported about seventeen million Italian lamps in 1961. They believed imported lights would eventually replace American-made ones due to tooling and wage costs, which were far too high in America to compete with Italy and Japan.

"Outdoor Glimmer Lights" marketed in 1961 sold for $14 and had twenty-five 2-inch flame-shaped bulbs which blinked in either crystal or multi-color sets.

At the American Toy Fair in New York City in 1968, outdoor decorations were promoted quite heavily. Poloron, for example, introduced new models in plastic candles, and other designs meant to brighten up yards and porches. Other molded plastic, illuminated decorations (including Santa Claus complete with reindeer, choir boys, and the ever-popular wreath) were promoted by Raylite Electric Corp., Leco Electric Co., and the L. A. Goodman Manufacturing Co. The Cortland Furniture Company displayed a large, corrugated cardboard Santa Claus—with a bright red, illuminated

nose. The Coney Island Plastic Company exhibited an illuminated plastic Santa measuring 63-inches in height and towering over most other Santa Claus decorations.

The Guilden Development Company displayed a colored plastic starburst shape that fit over an ordinary tree light bulb. This "Merry Glow Tree Ornament" was recommended for windows displays, since it could provide an effect of motion and light at a much lower cost than a motorized display. "Merry Midget" lights were heralded as the only midgets to be approved for outdoor use by the Underwriters' Laboratories, according to G.E., who also promoted a musical, revolving tree stand at the fair.

One sad note of this fair was the notable absence of bubble lights, save for Raylite, one of the very few manufacturers still offering bubble lights for sale.

Boxed set of three plastic bells, inside of which was a twinkling bulb. These bells were extremely popular and appeared on doors, in windows, and even on walls during this decade. $15-20 for complete boxed set.

Left:
Outdoor lights in intermediate size. Note the flame bulb and the use of paint inside so that the elements would not destroy the beautiful glowing colors. $5-10 for boxed set (in good condition).

Right:
Plastic Santa for use outdoors and indoors. Unmarked. Candelabra-base bulb fit into back shoulder area to light up figure. $15-20 each.

Plastic Santa with candy cane in 14" size. Dapol Industries. Candelabra-base bulb is inserted in back. $8-12.

Plastic snowman with wreath and cane. Empire Plastics Corporation. 1968. Candelabra-base bulb is inserted in back. $7-10.

Paramount manufactured Santa made from mid-1950s into early 1960s. Candelabra-base bulb fit into Santa's back. $25-35.

Large cone-shaped Santa, in back of which a candelabra-base bulb was inserted. $15-20.

Santa on reindeer. Hard plastic. Made from mid-1950s into mid-1960s. Candelabra-base bulb is inserted into back of reindeer's back $50-65 each.

Snowman into the back pack of which a candelabra-base bulb was inserted. $15-25.

Santa figures with hands in air. Candelabra-base bulb is inserted in the back of the toy pack of Santa Claus. $20-25 each.

Santa with Royal bubble light. Candelabra-base bulb. This unique Santa was available from 1958 to the mid-1960s. $45-55.

Plastic half-Santa with metal back into which the candelabra-base bulb was placed. Popular style through the early to mid-1960s. $20-25.

Late 1950s into 1960s spinners which were placed over electric lights. Heat of lights caused little foil fan to revolve and motion was then part of the tree. All U.S.A, $10-12 each except for domed shaped one with angel from West Germany, $20-25 each.

The 1970s—The Return to the Home-Crafting of Decorations

Historical Perspective of This Decade—We Delve into the Past

When President Richard Nixon threw the switch to illuminate the National Christmas Tree in December 1970, he turned on a dramatic floodlighting system around the Federal Triangle. Christmas 1972 was a success in that Americans were financially quite well-off and, as a result, spent considerably more purchasing both decorations and gifts for Christmas giving.

The 1970s witnessed a revival of home-crafted decorations as Americans sought to recapture the memories of times past, in which the family prepared together for their favorite time of the year. In an effort to heal family structures somewhat shattered by the turmoil of the late 1960s, Americans drew from the past and decided that family values were indeed important. They found Christmas to be one particular event for which they could prepare together as a family. Popular magazines such as *Better Homes and Gardens*, *Ladies' Home Journal*, and many other such home decorating magazines of the decade encouraged this with renewed publicity and directions for recreating ornaments like those made almost a century before. Thus this was a decade of either hand-crafted items or commercial ornaments which appeared hand-crafted; glass ornament sales slipped into the ground as the "Country" look in trees took root in the United States.

While American-made items were the mainstay of the 1970s tree decorations, our lighting of trees changed somewhat drastically in a most unexpected fashion. Foreign influences affected our decorating customs, though it was not the most positive of influences in the eyes of many. Though Christmas lighting was dim, the spirit was there in the 1970s during the energy shortage, which caused all Americans to think a bit about energy conservation. Reduced Christmas lighting occurred in many states. In Oregon, for example, Governor Tom McCall ordered a blackout of outdoor advertising lights because of a prolonged hydroelectric shortage in the Northwest in 1973. In New York, Christmas lights at Rockefeller Center and along the "Great White Way" continued to shine because, as Consolidated Edison told businessmen, cutting Christmas lighting in all of Rockefeller Center was equivalent only to shutting down four elevators. Bethlehem, Pennsylvania, cut back on its Christmas lighting by eighty percent and Patchogue, New York, eliminated all special holiday street lighting. Many other cities chose to stay lit. However, it became almost unpatriotic to light the outdoors in a large fashion. So, in an attempt to show their loyalty in those energy-conscious times, countless Americans chose to keep lights in storage.

In 1972 the Christmas lighting industry saw retail volume rise to $750 million and take a $200 million nose-dive in 1973. Although the Federal Energy Administration did not ban holiday lighting in 1974, the calls for conservation coupled with soaring costs on electricity and lights them-

selves took their toll. "You can't have the President telling people not to open the refrigerator more than three times a day, and then have lights blazing over all the streets," said Michael B. Grosso, executive director of New York's Fifth Avenue Association, which canceled its annual Christmas lighting display in 1974.

In 1974, several years' supply of lights were in inventory at retailers, manufacturers, and importers—one result of the ban having hit late in 1974. The Christmas Decorations Association tried in vain to put over its argument that midget tree bulbs used less electricity than ordinary light bulbs, and since many people turned off house lights to enhance the tree, a saving could actually result. As the years passed by, Americans turned slowly back to lighting their outdoor trees and homes once again, as well as their trees inside their homes. But it was a slow return to electric lighting, for countless Americans were deeply sobered by the energy crisis and just how it could affect their lives if it were to occur once again.

Prior to 1973, cut trees were donated for the Pageant of Peace in Washington, D.C. In that year, the National Arborist donated a 42-foot blue spruce from northern Pennsylvania so that it could serve as a permanent National Christmas Tree. Unfortunately, that tree began dying in 1976, and the following year, a new replacement tree was blown over during a windstorm. In 1978, a 40-foot tree was donated by an anonymous family in Maryland, and was transplanted to the Ellipse.

In 1975, The National Ornament and Electric Lights Christmas Association was founded to help promote and help businesses involved in Christmas retailing. Later the group was renamed: NOEL: The Christmas Decoration Association to better reflect an emphasis on the selling of all Christmas, not only lighting and ornaments.

In 1976, President Jimmy Carter exhorted the multitudes to go forth and shop, and that Americans did, increasing their Christmas purchases by almost five percent over the previous year. In 1976, Robert L. May, the creator Rudolph the Red-Nosed Reindeer, died. But before May died, he donated his original sketches and manuscript to Dartmouth College from which he had graduated. After his death, his children donated all the Rudolph memorabilia in their possession to Dartmouth. Each year, they display this collection to the public at Christmas.

In 1979, our National Christmas Tree was dark, except for one star at the top, because the hostages in Iran had yet to receive the gift of freedom from "the unwise men in the East."

Bernard and Jeanette Brenner on Christmas Day, 1977, in Mt. Calvary, Wisconsin, looking with pleasure as their daughter Marilyn and their children open their Christmas presents. $Priceless.

Left:
Al and Carmen Thiel on Christmas Day, 1971, in Sherwood, Wisconsin. $Priceless.

Right:
Marion Thiel on Christmas Day, 1971, in Sherwood, Wisconsin. Note proliferation of American-blown ornaments combined with lead tinsel and tinsel garlands. $Priceless.

Marion Thiel and Dan VanBerkel in 1976 standing by a heavily sheared pine tree so typical of this decade. Note use of thick gold garland and solid color ornaments. $Priceless.

Christmas, 1972. Lots of red satin ornaments hang on this tree with the old fashioned lead tinsel of an earlier decade. $3-5.

Christmas, 1973. One year later at the same house. Many of the same ornaments, but note the addition of some bright Polish blown ornaments. $3-5.

Christmas, 1972. Little girl modeling her new red coat brought by Santa Claus. $4-5.

David Brenner on Christmas Day, 1971, in Mt. Calvary, Wisconsin. $Priceless.

Our Cards

Currier & Ives cards enjoyed a strong recovery in theme during this decade. In the early 1970s, a number of Norman Rockwell designs were considered the rage as illustrations for our cards. It was a return-to-another-era card, a kind of saccharine Americana in which snow scenes and grandmother's house themes abounded. Immediately after Watergate, there was in incredible swing toward nostalgia. It was almost as we were attempting to swing from the stun of that event, and move radically from where we were.

An interesting method of sending Christmas greetings started in the early 1970s when newspapers began soliciting their readers to send Christmas greetings via the classified ads. Two or three lines of a Christmas verse were a way to communicate such sentiment to many people via a modern means.

There was an attempt to get back to sentiment, especially toward the end of the 1970s. A return to "good old days" with simpler memories soon became a part of card designs. It once again became quite fashionable to send Christmas in an era which quickly realized that telephone conversations were ephemeral whereas cards could be saved and savored time and time again. A renewed interest in greeting cards resulted in the late 1970s when Christmas cards returned to imitate many of the designs used in the early 1900s, especially those of the home-crafted type.

Boxed Christmas card assortments became more inexpensive and simpler than in previous decades in an attempt to continue to cater to the young. The familiar names involved in the manufacturing of Christmas cards continued in this decade. It should be noted that honeycomb was still a popular addition for Christmas cards as it was for Valentines as well. Devra of Brooklyn, New York, started to produce honeycomb in 1974 and Eureka of Paper Magic in Troy, Pennsylvania, started in 1979. Card companies who incorporated honeycomb onto their cards included American Greetings, C.A. Reed, Gibson, and Hallmark.

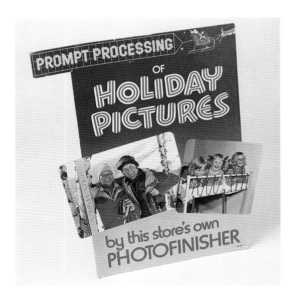

Advertisement for holiday pictures to be incorporated into Christmas cards, a very popular trend of the early part of this decade. $25-35.

Assortment of Christmas card styles very popular in the 1970s. $.50-.75 each.

Santa Claus printed stationary with envelopes for Santa to reply to the letters he was sent at Christmas. $1-2 for envelope and stationary.

Hallmark advent calendars to help families get ready for the spirit of Christmas. $3-4 each.

Assortment of magazines, books, and Christmas card display albums from this decade. $10-25 each.

Two Christmas comic books from the early 1970s. $4-6 each.

Late 1960s into early 1970s American-printed cards which doubled as Christmas ornaments. $4-5 each.

Assortment of Christmas story books and records from the late 1960s into the early 1970s. $3-5 each.

Large puzzle given as Christmas present in 1971. Whitman Publishing of Racine, Wisconsin. $10-15.

Our Trees

Live trees continued as a mainstay for countless Americans who found only the "real thing" to be their choice for a tree to decorate. The Scotch Pine continued to be the number one selling live tree during this decade. Almost 35 million trees were sold for the Christmas of 1972. Spruce and balsam followed as popular choices.

The National Tree continued its tradition in our nation's capital. In 1970, fifty-seven balsam firs, gifts of the American Mining Congress and Erie Mining Co., Hoyt Lakes, Minnesota, lined the Pathway of Peace when President Richard Nixon formally lit both the National tree and the trees symbolizing the nation's states and territories in a nationally-televised ceremony December 16.

Artificial trees gained new respectability during the 1970s when American Tree & Wreath, under the direction of Don Warning, then newly appointed national sales manager, in 1972 cut a stand-up thirty second commercial at a Dayton, Ohio, TV station. The spot was tagged with a local department store name and the next day, the store's entire stock of artificial trees was depleted. Thus it was quickly realized that television advertising was a powerful and potential means to promote their product. After four years of creative marketing and broadcast advertising, American Tree gained a 40% share of the market.

In 1971, U.S. consumers spent almost $90 million dollars for 4.5 million plastic trees compared with $210 million dollars for 35 million natural evergreens. The advantages of the plastic trees were many; trees were reusable, easy to put up, flame-retardant, and did not shed. Two other major artificial tree producers were Consolidated Novelty Co., Inc. and Carey-McPall, Co., a division of Marathon Mfg. Co.

Some of these trees came pre-assembled, but most consisted of a "trunk" pre-drilled to take "branches" that were color coded for easy assembly. The boughs were made of "needles" of extruded PVC interlaced with strands of wire. They strongly resembled long-bristled round brushes, thus collectors have coined the name "brush trees." To increase the convenience of artificial trees—their strongest attraction—manufacturers innovated such new trees as "Insta-Shape" by Mr. Christmas, which snapped into place when removed from its carton. American Tree promoted its "Mountain King," with clusters of branches that dropped into slots on the upper part of the trunk. Green was by far the best selling color in "Scotch pine," "balsam," and "Douglas fir." In 1975, the Woods-Sprite line of artificial trees introduced the Vienna Pine, in both up upswept shapes and in modified, upswept shapes. Carey-McPall Company, a division of the Marathon Manufacturing Company based in Philadelphia, was the producer of these trees.

Puelo's continued their rapid growth of the past decade into the 1970s. In an effort to encompass more of the holiday market, Puelo's began manufacturing satin ornaments, wreaths, and garlands. The year 1970 found the Puelo's feeling cramped again and operations were moved once more, this time to an 80,000 square foot facility. In 1972 Puelo's Novelty Company had become Puelo's Manufacturing Company.

While fresh trees continued to be very popular, *Consumer Bulletin* did warn us of a new trend: fresh trees being sprayed with a green vegetable dye before cutting to ensure a true green color. Thus, consumers were warned not to be misled by this color and forget to make that necessary fresh cut on the stump and submerse the tree in water for the entire duration of its stay in our homes. They also informed us that chemical fire-retardant materials sprayed onto these trees did not significantly reduce flammability.

The growing cycle for natural trees was about ten years. Over 35 million trees were sold in 1973. This harvest generated $90-million at the wholesale level and $210-million at retail. The plantation industry had four roles: growing the trees, wholesaling, shipping to markets, and retailing on lots. Even though there were four to five major species of trees, Scotch Pine was the tree of choice in the early 1970s.

Since aluminum trees were still marketed, we were warned that using lights on such a tree was a hazard. Sharp metal edges could cut through electric cord insulation, or the tip of the metal "needles" could contact an electrically charged component, such as a lamp holder, a partly exposed lamp base, or a bare spot on a wire. Therefore, the metal tree could become electrically charged and present a threat to the life of anyone who might touch the tree and a grounded object simultaneously (a TV set, radiator, water pipe, etc.). They recommended using a floodlight placed some distance from the tree. They also warned consumers that, even though trees were also made of plastic, these trees had metal limbs, and could also become electrically charged and quite dangerous.

Artificial trees gained new status through various marketing strategies. Jonathan Gubin, president of Jonathan Advertising, New York, took on an advertising campaign for the American Tree & Wreath division of American Technical Industries. In the early part of this decade, the artificial tree market consisted of half a dozen or so highly competitive manufacturers who slugged it out in a price war, with most of the sales being in the lower end tree price range. In 1972, Don Warning, newly appointed sales manager for American Tree, produced a stand-up, 30-minute commercial in Dayton, Ohio. He promoted their Mountain King, a flame retardant $49.95 tree in a spot which identified a local store. The next day the store sold completely out of this model. Don Warning then hired Gubin to produce advertising for his tree company. A commercial featuring a woodsman and his son searching a forest for the perfect tree was run in twenty-five markets. In this commercial, the son points and the father nods in agreement. The woodsman lays aside his ax and takes apart a completely assembled Mountain King tree. Mountain King tree sales soared, and legitimate marketing rather than competitive price cutting led to some interesting results. Both retailers and their customers upgraded the quality and price of their trees. Four years of creative marketing and broadcast advertising provided American Tree a forty percent share of the market and Mountain King with a ten percent share of market in dollar volume. In 1977, Marathon Carey-McFall Company absorbed the sales organization of Marathon Franke Company, the nation's oldest manufacturer of Christmas decorations, including tinsel, garlands, icicles, glass balls, and sundries.

In 1979, retailers across the country reported increased demand and shortages in supply of natural Christmas trees. For the second straight year, decreasing enthusiasm for artificial trees, plus droughts in some areas helped to create the shortage. Thirty million trees were harvested in 1979, with shortages of up to one million trees predicted. The swing back to natural trees was thought to be a reaction to the petroleum shortage (needed to manufacture artificial trees) and America's renewed interest in the environment and ecology. Regardless, for Americans who did revert to an artificial tree, it was an expensive one, since these trees were more realistic and better mirrored those grown outdoors.

Aluminum Trees still sold into the early 1970s. Soon to be a dying fad, these did not sell very well. Left to right: $100-125; $70-90; $145-165.

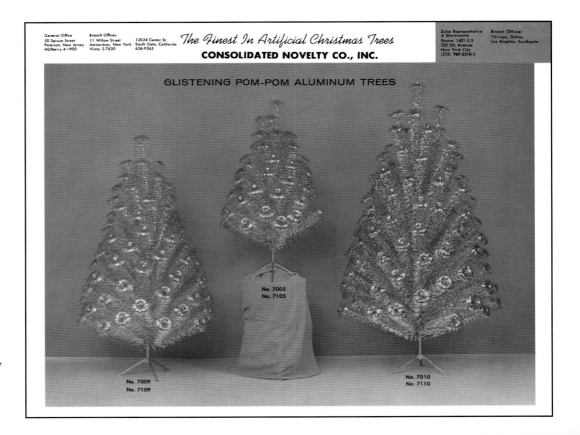

General Office
50 Spruce Street
Paterson, New Jersey
MUlberry 4-1900

Branch Offices:
11 Willow Street
Amsterdam, New York
Victor 2-7630

12024 Center St,
South Gate, California
636-9265

The Finest In Artificial Christmas Trees
CONSOLIDATED NOVELTY CO., INC.

Sales Representative
& Showrooms
Rooms 1401-3-5
200 5th Avenue
New York City
(212) 989-2510-1

Branch Offices:
Chicago, Dallas,
Los Angeles, Southgate

GLISTENING POM-POM ALUMINUM TREES

No. 7005
No. 7105

No. 7009
No. 7109

No. 7010
No. 7110

The Finest In Artificial Christmas Trees

CONSOLIDATED NOVELTY CO., INC.

VINYL TREES—FLAME RETARDANT—REALISTICALLY BEAUTIFUL—EASY TO TRIM

No. AF48 — 4 ft.
No. AF49 — 4½ ft.
No. AF50 — 6 ft.
No. AF51 — 7 ft.

No. 6094 — 4½ ft.
No. 6096 — 6 ft.
No. 6097 — 7 ft.

No. 3084 — 4½ ft.
No. 3086 — 6 ft.
No. 3087 — 7½ ft.
No. 3088 — 8 ft.

Vinyl Trees marketed in the early 1970s by Consolidated Novelty Co., Inc. Left to right: $35-45; $15-20; $65-75.

How We Decorated Our Homes and Trees

When country styles and colors became popular in home furnishings in the 1970s, Kurt S. Adler, Inc. unveiled the first ornaments with "Country" motifs and colorations. From that point on, the company continued to create decorations with innovative designs such as Victorian, Contemporary, Folk art, and many others. Since the early 1970s, the firm has utilized the unique talents of its art director and veteran designer, Marjorie Grace Rothenberg, to introduce a variety of Christmas themes—each included ornaments and accessories that have been saved by collectors and passed down from generation to generation in their families.

Many Americans began to think of their trees as very personal experiences, which should not be decorated with items off the assembly line. Therefore, many magazines gave directions for producing handwork ornaments such as homemade dolls, needlepoint figures, pretzels strung on gold cord, gingerbread cookies, popcorn strings, and even cranberry chains. Recipes and how-to directions for cookie and popcorn ornaments abounded in the mid-1970s, in what was a resurgence of the home-crafted look for our trees.

One of the more intriguing twists on ornaments appeared in the late 1970s when ladies magazines and craft publications suggested that people make ornaments by blowing up a balloon to the size of the desired ornament. Then string, heavy thread, or yarn was dipped in a pan of liquid starch (in full strength). This was wrapped around the balloon, leaving spaces, allowing for some designs. Subsequently, a piece of unstarched string was tied around the balloon, which was hung and left to dry for several hours. When the thread or string was dry, a pin broke the balloon. Once the broken balloon was removed, the lacy ball was spray-painted or decorated with colored embroidery thread designs. Countless variations and examples were illustrated, producing a frenzy of this type of decoration for about two years.

Christmas china continued to be popular with people who used these festive dishes during the Christmas season. Most of this china was made in Japan and most all was extremely affordable, which led to its popularity as well.

Lefton holly china. 1970-1971. This pattern followed the 1960s green berry pattern. Salt and pepper, $35-40; coffee cup, $10-12; coffee pot with cover, $55-65; creamer and sugar with cover set, $40-45; three compartment candy dish, $30-35; simple leaf candy dish, $10-15.

Lefton holly china in a new green variation for this decade. Toothpick holder, $12-15. Large vase, $25-30.

Corning Ware made from late 1970s into early 1980s. Different themes for each setting. $15-20 per place setting.

Greenish-brown china with red poinsettia decoration. An Enesco import. Salt and pepper shakers, $8-10; napkin holder, $45-55; cookie jar, $30-35.

Two Christmas mugs. Left, USA. $3-5. Right, Johnson Brothers of England. $5-7.

Christmas china with tree loaded with presents and toys. Marked "Plummer, LTD New York." Large dinner plate, $5-7. Small plate, $3-5.

Holt-Howard Santa candle holder. $10-15.

USA china with red poinsettia transfer. $10-15 for place setting.

Holt-Howard ash tray. $15-18.

Left:
Marked "Japan," ceramic musical box. Santa rotates as "Jingle Bells" is played by wind-up key in bottom. $40-45.

Santa banks continued to be popular choices for presents. Employing the same mold as in the previous decade, these Santa Claus banks were not painted quite as perfectly. $15-18 each.

Salt and pepper shakers in shapes of Rockets with Santa. $15-20.

Santa Claus kissing Mrs. Santa Claus (Japan) glued to a wooden sled with plastic greenery indicative of the late 1970s style. $5-7.

Santa egg cups with cloth cap meant to keep egg warm while being served. Marked "Japan" on bottom. $20-25 for complete set of two.

Large teapot from Japan. Note tiny cup in his hands. $12-15.

American Influences on Glass Ornaments

While European ornaments gained popularity at a quicker pace, American businessmen sought to provide such products created in this country. Most of the problem behind our poor efforts resulted from a lack of the craftsmanship that only the Europeans seemed to be able to create. Therefore, American business executives soon realized that their share of the glass market was never to be gained in thin, fancy glass ornaments. Thus it was that creative individuals turned to combine our present technology with the concept of limited editions, a soon-to-become fad of the 1970s which continued quite successfully into the 1980s.

These early beginnings go back to 1972, when Corning announced a new decorating process permitting art work prints and photographs to be permanently adhered to the ornaments. Color reproductions were printed on a plastic sleeve and slipped over the ornament which shrank, once heat was applied. As a result of this decorating technique, Corning embarked upon a sales campaign to market ornaments using the Corning name, while still supplying bulb blanks to the decorator firms. This move was initially a good one for Corning, selling over 9.5-million ornaments under their own name in 1973.

Corning introduced these conventional glass ornaments in solid colors and decorated finishes in a variety of assortments for sale at the retail level. One such collection was a series of four Currier and Ives scenes on 3 1/4-inch ornaments. In the 1970s, they produced many different ornaments on many different themes including "The Ferris Ornament Collection" based on early American oil paintings; "Walt Disney Ornaments" based on Disney characters; and "Chuck Ripper's Famous American Birds" based on his depictions of American birds. Corning did this to increase the sales of domestic glass ornaments, which had shown a gradual decline in the recent past.

By 1976, many of Corning's customers were experiencing pricing problems. It was difficult to buy from Corning and also compete with them on the open market. Therefore, in October 1976, Corning discontinued their direct retail sales, but retained their decorator customers up until 1981.

In anticipation of our country's Bicentennial year, Marathon Franke Co. put together a line of tinsel garlands and tree ornaments in red, white, and blue. These red, white, and blue balls included designs of Old Glory, the American Eagle Emblem, and a series of Stars and Stripes. Accompanying these balls were a set of bells decorated in red, white, and blue stripes.

In 1977 Shiny Brite packaged new combinations of satin-wrapped ornaments and glass in the same box. Also new that year were individually boxed starter kits which contained various sizes of ornaments in the same finish. The kits came in decorated glass, shining glass, and satin-wrapped.

The P.M. Manufacturing Company of Los Angeles produced glow-in-the-dark ornaments. They were created in the shapes of Santa Claus, angels, candy canes, trees, bells, candles, and even stars. According to an advertisement in 1970, a motion picture producer accidentally discovered this effect while investigating special effects for a science fiction movie. Researching phosphorescent materials, he found that hand painting and silk-screening this material onto a surface was often unsatisfactory and always costly. He developed a new way of using laminated metallic inserts and injection molding to create these new type ornaments. A set of 72 "Magi-Glo" ornaments in an average 3-inch size sold for $3.50.

While "Hallmark" meant greeting cards to almost all Americans, their entry into the decorations industry was most interesting. Capitalizing on their solid reputation for paper products, Hallmark experimented with creating ornaments for our trees. In 1973, Hallmark introduced its line of Keepsake Ornaments. The talented design staff deviated from the plain colored glass balls by printing traditional holiday scenes on sleeves fitted over the balls. Since then Hallmark has added a number of different styles and figural shapes to their lines. In 1975, molded plastic ornaments which simulated wood were added to the line of glass spheres. The year 1977 was one of tremendous expansion for their collection, with three new ornament formats—sewn ornaments with silk-screened designs, acrylic ornaments, and ornaments with the look of stained glass. Two new commemorative ball ornaments for "Teacher" and "Special Friend" were added in 1979. By then Baby's First Christmas satin ball ornaments had become solid sellers. Ball ornaments were given new packages in 1979 and nearly sixty percent of the ornaments were dated.

It took two years to create an ornament. At the starting point, the designers and market planners visited with different selected groups of twenty to thirty customers, surveyed different market trends, and traveled to different marketplaces throughout the world. With all the research in place, a meeting was held where the decisions on what to include in the product lines were made. After an idea was chosen for the line, it was returned to the artist to be finished. From the time an artist began to sculpt an ornament to the time it was finished, each individual ornament went through as many as seventy-five steps.

While many American-produced ornaments were sold only at Christmas, there was a small, select group of year-around Christmas stores in existence in this decade. One of the first and the largest was Bronner's. While Bronner's of Frankenmuth, Michigan, had been in existence for quite a few years, it was in this decade that numerous travel magazines and newspapers began to herald this store as being a unique and wonderful place to visit.

Wallace Bronner started this business as a sign painter in 1943, at the age of sixteen. In 1951 he painted holiday designs on cardboard panels for the city of Clare, Michigan, and the project was so successful that the merchants placed a duplicate order the following year. After the second order, it occurred to Bronner that surely other cities might be interested in decorations of a similar nature. It was then that the business was started.

At first it was more of a sideline business. Bronner would occasionally display Christmas products at a town hall or school. However, Wally and his wife, Irene, added a complete line of decorations and gifts for the home in 1960. After attending his first International Trade Fair in Europe in 1965, Bronner began importing Christmas merchandise. Thus, in 1966, Frankenmuth welcomed the expansion of the Christmas business to include Bronner's Tannenbaum Shop. Formerly home to the Frankenmuth Bank, The Tannenbaum Shop was located across the street from Bronner's original store building, constructed by Wally's father Herman, a stone mason, in 1954.

Their personalized ornament line commenced in 1967. Soon after, they began patenting their own Christmas decorations—including their famous life-size, fiberglass nativity scenes. Before long the Tannenbaum Shop was overflowing, and Bronner opened the Bavarian Corner (next to the original shop) in 1971. In 1977, Bronner's consolidated under one roof at 25 Christmas Lane at the south end of Frankenmuth.

Wally Bronner was one of the first American year-around Christmas stores to stock old-fashioned ornaments made in Europe, which reminded people of those their grandmothers had on their trees. In the early 1970s, this store usually had over one thousand different ornaments on display, covering three basic holiday themes—holiday, religious, and toyland. His early importation of Italian ornaments helped to solidify their popularity in the United States.

Rayon-covered satin balls and bells, very popular in late 1970s. $.50-1.00 each.

Home-crafted ornaments made from Styrofoam bases, to which was applied beads and other decorative trims. Most of this type were sold in kits and women and children spent the months preceding Christmas making their own ornaments and ornaments which they gave as presents. $4-5 each.

More elaborate examples of home-crafted ornaments so very popular in this decade in our attempt to duplicate some of the Victorian very-lavishly trimmed ornaments. $8-10 each.

More unusual satin-covered Styrofoam ornaments with different themes. These types of collector's yearly series foreshadowed the glass collector's craze to follow in the next decades. $5-6 each.

Boxed sets of American ornaments typical of this decade. Very common, they were made in huge quantities. $1-3 per boxed set.

European Influences on Our Glass Ornaments

Italy Increases Production of Glass Figural Ornaments for the United States

One European glass type of ornament did enjoy great success in this decade and that was the figural-type ornament manufactured in Italy. Italian glass ornaments continued to capture the hearts of Americans and they flocked to specialty stores and high-fashion department stores to purchase in single numbers some very elaborate and hand-blown decorations. In the 1970s, unsilvered muted colored figurals became the most common. Most often ornaments were dipped in a single soft pastel color and then details added with black and other dark colored paints. Today more unsilvered than silvered figurals are being imported. Even though Italian figurals are fairly recent, subject material does help in dating them. Since cartoon characters and other popular personalities are an indication of American interest, they were made only when these subjects were popular. Therefore, the Pink Panther and other such subjects help to pin down a particular time frame. Since the 1970s, the Italians have especially capitalized on appealing to America's youth and the majority of the ornaments created since then are of animals, fairy tale personalities, and cartoon characters.

The Italians have also become quite famous for their hand-painted spheres and teardrop shaped ornaments. Maria Luisa De Carlini has for a great number of years hand painted a variety of ornaments for Bronner's Christmas Wonderland in Frankenmuth, Michigan, as well as for a few other importers. Maria Luisa is especially known for her religious themes. Undoubtedly she would have continued to add much to the artistic line of Carlini had she not died at an early age from cancer in the 1970s. Bronner's of Frankenmuth, Michigan, became the largest importer of these Italian figurals and other Italian-crafted glass ornaments during this decade. By the late 1970s, Bronner's artist-in residence, Connie V. Larson, sketched a particular scene for an ornament, created an ink drawing, filmed it, and then sent it to Italy with the exact specifications so Italian artists could hand paint each one according to the specified directions.

Italian ornaments blown from the early-1960s on into the mid-1970s. Difficult to ascribe to specific years as no catalogs were issued illustrating these ornaments nor are there very well documented importation records. Left to right, top to bottom: Clown with red hair, $85-95; pink elephant, $75-85; Clown with wine flask, $70-80; Charlie Brown (could date back to early 1960s), $125-135; wizard with gold paper stars, $85-95; Lucy (could ate back to early 1960s), $125-135.

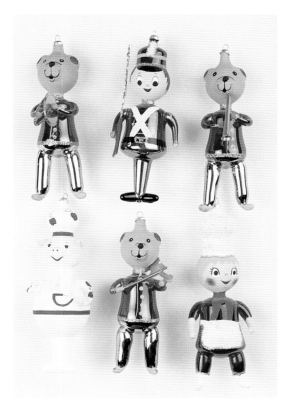

Italian ornaments of 1970s vintage. Left to right, top to bottom: Bear with cymbals, $85-95; Soldier with gun, $70-80; Bear with horn, $85-95, Baker's pig in chef's garb, $75-85; Bear with fiddle, $85-95 (complete set of bears together, $325-350); Chef with apron and hat, $75-85.

Italian ornaments blown between mid-1960s and mid-1970s. Left to right, top to bottom: Little chick with extended legs, $75-85; Cat with white face, $85-95; Sailor with pipe, $100-10; Bear with chenille tail, $70-80; Rabbit with floppy ears, $110-120; Martian with metal antennas, $125-135; Little boy with tuxedo, $70-80; Little space boy sitting on quarter moon, $135-145.

Mid-1970s Italian blown ornaments all from white glass. Left to right, top to bottom: Drama figure with open eyes, $85-95; Italian drama comic figure with glass cap, and glasses, $90-100; Drama figure with tear-dropped eyes, $85-95; Neil Armstrong, $100-110; Dancing pirouette, $75-85.

Jonah in the Whale, a popular Italian figural made from late 1950s into early 1970s. $100-110.

Dwarfs from Snow White series. Italian blown from early 1960s into early 1970s. $95-110 each.

Mexican dancers blown in Italy from mid-1960s into early 1970s. $75-85.

Germany Continues to Produce Glass Ornaments

The "Oberfrankische Glas und Spielzeug" (toy goods) at ist Neustadt near Coburg was a cooperative business providing glass, paints, and molds to cottage workers. In 1948, Fritz Rempel, a teacher, founded Oberfrankische Glas und Spielzeug. His idea was born from the fact that in this year glass blowers were bringing their ornaments in baskets to the still open Soviet border to Neustad to barter for food and money. Oberfrankische Glas commenced the distribution of glasswares on a seasonal basis and delivered them to customers. Their business florished with Woolworth's, Montgomery Ward, Sears Roebuck, and Kresge's. Rempel's first showroom was actually his living room in his modest home. In 1962, it was evident that the Russians would keep the border with West Germany completely closed. Rempel persuaded glass blowers to escape over the border at night so that they could work for him. The company continued to grow over the years.

Oberfrankische Glass continued to grow and flourish as a major distributor of glass tree ornaments until the sudden death of its owner, Fritz Rempel. His son, Ralf, took over the business and took it in a new direction. Ralf Rempel built a production factory, allowing the company to make its own glass ornaments and even the cardboard boxes to merchandise these glass creations.

Krebs & Sohn reached across the ocean in the 1970s to establish an ornament factory in Roswell, New Mexico. Situated in Rosenheim, Germany, their entry into American business is quite interesting. Their son, Eberhard, came to study English at the University of New Mexico to improve his English skills, which the family saw as essential to the continued success of their ornament manufacturing business. Actually, the family had been interested for years in establishing a factory in America. Many possible sites had been previously explored, but Eberhard's arrival in New Mexico to study the English language caused his family to consider this state as a possible site. As a result, their American plant was started in New Mexico in 1973 to take advantage of the dry climate of the area which allowed the lacquers used to dry quickly. The choice of sites was also due, in part, to the surplus labor market available in the area. Eberhard's brother, Wolfgang, came to the United States to assist in the setting up of the operation. Once it was firmly established, Wolfgang returned to Germany and left his brother, Eberhard, in charge.

During this decade, ornaments continued to be produced in East Germany. What continued were the government's continued efforts to form a huge state-owned cooperative in the Christmas ornaments industry. In April 1972, the PGH (Produktionsgenossenschaft Handwerk) and the BSB (Betrieb mit staatlicher Beteiligung) were transformed into state owned companies. The new company VEB (Volkseigener Betrieb) was then responsible not only for the production, but for the centrally organized marketing of all the Christmas decorations within the group of Christmas decoration producing companies. In 1972, the following half-state owned distributors joined the VEB: Bernhard Matthai, KG Greiner & Co., Richard Roos, E. O. Walter, and Oskar Scheler. In September 1978, a training school for glass blowers graduated thirty-five new craftsmen.

In 1979, the Baumschmuck (Christmas Tree Decorations) department of the cooperative was brought into the central industry. The aim was to step by step, in concentrated measures, connect all of the companies into a so-called "combined cooperative." Villages and places in the Lauscha region that played a role in these combined cooperatives included Meiningen, Ernstthal, Steinheid, Haselbach, Steinach, Sonneberg, and Ilmenau.

Metallverarbeitung (Metal Processing) Lauscha was a major part of the Christmas industry in this decade. It was founded in 1930. The founder, the master toolmaker Max Greiner-Bechert, came from a family business that had come up in the second half of the nineteenth century, supplying the production of glass made Christmas ornaments with the metal caps for ornaments, clamps for birds, clip-on candleholders, and chimes which revolved and rang with candles.

Max Greiner-Bechert used the knowledge that he had acquired in preparation of his master exam in Nürnberg (Nuremberg), for the construction and production of automatic machines, for making parts of Christmas tree decorations and toys in the company. At every economic turn, he was able to adapt the production of his own toolmaking department to counter the effects that the worldwide economic crisis had on these various items. Besides the permanent production of metal caps and clip-on holders for birds and mushrooms, the company made molds and mold holders for the glass processing in the glasswork factories and for the cottage workers which produced Christmas ornaments and various glass decorations. He constructed and produced metal parts for the production of new toys for various Sonneberg companies and supplied these companies with the needed machinery to produce quality Christmas dolls and toys.

After 1945, the production of every-day goods for the East German population started, like nails made from tin cans, jewelry made of metal waste, and other items. Later, Metallverarbeitung (Metal Processing) Lauscha specialized in the production of metal jewelry, candlesticks, metal icicles (the spiral kind duplicated in the United States), toy parts, and cases for lipsticks. With his son, an engineer for cutting tools and stamp machines who joined the company in 1949, in 1955 a so-called partnership was formed. During the following years, their production line was enlarged by the company-owned designs: ball-shaped bells, skewers, and holders for of blown vases and racks for cognac glasses and fruit skewers for the glass industry were made.

On April 19th, 1972, the company was sold to the state and the VEB Metallverarbeitung *(Metal Processing)* Lauscha was formed. In closed teamwork with the VEB Kunstglas *(Artistic Glass)* Gehren and the VEB Farbglaswerk *(Colored Glass Factory)* Lauscha, the technological base for producing metal parts for paraffin lamps, table lamps, and hanging lamps were made in the company and its production started. The produced line was enlarged for the Christmas tree decorations industry. On January 1st, 1977, the company, with its twenty-two employees, was affiliated to the VEB Thüringer Glasschmuck *(Thuringian Christmas decorations)* Lauscha.

VEB Baumschmuck *(Christmas Tree Decorations)* Steinheid was another major company who played a role in the production of Christmas decorations in East Germany. In neighboring Steinheid, this company was founded on June 1st, 1957, when sixteen friends and colleagues teamed up to make the first cooperative of the Christmas ornaments producing craft that was called "Heinrich Rau" from 1962 on. Their union was an advanced step, the importance of which is only realized by those persons who had survived and fashioned the 1950s in a conscious way. Under the conditions of the "State of workers and farmers," the advantages of the socialist means of production from now on could come into force for the glassblowers from the formerly depressed area too. They made use of this opportunity, and after ten years, 650 members and employees belonged to the cooperative.

During the first years since the cooperative was founded, its members realized that a fundamental improvement of the glassblowers' social situation wasn't possible to reach under the conditions of the traditional, decentralized home workers' production means. Only by the use of modern production technologies in central production places, could an improvement in productivity be possible. Therefore the building in the Neuhäuser Straße *(Neuhaus Road)* that had been taken over by the VEB Thüringer Christbaumschmuck *(Thuringian Christmas Decorations)* in 1960, was expanded and used.

Changed automatic ampoule machines were used for making glass beads termed "little pieces" by the Germans. Later glass products were made on flask blowing machines and silver plating and varnishing machines as well as assembly lines for drawing and drying that partly had been developed and made in the town locksmith's shop.

The production cooperative owned a common credit fund and gave the money to build the story production building with an area of 1,100 square meters (about 1/4 acre). They enlarged a building for the first "production place" (i.e., factory) in the history of Siegmundsburg with twenty-five jobs reconstructing old buildings, financing the technological equipment for improving the working and living conditions of the employees in Steinheid.

By the use of the so-called Olivotto machines, blown glass spheres were produced on which new stamping, silk-screen-printing, and gluing technologies were employed by the production cooperative. At the end of the 1960s, the employees reached outstanding results with a short-term change of the complete export range. Hereby, the experiences that had been collected during the business trips abroad were used in production. For the first time, Germans were collecting data on trends and social customs which would help them in decorating ornaments which would be very desirable and salable in the American market.

On April 24, 1972, the production cooperative was changed into VEB Baumschmuck *(Tree Decorations)* Steinheid. During the following years the company got extensive financial means for further improvement of the working and living conditions of its employees that mainly were used for the following investments:

• erecting a building with a company kitchen and canteen for 200 persons;
• equipping a common room in the production place Siegmundsburg;
• installing bathrooms;
• building two production and storage halls;
• building a fence and a lake for the fire brigade;
• building garages;
• insetting a three-color silk-screen printing facility and two more *circle spraying machines*.

After the completion of the new school, that was situated close to the company, in 1976, the company kitchen also supplied the students of the school with meals. Most of these students were children of the glassblowers' families.

For their efforts in building the socialist society in the GDR, the former production cooperative was awarded with honorary diplomas of the GDR communist party several times and the VEB got the award "Banner of work" in 1977. During the Autumn Fair in 1977, the company was awarded with the first gold medal for Christmas decorations made of glass.

Deserving employees were honored for outstanding results in the socialist competition and for strengthening the GDR with high awards by the state.

Due to economic reorganizations on the government's part, on January 1, 1978, the VEB Dekofrüchte *(Decorating Fruit)*, and on January 1, 1979, the VEB Schmuckwaren *(Jewelry)* Lichte, were affiliated to the company. During the following years, both extensive reconstruction works and a change of the power supply were started in this part of the company.

After taking over the companies of the leading department, Tree Decorations, by the centrally led industries, the new economic management, the VEB Kombinat Technisches Glas *(Technological Glass)* Ilmenau, continued the concentration of production and the creation of bigger economic units. This ultimately resulted in unification with the VEB Thüringer Glasschmuck *(Thuringian Glass Decorations)* Lauscha on January 1, 1984.

Glass fruit and cotton wool fruit were important export items before World War II. Their production continued in the period after World War II and into the 1970s. VEB Deco-Früchte *(Decoration Fruit)* Lichte was founded in 1876 by Carl Meusel. With four employees he started the production of decorative fruit made of glass. In 1898, the production line was enlarged to include cotton-wool fruit.

Over the years, the product range was enlarged more and more, with items ranging from grapes as small as a pin to giant grapes for decorating shop windows. The main products were decorations articles for the advent and Christmas season. The company, meanwhile, with more than fifty employees, has been presenting these goods at the Leipzig Fair. While in existence since the middle ages, during GDR times it was just as important for eastern Europe, since Leipzig was behind the Iron Curtain.

Together with the old product line, the company was managed under private ownership after World War II. In 1959, the state's participation started with the VEB Kunstblume *(Artificial Flower)* Sebnitz as a companion company. Overtaken as national property in 1972, as VEBDeko-Früchte *(Decoration Fruit)* Lichte, the company was affiliated to the VEB Baumschmuck *(Tree Decoration)* Steinheid due to economic organizing measures. One year later, the VEB Schmuckwaren *(Jewelry)* Lichte followed also and was joined to this government-owned cooperative. This company had been managed temporarily by the original management of the company and had been set up from the HSB Heinrich Heinz KG – Pearl and Button Factory.

The articles that had been produced included foil berries and cotton-wool fruit which were sold in East Germany. Some were also exported as Christmas tree decorations, with artificial flowers for trim; but, their cost was prohibitive due to trade barriers and export taxes in place for East Germany.

Under socialist production conditions, several innovations for the mechanization of the working process were used: automatic machines for making smaller glass balls, cotton-wool turntable machines that had been made by the company itself, an automatic machine for blowing glass with a three times higher efficiency that had been created and developed by the company to increase the productivity of work, and others. Extensive investments have been made on the company's own initiative by its workers to enlarge the production and storage capacities.

To open up working power reserves in Schmiedefeld and Sommersdorf, new production places were built, supplying products for the Christmas tree decorations industry started there. With 130 employees, the production department Lichte was the only production factory in Geiersthal in existence in the mid-1970s through the 1980s.

By the end of this decade, many companies quickly woke up to the fact that German manufactured ornaments were "hot" sales items. Commodore Manufacturing Company of New York offered a line of German ornaments including over 150 styles. Traditional coffee pots, tea kettles, soldiers, clowns, and tear drops were among the most popular. These popular ornaments were also marketed in four-color window boxes and were packaged in vacuum-formed trays, packaging that helped to promote them.

Two folk art ornaments blown by Gedania in Gdansk, Poland, in the early 1970s. $25-30 each.

Animal figural ornaments blown by Gedania in Gdansk, Poland, in the mid-1970s. $25-35 each.

Austrian-blown ornaments with plastic tops from 1970s. $1-3 each.

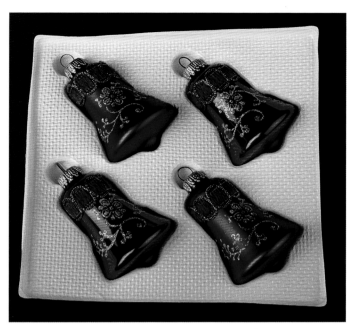

Box of four bells made by Krebs in Rosenheim, West Germany, during this decade. $4-5 for boxed set.

Candy Containers

While boxed assortments of chocolates continued in popularity, tins containing hard candies, chocolates, and nuts also gained strong sales as Americans now more than ever were concerned with large quantities of whatever confections and "Christmas goodies" they purchased for their family and friends. While not a container, clear plastic trees in 12-inch sizes were sold. On the tips of each branch, families put colored gumdrops, both as decorations and as treats for their guests.

Thin plastic see-through body containers were filled with tiny bits of candy and were sold in sets of five by Sears Roebuck in 1972. A snowman, clown, Santa, dog, and lantern were included for the price of 99 cents. One other very popular style included plastic spheres, one half of which was opaque and the other half clear. Parting in the middle, they were filled with a small assortment of candy and cracker jack-type toys. Once filled, they were being hung from the tree by means of a tiny molded plastic circle at the top of each ornament.

West German blown ornaments in variety of shapes, all stenciled heavily with gold glitter and brocade decorating so typical of this decade to reflect home-fashioned look. $1-3 each.

Plastic ornaments which separated. Some were filled with plastic decorations while others were filled with candy and tiny toys for children. Separated in middle. $2-3 each.

Candy and cookie tins. All from the 1970s period. $7-10 each.

Made in Japan, ornaments with cardboard feet. Insides of cone were filled with tiny pieces of candy and miniature toys. An advertising ornament used by companies to promote their stores or services in the early 1970s. $10-15 each.

Tinsel Icicles and Tinsel Garlands

Lead icicles or tinsel disappeared from the market when the federal government banned traditional lead-foil icicles in 1971, calling them "a threat to the health of the children of the nation." Even through there was not a documented case of lead poisoning, our government took this very strong stand. From here on, icicles were made of plastic and cellophane. The icicle machines swallowed foil at one end and disgorged streams of tinsel from the other end at a rate which kept several workers busy sealing the icicles in black packages bearing National Tinsel's rainbow symbol. The invasion of the decoration market by European and Asian firms killed off the "frill" side of National's line—elaborate ornaments that were almost sixty percent of their business previous to this time.

Plastic and cellophane-type tinsel were the only types of tinsel icicles available to Americans during this decade. Tinsel became popular in the 1970s as decorators attempted to add more of an old-fashioned look to their trees, now decorated with those ever so popular home-crafted type ornaments. Tinsel garlands continued to get thicker and wider as we decorated with few ornaments and more tinsel garlands, which sparkled and gave more glitter to trees decorated with midget lights. Widths of up to four-inches were sold with the two and three-inch varieties being the most popular. While silver and gold were the predominant colors, wild colors such as purple, lavender, pink, and green appeared in an attempt to jolt those traditionalists.

Two types of machines made garlands. One type spun heavy, wire-centered garlands—used primarily for displays in stores and public buildings—three or four at a time. The other type serrated narrow foil into whiskers, sewed or wove foil and thread together, and spun out a garland that looked just like cotton candy, and had the same velvety feel.

National Tinsel's new line, introduced in 1976, offered a three-ply thickness and gave buyers the opportunity to step up from standard one and two-ply tinsel to a fuller, heavier garland. These three-ply garlands were offered in a variety of lengths, widths, and colors.

Traditional garland sold by National Tinsel in 1970. $3-5 for box.

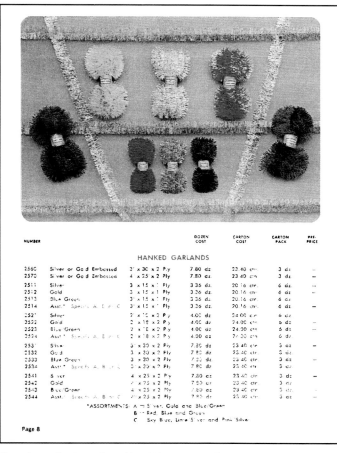

Traditional silver-colored roping from the 1970s. $3-5 for boxed set.

Experimental colors released in 1973, meant to give a new impetus to the sale of tinsel garlands. Note the very bright and unusual colors. $4-5 for box.

18 FT. (6 YDS.) LONG
1-3/4 IN. WIDE-2 PLY

Tinsel garland in very elaborate gold and red color variation. Late 1970s. $3-5 for boxed set.

Left:
Green tinsel roping, typical of the different color variations used to entice people to purchase this roping. $4-6 in original box.

Plastic Decorations

Since electric lights were dimmed in the early 1970s, some interesting ornaments were produced which would give a little "sparkle" to the tree. One popular alternative was "Magi-Glo" ornaments in red, white, blue, and green manufactured by P.M. Manufacturing of California. The most unique "Magi-Glo" feature was the fact that these metallic laminated plastic ornaments glowed in the dark. The figures included candles, Santa Claus, angels, stars, candy canes, bells, and trees. Plastic decorations continued to be popular alternatives, especially for young married couples with children who purchased the bulk of these decorations. Spheres, pear shapes filled with plastic scenes, and prism-shaped ornaments in red, blue, gold, and silver gained some respectability in the late 1970s, as they combined quite well with satin and Styrofoam decorations. Intrigued by the "unbreakable" nature of these decorations, young Americans purchased thousands of these ornaments; but, history also records that most of them were hung at the bottom of the tree, reserving the top-most branches for favorite, fragile glass treasures.

Thousands upon thousands of felt ornaments, in shapes of Santas, angels, and elf heads, were imported from Japan, all of which contained a plastic face animated with painted eyes, cheeks, and mouth. Other plastic imports included the Della-Robbia fruit and nut assortments. Assorted apples, oranges, bananas, grapes, and walnuts were bunched and finished with glossy leaves. Not only available in bunches to attach to the boughs, decorators could purchase entire chains of this fruit in lengths of up to 9-feet.

Even the crystal look, captured in the white trees of the early 1900s and revived in the 1960s, found renewed interest in the late 1970s as consumers bought sets of crystal plastic garlands, crystal snowflakes, crystal prisms to simulate icicles, and white glittered Styrofoam balls, all of which combined to appear more natural than some of the bright and almost gaudy sequined-look Styrofoam satin balls. Rauch Industries continued to be a viable force in the ornament business by acquiring the Essex Frank Company, adding tinsel garlands and Christmas aerosols to the line. In 1993, Rauch purchased Holiday Products, manufacturers of tree skirts, stockings, and Santa suits. Marshal Rauch continued as CEO with his three children, Marc, Peter, and Ingrid, as officers of this company. In 1998, Rauch Industries became a division of Syratech, and became the largest manufacturer of Christmas tree ornaments in the world, producing over 1,200,000 ornaments per day in fifty-two colors and eight sizes.

Artform Industries, a subsidiary of Cindarn Plastics in Portsmouth, Virginia, produced silk-screened and vacuum formed plastic plaques for all seasons, but primarily for Christmas.

Abe Damast, president of Commodore Manufacturing Corporation, reported in 1975 that plastics, formerly used as the principal material for ornaments, was being replaced by new materials such as woods, corn husk, metal, and cloth fabrics. Damast recorded this as a significant change in production. Keeping with that trend, Commodore concentrated on birds, soldiers, animals, and other tree decorations made from wood. Dolls, wreaths, and garlands were made from corn husk. In metal there were also many new styles.

A Closer Look at Christmas Ornaments and Decorations For Our Trees

Felt-covered plastic ornaments from Japan, all of which reflected home-crafted look so popular. Rather than making our own, we turned to commercial manufacturers to do our work for us. $2-4 each.

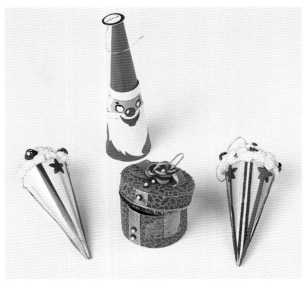

Japan-manufactured home-crafted ornaments including ice cream cones, gift box with detachable cover, and Santa Claus cone. $3-5 each.

Felt over Styrofoam base ornaments from Japan, which reflected the home-crafted look but made a statement indicating we needed to get back to the creation of our own ornaments. $3-4 each.

Elves made of flannel, cotton, plastic, and felt from Japan. Made in early 1970s through later part of this decade. $2-5 each.

Larger 6" fabric and straw ornament typical of the home-crafted look so very popular in this decade. $3-5 each.

Plastic star midget light tree top from early 1970s. $5-8 with box.

American blown tree top, very typical of the simple look of this decade. $3-4 for top and box.

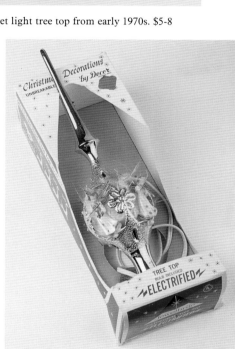

Early 1970s electrified tree top with plastic angel and spun glass decorative effects which help to give an unusual glow to this top. $5-7 for top and box.

Angel tree top with candles (midget lights) in both hands and midget lights hid in her shirt to give her a glowing effect when placed at top of the tree. $5-7.

Manitowoc Tinsel tree top features Santa with a spun glass curly beard. $5-6 for top and box.

Styrofoam ornaments made to imitate edible cookies which were to hang on tree. These were intended for those who wished to recycle their cookies from year to year. $1-2 each.

Wooden based ornaments made following directions found in women's magazines of the decade. Covered with satin, sequins, and braiding, these ornaments took on a home-crafted look which made the neighbors envious. $2-5 each.

Plastic musical instruments made from the same molds used in the 1960s, but this decade found a simple gold flashing, just the type to go with the colorful home-crafted ornaments finding their way to the tree. Made in Japan. $1-3 each.

Plastic snowflakes from early 1970s. White plastic was heavily glued and heavy amounts of silver glitter were then applied on both sides. These snowflakes made in the U.S. then blended well with the more colorful home-crafted ornaments. $5-6 each.

A popular plastic ornament type which continued to be produced into the early 1970s to complement the home-crafted heavily decorated ornaments. $1-2 each.

Under Our Trees

In the early 1970s, Roman Religious Goods, founded by Ron Jedlinski, imported religious items from Italy. In 1973, his company became the exclusive distributor for Fontanini Heirloom Nativities. With this splendid line, Jedlinski started his venture into the Christmas market. His entrance into the import business had started in a previous decade. While stationed in Barcelona, Spain, he began his first imports of religious figurines. Upon his discharge from the Navy in 1963, Jedlinski formed his company, importing religious gifts and figurines. Many companies were leaving the religious market due to the influence of the 1962 Vatican council and resulting abandonment of Catholic tradition. Going against the tide, Jedlinski entered this market. As a result, he did much to ensure the survival of these very important religious symbols of Christmas.

Italy was the primary supplier of these crèche figures as their painting detail and colors were unsurpassed by the Japanese and German painters of this period. Most of the German creators of such items were behind the Iron Curtain and Japanese goods just never had the detail of the European varieties. Their price, however, was an incentive for many American families who wished to have a crèche scene for their homes.

Village Houses

While the tradition of placing a village underneath the tree somewhat diminished during this period, American and Japanese manufacturers did continue to provide some very simple and affordable sets.

Cardboard continued to be the choice for the traditionalists and plastic became the choice of the modern family. A nine-piece Alpine set sold for $4.39 in 1976 and included eight houses and a high-steeple church. Miniature lights snapped into each house, giving-off a warm glow of "stained glass." The 22-inch cord used only 17 watts and plugged into any wall outlet. Over ninety-five percent of the cardboard houses were manufactured in Japan, and were painted with a minimum of detail.

Animals and Figures

Barclay reissued its hand-painted villagers in 1970. Two to three inches tall, they were hand cast of lead alloy. There were thirteen pieces: two skaters on an aluminum foil pond, two skiers on a cotton "ski slope," a couple in a horse-drawn sleigh, a woman on a sled, and a man pulling two children on a sled. Sears sold this set for $2.98.

Papier-mâché boots continued to be made into the earlier part of this decade. At this time, they were primarily airbrushed a red color with a white band at the top. The larger sizes merely were painted red. Between 1965 and 1975, most American red papier-mâché boots were sold by Carry-lite of Milwaukee, Wisconsin. In 1976, Carry-lite of Milwaukee, Wisconsin, went out of business and most of the molds were sold for scrap.

Early 1970s wax candles which continued to be popular favors and table place setting decorations for Christmas dinners. $1-3 each.

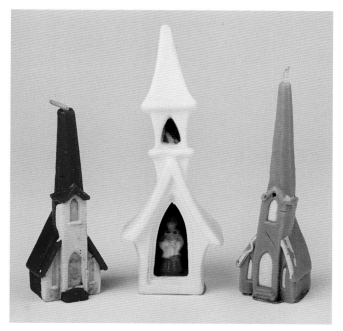

Church themed wax candle decorations for home and school use. Many of these were given as presents by teachers to their students after Christmas programs as the candy boxes disappeared. $1-3 each.

Large 8" to 10" wax candles from mid-1970s for Christmas decorating. $5-7 each.

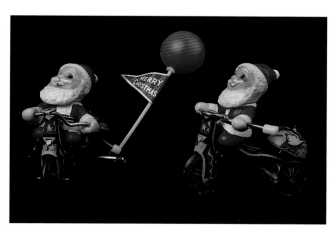

Wind-up metal toys with plastic-headed Santa Claus from the late 1970s into early 1980s. $25-35 each.

Santa push button puppet from mid-1970s. 4" U.S. $8-10.

68

Santa push button puppet made from mid-1960s through the early part of this decade. $10-15.

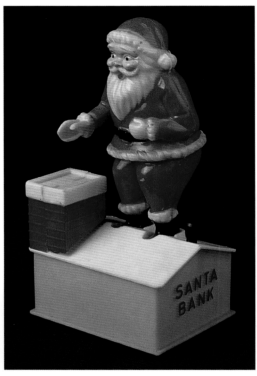

Early 1970s hard plastic bank. Coin was placed in Santa's hand, and when a button on the back of the roof was pushed, the chimney opened and the coin was dropped in by Santa. $30-40.

Musical hard rubber wall hanging with cotton beard. When a hidden button (under beard) was pushed, musical notes were heard. $15-20.

Hard rubber bank for saving money to buy presents for the next Christmas season. U.S. $10-15.

Soft rubber squeaker toys meant to be taken into bathtubs by children. They floated and made wonderful noises when their tummies were pushed. Sani-Toy Company, U.S. $6-10 each.

Left:
Sani-Toys but meant more for play outside of bathtub since these were elaborately painted and also squeaked when their tummies were pushed. $10-15 each.

Right:
Ceramic bottle made in Japan, but contents are gone and unknown. Quite possibly a bottle filled with liquor after being imported. Early 1970s. $25-35.

Variety of toys from mid-1970s into the early part of the next decade. All are of hard plastic and all were manufactured in Japan or Taiwan. $5-10 each.

Japanese-manufactured Santa dolls from early 1970s. Made of felt, they sported hard plastic boots, cotton beards, and soft plastic faces. $5-7 each.

Early 1970s mail box for children's greeting cards. $45-55.

70

Indoor Electric Lighting of
Our Trees and Homes

While midget lights all but captured the imagination of most Americans, countless others clung to tradition, getting out their candelabra lights and even bubble lights during this decade. The bubble light's popularity decreased in the late 1960s through the 1970s, but they were not forgotten completely. They were revived in candelabra form, but not successfully, lacking the color variety of the early midget style. Midget bubble lights were being offered, but were somewhat lost on a large tree. Still, they made an impression upon the generation who missed the heyday of the bubble light.

For those using candelabra lights, there were enticements to purchase figural lights like those made in years past. Figurals made in the early 1970s were the Walt Disney sets in both miniature and candelabra. The Walt Disney Corporation did not give permission for these sets being produced and so they could not be marketed. The molding was actually good for the time, but lacked the personality of the earlier sets from the 1930s. Christmas tree bulbs developed by General Electric's Lamp Division for the 1979 season made use of a transparent, colored plastic in a new way and provided the traditional sparkle, while costing less to make and using less energy. The bulb was injection blow molded of butadiene styrene. The bulb was fluted and wrinkled to disperse the light coming from a tiny tubular light source placed inside it. The high efficiency of light transmission of the material allowed the small light source to provide the effect of a larger bulb. Butadiene styrene was chosen because it combined a high degree of clarity with toughness. It was colored in all the traditional holiday colors while retaining its transparency. This eliminated problems that were common with all other lighting products, which were coated and tended to chip and peel.

NOMA-World reintroduced bubble lights in 1975. According to Robert J. Braasch, vice president of sales, "We are keeping in the spirit of this Bicentennial, traditional-inspired period. This type of home décor lighting reflects the basic spirit on which our traditions pivot." Top of the line leaders in this exclusive NOMA category were #2502 (8 lite), C6 Series Bubble Lites, and the #2807 (7 lite) C7 Multiple Bubble Lites. Albert V. Sadacca, president and executive officer of NOMA-World, announced that it agreed in principle to sell all of its stock to INTERPHOTO in February 1975. Sadacca and his brothers were the original founders of NOMA LITES, which was the largest independent manufacturer, importer, and distributor of Christmas tree lights in the country. Sadacca saw the need for product diversification, strengthening its operating base into the toys, hardware, and house ware fields.

John T. Sutler, a lighting specialist with General Electric Co., who annually designed the holiday lighting for the National Christmas Tree emphasized, "decorate tastefully, not wastefully." He further pointed out that "a display of 50 conventional Christmas lights costs less than a dime to burn for five hours a day." Sutler suggested using light bulbs in the same color family. Cool colors such as blue and green as well as warm colors such as red, orange, yellow, and white were to be mixed together for a different artistic effect. When it came to using a floodlight for showing off evergreens, Sutler recommended avoiding red, yellow, amber, and pink lamps, which would turn the tree a muddy brown color. Blue, green, or blue-white would enhance the evergreen colors.

Midget lights changed somewhat this decade in that it was almost universal to have "push in" lamps housed in plastic bases with the two lamp wires folded back against each side of the base. The base was then pushed into a socket where the wires made contact with the base connection. However, the lamps were still wired in an intermediate series basis and sets were not foolproof. The wire was thin and broke easily, and it was more frustrating going through 35 or 50 lamps to find the problem than it had been with the old-fashioned eight. Consequently, consumers who didn't have the time, patience, or knowledge to check for the problem trashed thousands of these sets each year. Midget lights were popular due to their light weight, versatility, low price, and many now were being made weatherproof for outdoor use.

Americans continued to search for "new" ideas and promoted sets with plastic covers of people animals, fruits, etc., over the midget lamps. GE's midget lamp line, "Merry Midget," included plastic covers of Santas, post lamps, kerosene lamps, and tinsel sprays. But their most unusual midget lamp product was the "Twinklettes." Twenty light sets consisted of ten regular midget lamps and the specially constructed twinkle lamps, which blinked on and off but left the regular lights burning constantly, giving a pleasant variety to midget twinkle lamp sets. Another interesting development was the "Drape-A-Lite" set, where lights fell quickly into shape by simply placing an add-on connector on the tree top and subsequently draping lines of lights around the tree from top to bottom in six-foot lengths for six to eight-foot trees.

NOMA introduced a 20-lite fancy set employing "Mini Globes," each bulb looking like a bubble of light. They also introduced a fiber optic tree in a seven-foot size. Their 50,000 ever changing points of light created a fabulous light display, changing in four colors.

Little that was new really gained popularity with the American consumer in the 1970s. If anything it could be said that the "theme trees," where a certain decorating effect was sought, got their start in this decade. However, the 1970s did set the stage for the explosion of interest in Christmas decorating which lay ahead in the 1980s.

In November 1977, the National Consumers League submitted to the Consumer Product Safety Commission its recommended safety standards for midget Christmas tree lights. In that year, between 30 and 40 million midget light strings were on the U.S. market. The light circuit on these strings carried small amounts of current, about 150ma. However, there were concerns that a short-circuit condition could cause a disastrous fire. They also feared that several bulbs in a set might fail in swift succession, forcing the remaining bulbs to carry too much current and subsequently overheat. Or, if some bulbs failed, the bulbs that remain lighted could cascade out, leaving the string operating primarily or exclusively on the shunts in the bulbs. Because shunts generally have a lower resistance than filaments in the bulbs, excess current would flow through the string, causing the insulation to heat to the melting point before either the shunts or the house circuit breaker opened.

"Lighted Ice" boxed set of candelabra base bulbs so popular that they continued to sell very well into the 1970s. $15-20 for boxed set.

Late 1970s GE "Lighted Ice" bulbs. When lit, their colors radiated through the cracked crystals glued to the colored candelabra base bulbs. $15-20 for set.

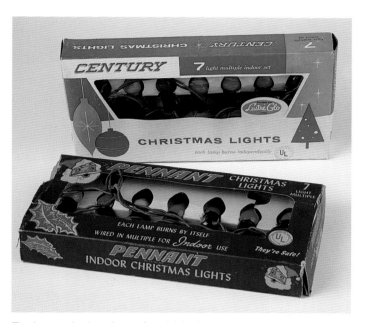

Two inexpensive boxed sets of candelabra base bulbs which still sold quite well in spite of the competitive midget lights. $5-7 for boxed set.

Ever popular NOMA LITEs for indoor decorating. $5-8 for boxed set.

Standard base decorative lights from late 1970s from GE which was a variation on their ever popular "Lighted Ice" sets. $15-20 for boxed set.

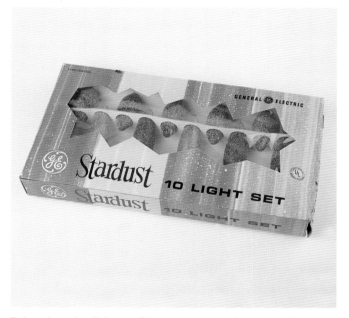

Poinsettia midget light set of the type so popular in this decade. Japan. $15-20 for set.

Early 1970s set of Italian midget lights in snap-on candle shapes. $20-30 for boxed set.

Set of Angel midget lights. Japan. $25-35 for boxed set.

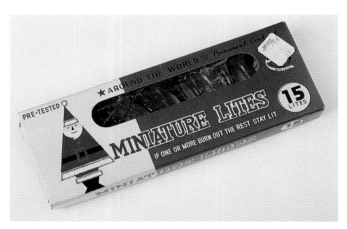

Midget lights advertised as "miniature lights," where if one burned out, the others would stay lit. $5-7 for boxed set.

A 1972 patented motion lamp made of plastic. Shade revolves from heat of bulb inside which illuminates holiday themes. $45-55.

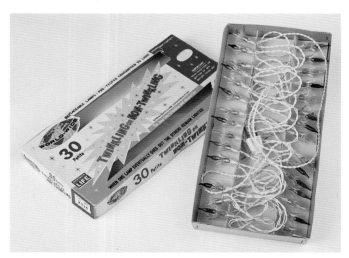

Twinkling and non-twinkling midget light set produced from mid-1960s and sold into early 1970s. $10-15 for boxed set.

Electrified table decoration. House windows light up from candelabra base bulb inserted in back. $10-15 complete with box.

Early 1970s lighted table decoration from Japan. Celluloid Santa, brush trees, and little elves in windows of house. $20-25.

Outdoor Electric Lighting

When President Nixon turned lights out on Christmas 1972, the trim-a-tree industry suffered greatly. The Christmas lighting industry took a nose-dive during the 1973 winter's energy crisis. Although the Federal Energy Administration did not ban holiday lighting, the calls for conservation and the soaring costs of electricity and lights themselves all took a toll. "You can't have the President telling people not to open the refrigerator more than three times a day, and then have lights blazing all over the streets," stated Michael B. Grosso, executive director of New York's Fifth Avenue Association, which, after fifteen years, canceled its annual display. The American Decorators Association and the General Electric Company, whose Cleveland based lamp division made most of the nation's domestically produced Christmas bulbs, released the fact that several years' supply were in inventory at retailers, manufacturers, and importers—one result of the 1973 ban having hit late in the year.

During this energy-conscious age, bulb ratings were stepped down two watts each while their brightness was enhanced by the introduction of transparent color coatings. These transparent coatings, by absorbing less heat, also became safer and cooler to the touch. C7 1/2 were 7-W and the C9s were 9W lamps.

Retailers told Americans that midget tree bulbs used less electricity than regular light bulbs, and, since many people turned off house lights to enhance the tree, a savings could actually result. Many magazines provided us with ideas of how to decorate without lights. They suggested that we trim the tree with light-reflecting ornaments such as small mirrors, glittery bulbs, and gold or silver foil and tinsel. Tree branches could be sprayed with glittery paint, brightly colored Christmas cookies could be hung from these branches, and even popcorn strings would lighten the tree. White or near white decorations would appear extra bright against a dark green background. They further suggested that a small room fan be placed near the tree and be operated at low speed to give an extra glimmer to the tree.

NOEL (National Ornament & Electric Lights Christmas Association) donated lights to light up the Madison Square Park tree with over 3,652 lights. To dramatize the money-saving aspects of lighting trees, Tom Congalton, president, presented a check for $48.24 (which reflected the total cost of electricity for the entire Christmas season) to the Recreation Commissioner, Joseph P. Davidson. So successful was this campaign, and other such promotional efforts, that the lighting industry was able to draw itself out of the dumps. In 1976, most stores reported selling out of electric lights, in some cases almost two weeks before Christmas. Retailers looked to the Carter administration for help with promoting the outdoor decorating of American homes once again like the period before the energy crisis.

John S. Suter, a lighting specialist with the General Electric Company who regularly designed the holiday lighting for the National Christmas Tree near the White House, provided some decorating hints for using midget lights in a November 1976 issue of *Hardware Age.* He suggested light bulbs in the same color family. Cool colors such as blue and green, and warm colors such as red, orange, yellow, and white for suggested for outdoor decorating which was seen from afar. Stutter further suggested that deciduous trees be floodlighted from a single direction to give the tree a definite highlight and shadow pattern. He suggested that shiny ornaments be placed in the tree and then the floodlight be placed directly below to help visually anchor the tree to the ground. Outdoor floodlights were extremely popular in the 1970s for Americans as they lighted their evergreens, other trees, and even the magnificent, elaborate wooden displays which often included Santa in a sleigh complete with reindeer, nativity figures in a scene, carolers and snowmen in various musical poses, and even trios of angels blowing trumpets.

Between 30 and 40 million midget light sets appeared on the U.S. markets in 1977. As a result, new standards for Miniature Electric Christmas Tree Lights and Decorations in 1977 addressed hazards associated with electric shocks and fires. New requirements include mandatory testing of parts such as plugs, connectors, and wires for strength of connections and exposed sources of hazards as well as all products being required to be permanently identified with a name and/or code number of the manufacturer. A life test was added to ensure that the product was not subject to thermal deterioration which could lead to an unsafe condition. A seal or mark signifying such conformance identified all products which conformed to these new standards.

In 1979, General Electric developed a transparent, colored plastic in a new way, and provided the traditional sparkle while reducing manufacturing costs and using less energy. This C 7 1/2 bulb was injection blow molded of butadiene styrene. The bulb was fluted and wrinkled to disperse the light coming from a tiny tubular light source placed inside it. It was virtually unbreakable and cool to the touch. Butadiene styrene was chosen because it combined a high degree of clarity with toughness. The material could be colored in all the traditional holiday colors while retaining its transparency. This eliminated problems common with other bulbs, which were coated and tended to chip and peel. A twenty-caavity mold was employed for bulb production, the largest number of cavities every made in one mold. The record had been twelve.

Empire Plastics Corp. Large 14" Santa into the back of which a candelabra base bulb is inserted. $10-15.

Unmarked hard plastic Santa with sack over back. Electrified by a candelabra base bulb. $8-12.

Angel from 1972. Empire Plastics Corp. 14", $8-10.

Pair of Empire Plastics Corp. Santa figures. Both electrified and used in windows, outside on sidewalks, and even on the edges of roofs. $10-15 each.

Historical Perspective—
Return to European Traditions

In the 1980s, rather than reaching into the future for innovative ideas for Christmas decorating, Americans turned to the past and returned to the old-fashioned decorations of the early 1900s. They returned to this past by purchasing thousands of different ornaments, house decorations, and even artificial trees like those they remembered at their grandparents' houses. In the attempt to recapture the essence of "Christmas Past," this decade perpetuated past Christmas celebrations by using "new" versions of past designs. European decorations once again took on new significance as importers sought high-quality products like those made before World War II. This decade gave new impetus to decorating as countless Americans spent more and more dollars to lavishly decorate their homes. As a result, "Trim-a-Home" departments in stores boasted a sales productivity exceeding $200 per square foot. Thus most stores devoted 500-1,000 square feet to this seasonal display, which was generally set up by October 15 of each fall. American retailers set up early in an attempt to sell as much as possible to a nation which now reached into the past for inspiration. The late 1980s proved to be a golden age for Christmas retailers. Sales were strong despite economic slowdowns and scares.

Most Christmas departments contained few recognizable brands, with at least 50% of this merchandise imported (as much as 90% in some of the larger stores). Retailers shopped Europe, Asia, and United States gift shows throughout the year, planning and buying for this brief, two-and-a-half month department which hoped for an 85%-95% sell-through by December 25. While the previous trend was to sell ornaments by the box, it became evident that this would not work in the 1980s. Americans had complete sets of decorations and many consumers wanted to add one or two each year when they spotted something nice. Americans would rather buy one nice ornament than three or four ordinary ones. They sought ornaments which could be kept in the family and passed from generation to generation.

The best sales were gained by department stores which decorated by themes. Some popular themes included Old World/Victorian, Santa/whimsical, teddy bears, painted wood, gold, silver, brass, plaid, and the traditional holiday colors: red, white, and green. There is no doubt that the 1980s was a decade of "trends." Americans more than ever followed fad after fad in this decade, as certain colors and decorating schemes captured their interests. While nostalgia was in, it gained its own identity with "Country," "Western," and "Southwestern" additions, as each "theme" took its place in decorating trends. Ever-popular was the Victorian look, as well as a medieval style focusing on royalty, castles, and romance. Electronic "gizmos" were in vogue and Americans rushed to buy the latest Santa, be he beating some drums, driving a car, or walking across the floor. In 1983, the most popular buy among retailers was the walking Santa Claus that rang a bell. Made in Taiwan, this toy retailed for $10 in discount stores and for $20 in department stores.

By 1989 two major new themes emerged. One was a "Legendary Christmas," with a mystical, medieval look with castles, angels, and unicorns, incorporating lots of creams and golds. The other was a "Christmas in the Colonies," focusing on Williamsburg and using Williamsburg blues and creams. Especially popular in glass figurals at the end of the decade were animals, with a shift toward forest animals and related objects. Squirrels, mice, and walnuts were extremely popular.

New England families spent the most on Christmas in the middle part of this decade. A study by the Consumer Research Center found that New England families spent an average of $387 in 1986. Ranking next were the Middle Atlantic states, where the average was $360, the Pacific Coast ($323), and the lowest spending area, the Rocky Mountain region ($283). Households in the 45 to 54 age group were the largest purchasers of Christmas items.

In 1980, the National Christmas Tree was only fully lighted for 417 seconds—one second for each day the hostages had been held in captivity. In 1984, the nativity scene was reinstated as being historically and legally appropriate for display during the Pageant of Peace in light of a U.S. Supreme Court decision. This nativity scene had been discontinued in 1973 after the U.S. Court of Appeals for the District of Columbia Circuit decided an argument based upon U.S. Constitutional rights of religious freedom.

In 1982, Rennoc Corporation sponsored a float in the Macy's Thanksgiving Day Parade which celebrated the legend of St. Nicholas and the stocking tradition. The float,

which was seen by millions of people, consisted of ten life-sized, Christmas stocking characters in an entourage headed by Santa Claus.

Two days before Christmas 1985, in Chicago, a man who changed his name to Santa C. Claus died. Five years earlier, Claus changed his name from LeRoy Scholtz. He lived in a red and white house in North Pole, New York, near Lake Placid, where he worked from 1970 to 1979 at a theme park called Santa's Workshop. In his last years, he spent most of his time traveling and making appearances as Santa. Interestingly enough, his natural white hair and beard helped to convince many that he really was Santa Claus.

In this decade, ornaments became the number one Christmas collectible. With an increased emphasis on nostalgic, family-centered Christmases, ornaments were no longer perceived as merely decorative but were invested with feelings of family, tradition, and seasonal memories. More single ornaments were sold than ever before and the individual price for these single ornaments was quite high. To feed this appetite for "old-fashioned-themed decorations," countless importing firms, as well as artisans of the United States, either found their beginnings in this decade or experienced a new spurt of growth. Decorating for Christmas gained immense popularity with Americans, who almost seemed to imitate their earlier Victorian counterparts with a "the more, the better" philosophy.

In 1985, President Bush directed that the lights on the National Christmas Tree be turned down momentarily in support of American hostages in Lebanon and their families at home.

In the mid-1980s, American importers turned more and more to Japan, Taiwan, and Hong Kong. In 1985, imports from these countries had risen over twenty-five percent from the year before. Taiwan was particularly well known for Christmas light sets and novelties such as wooden decorations and unusual garlands. Hong Kong was known for polyethylene garlands and trees, Japan for its metallic film, and Bangkok for its brass ornaments.

Taiwan was still the number one source at the end of the 1980s; but, there was a perceptible shift in Christmas manufacturing underway toward other developing countries, notably The People's Republic of China, Thailand, and the Philippines. Taiwan's economy and labor costs were the principal reasons for this shift. Like Japan before it, Taiwan had moved from being a struggling, developing nation to being a leader in high technology industries such as computers. The shift from Taiwan to The People's Republic of China mirrored the same shift from Japan to Taiwan the previous decade. "Companies want to upgrade their products, so they are trying to get rid of labor-intensive industries. But it will take a while to do this. One way they may be able to stay in the Christmas industry is to design new machinery which could off set labor costs," observed Tom Lin, director of the Far East Trade Service, Inc. in 1989. U.S.-based Christmas suppliers imported more goods from Asia than ever before. High-end suppliers were still importing from European countries, such as West Germany, for crystal ornaments and nutcrackers, and Czechoslovakia and Poland for glass pieces. A few companies had suppliers in Mexico, but internal political regulations and quality problems kept Mexico off the list of primary Christmas supplier nations. By the end of the decade, seventy-five percent of the imports came from Taiwan. About twenty percent were manufactured in mainland China, Thailand, and the Philippines, with the remainder coming from Europe, Japan, Hong Kong, Mexico, South America, and other places.

The 1980s saw a revival of department store displays like those of earlier decades. Designers singled out B. Altman & Company, Lord & Taylor, and Sakes Fifth Avenue in New York as having some of the most beautiful Christmas displays in the country. B. Altman & Co. displayed "The Story of the Kissing Cousins" set in post-Victorian period, and featured a window for the four seasons, ending with an elaborate Christmas part scene complete with a decorated tree, fireplace, and stacks of gifts. Lord & Taylor featured "New York City Landmarks" including the Peter Stuyvestant house, the Robert Murray House, and the William H. Vanderbilt mansion.

Outdoor holiday light festivals continued to expand across America. Two of the largest city light shows were in Kansas City and Niagara Falls. Kansas City, Missouri, was the first shopping district in the country to have outdoor decorative lighting, starting in the late 1920s. In 1983 over 152,000 lights were strung on forty-six miles of wiring. This annual installation required a five-man crew to work 3,000 man-hours over a period of ninety days. The display was lit from Thanksgiving Day to January 2nd.

A similar holiday event in Niagara Falls, New York, commenced in 1981. Over 400,000 lights, painted and lighted displays, and a center of focus on the Rainbow Center shopping area helped to create a Christmas fantasy which attracted much attention from locals as well as tourists. Opening night on Thanksgiving Day drew over 20,000 people.

Christmas Crackers enjoyed renewed popularity in this decade. In recent years College Crackers has purchased several smaller companies producing crackers: Batger's Harlequin Crackers and Rainbow Crackers. In the1980s, a small revival of crackers occurred with new topical designs and concepts appearing on the market. Some recognizable trademarks are Smiths, Caleys, Neilsens, Mansells, Bounty, Unique, Bender, Mason, and College.

Early 1980s photo of Christmas in St. Luke's Church in Watertown, Wisconsin. Greeting card. $2-4.

Sanctuary St. Joseph's Co-Cathedral Catholic Church. St. Joseph, Missouri. December 1985 postcard. $3-5.

Right:
Christmas, 1980 at the Brenner's. Left to right: Karen, Linda, Susie, Julie, and Janet. Paula is seated in middle. Note use of the old traditional German pre-World War II ornaments. $Priceless.

Our Saviour's United Church of Christ. Ripon, Wisconsin, 1983. Elegant example of Lutheran tradition of "Chrismons" (Christ's monograms-church symbols). Greeting card. $2-3.

Right:
Christmas, 1984 in rural Wisconsin. $2-3.

Christmas, 1989 in Princeton, Wisconsin. Left to right: Sister Virginia, Jeanette (Reinl) Brenner, Elizabeth Reinl, Shirley (Reinl) Roehrig, and Dick Roehrig all enjoy the Brenner's Christmas tree.

Aaron Baltz in front of his Christmas tree in Malone, Wisconsin, 1982. Note proliferation of European ornaments collected by his mother. $Priceless.

Christmas, 1985 in Princeton. Bob and Sharon Brenner enjoying the 14-foot Christmas tree in their stairwell. $Priceless.

Our Trees

The National Christmas Tree Growers Association, headquartered in Milwaukee, Wisconsin, stated that about 450,000 acres were devoted to tree production in the United States in the late 1980s. That represented about 15,000 individuals who grew the trees and no other crops. The industry generated about $70-million annually at the retail level and provided more than 100,000 part-time and about 7,500 year-around jobs. A Purdue University Extension Service officer estimated that an acre of growing Christmas trees produced daily oxygen requirements for eighteen people. In 1980, live trees sold from $3 to $5 dollars a foot, causing many to seriously look at purchasing an artificial tree which could be used in successive years.

Artificial trees continued to gain popularity in this decade with consumers much more interested in upscale trees which included more branches and a more realistic appearance. There was a considerable increase in the sales of tabletop trees in the two-foot and four-foot sizes as they were perfect sizes for apartments and institutions. In order to promote the sale of artificial trees, American Tree educated consumers in how to properly set up, shape, and decorate their artificial tree for maximum beauty. The company produced a twelve-page how-to customer manual which it made available to retailers for point-of-sale use. The company also sponsored a decorate-a-tree contest, featured in *Family Circle* magazine which drew over 100,000 responses. In the early 1980s, imports were a small factor in the artificial tree market due to high freight and quality control. In 1982, Marathon Carey-McFall Co. discontinued its artificial tree business, selling the remaining manufacturing equipment and inventory to American Technical Industries, Inc., a division of Papercraft.

A new development in Germany revolutionized the artificial tree market in the early 1980s when they developed short, soft-needled balsam and spruce trees, referred to as "Black Forest" trees. Their incredible realism and natural beauty attracted the attention of American importers. However, importers questioned whether or not Americans would purchase such an expensive tree as these trees were more labor intensive. However, they soon realized that the key to a consumer purchasing a tree was its realistic look. Americans were "put off" by the artificiality of the bottle brush tree.

This innovation came at a time when more and more Americans were switching from live to artificial trees; but, Americans were searching for a "non-artificial" look rather than the traditional bottle brush tree. In 1983, 33 million American homes put up an artificial tree compared with 17.4 million in 1969. Hudson Valley Tree, Inc. had such faith in these short needled varieties that they made a short-needled balsam fir utilizing a solid steel core with branches bound on with filament colored brown and green. Other manufacturers quickly followed suit as Americans were more than willing to pay that extra price for a more realistic-looking artificial tree.

Terry Hermanson, president of Mr. Christmas (and son of current owner), in 1984 predicted the demise of the bottle brush tree when he stated, "The bottle-brush tree is going to be history. People are buying the new looks—fir trees, deluxe trees." Three million artificial trees were sold in 1985 as compared to 30 million real trees. Over forty percent of the sales were to families who already owned one artificial tree and wished to decorate a second, and, in some cases, even a third one. Mr. Christmas began manufacturing ornaments in the late 1950s and artificial trees a few years later by owner Merill Hermanson. Among the firm's firsts was its development of an artificial tree with a real wood trunk.

In the middle of this decade, artificial trees continued their excellent sales. Kurt S. Adler introduced an entire line of German Black Forest trees, following the company's move to silk construction. Mr. Christmas introduced a new tree of the spruce variety, which retailed in the $75-200 dollar range. Companies involved in the artificial tree business included American Tree, Barcana, Commodore Manufacturing, Hudson Valley Tree, Mr. Christmas, Puleo's Mfg., and Rynveld's. In fact, Hudson Valley Tree, Inc. expanded from four employees to over 400 in four short years. In 1985, artificial trees accounted for twenty-five percent of Christmas decoration sales. Retailers quickly discovered that when they decorated the trees in various themes, and placed these theme ornaments below the tree or very near it, sales of both trees and decorations proliferated. By 1989, the majority of artificial tree buyers were repeat customers. According to Jeff Wilner of Mr. Christmas, "Artificial tree users buy natural trees every four years or so, but then they remember all the trouble associated with real trees, and contentedly go back to artificial trees." One of the keys to successful sales was shaping the trees somewhat differently. Tabletop trees as well as floor-to-ceiling trees came in narrow widths which helped fit trees into a small space.

Artificial tree suppliers like Mr. Christmas, Inc. and Puleo's had both domestic and foreign factories. They produced hard-to-ship trees in the United States and the more expensive hard-to-produce trees in the Orient. While most of the items were manufactured in Hong Kong and Taiwan, there was a noticeable shift to mainland China.

Our electronic age was reflected in Radio Electronics, when, in 1987, they provided complete instructions for an electronic Christmas tree composed of a tree-shaped printed circuit board outlined by randomly blinking red, green, and yellow LED's. The base held two AA-batteries with a PC board sandwiched between the base and the tree portion.

One of the most interesting trends was renewed interest in feather trees, spurred in part by historic photographs which chronicled their use. A further impetus to their popularity arose from the "country look" which gained great popularity in this decade. Added to all of this was the fact that these trees were very difficult for collectors to locate and often times these antique trees were not in the best of condition.

Therefore, in the 1980s, a number of individuals commenced to recreate the feather trees of past times. One such individual was Carol Eggert, of Cedarburg, Wisconsin, who made trees in 19, 30, and 36-inch sizes employing feathers, wire branches, wood dowels, and wooden-turned bases. She used turkey feathers, stripped from the quills, dyed with a product usually used to color wool, then wrapped on the branches in the same manner as the old, original trees. Carol Eggert produced trees in green, blue, lavender, white, and silver.

Another early pioneer in the resurgence in feather tree manufacturing was Robert Treadway of North Salem, New York. Treadway led the way through the founding of Crispin Treadway in the early 1980s, devoted to reproducing feather trees like those manufactured in Germany before World War II. With either red berries or candleholders at the ends, his products were recognizable by the red turned pots in which he placed his feather trees. First produced in this country by cottage workers in upper New York State, he eventually turned to Taiwan for the manufacturing of trees to cut down prices to make his trees more affordable. Countless other American manufacturers began feather tree production in the mid- to late 1980s and, while it is impossible to document all of them, certain companies did obtain a strong reputation for quality. But it was Robert Treadway who forged the path.

Robert Treadway tree on left, $75-90. Made in Japan brush tree on right, $30-35.

- convenience construction
- 4" diameter branch
- 3½ - 7½' height
- available in blue or green
- matching wreaths available
- CPG-75 shown

"California Pine" artificial trees as marketed by Puleo's in 1980s. $20-30 each.

- convenience construction
- 2¾" diameter branch
- 4½ - 7½' height
- available in blue or green
- MWG-75 shown

"Midwestern Spruce" as marketed by Puleo's in 1980s. $25-35.

Our Cards

An interview with George L. Parker, vice-president of Hallmark cards in December 1982, revealed some interesting trends to come in this decade. At that time Hallmark was the largest Christmas card company and the number one greeting card company in the world. There were over 672 people in his division—of whom 450 were artists—who labored year-round, and years in advance, to figure out exactly what we were thinking and what we believed, as reflected in what we chose to buy to communicate in our annual Christmas card sending.

In this decade cards illustrated Santa playing golf, jogging, and playing tennis. Animals were popular themes of this decade — Garfield led the pack of cats while dogs and even Miss Piggy, enjoyed her popularity, were immortalized on cards. Black was a great color in the early 1980s. Christmas card sales increased both in unit and dollar volume in 1987. This increase was attributed to families and friends spread out not only in our country, but abroad as well. Also, the primary card consumers—women—were in the work force and had more discretionary income than in the past. Pearl leaf and parchment stock was the designs of choice with consumers moving away from the red and green to Wedgwood blue, silver, and cloisonné. Americana, wildlife, scenic, and Christmas traditionals continued to be the most popular. Hallmark Cards commenced retailing juvenile boxed cards for children to exchange; regional cards featuring cityscapes of metropolises like New York, San Francisco, and Washington D.C. and coastal, rural and desert motifs; and business greeting cards, some of which held business cards.

New colorations and finishes such as hot pink, ice blue, burgundy, crystal green, Paine's gray, pearl zing, hot embossing, suede looks, foil, multi-textures, leaf-stamping, and hot stamping were in evidence in abundance for the Christmas of 1988.

Examples of cards from the 1980s. The ones on the right are hand colored. $1-2 each.

Childrens' books from the 1980s. All printed in China. $2-5 each.

Trio of candy and cookie tins from this decade. All USA made. $5-7 each.

How We Decorated Our Homes and Trees

The traditional red, green, and white continued in popularity, but alternative colors such as apricot, plum, purples, and earth tones caught the eyes of many Christmas decorations purchasers in the early part of this decade. Another trend that emerged in this decade was the licensing characters in the selling of Christmas decorations. E.T. made his debut in 1982; other characters included the Smurfs, the Flintstones, Ziggy, and Garfield.

Much of our tinsel garland and roping came from Wisconsin. PSI of Belgium, Wisconsin, was a division of Holiday Trims, formerly based in Manitowoc, Wisconsin, which produced tinsel garlands in thirty standards colors in a variety of lengths and thickness. Another division—the former Jensen-Fisher Corporation, once based in Los Angeles—produced artificial trees and wreaths. PSI targeted its sales toward the higher end of the market, catering to the "fancier stuff." In 1969, Scott Blade first invested in PSI, then a small business located in Port Washington which at that time produced silk-screened door posters. Blade, who took full control of PSI in 1979, held the title of president and board chairman. He operated the business with his two sons, Curt and Scott, along with twenty-five to fifty employees, depending upon demands.

Individual gift ornaments such as those produced by Hallmark and American Greetings were popular choices for Christmas presents in this decade. Prices ran from $3 to $10 dollars each. Ribbon as a tree decoration quickly became the fad and many companies even produced ready-made bows for quick tree decorating. Theme-decorating was another trend—coordinating color and theme throughout the home—and this concept grew with each passing year of this decade. Popular themes included the Muppets, Super Heroes, wooden, Christmas goodies, gold, and silver. Lots of improvisations occurred as well, utilizing silk flowers, baby's breath, ribbon bows, and other decorative trims on trees. Glass as well as satin ornaments in solid colors were sold by the thousands to help carry out color themes on trees. One other trend continued to emerge—novelty ornaments (or figural ornaments as collectors refer to them). Santa Claus, pinecones, umbrellas, cars, and multitudes of figural shapes made up almost sixty percent of the market in the early 1980s, with glass balls being about twenty-five percent and satin fifteen percent. The most popular colors were red, silver, and gold. Individually boxed ornaments were the real growth segment of the ornament business in the early part of this decade. Glass represented seventy percent of the sales in ornaments, with a sharp decline in satin ornament sales. The bulk of glass ornaments sold in the $2 to $4 dollar range.

Animated musical dolls, cookie baking Santas, whirling skaters, and other such figures, previously limited to store displays, started to be used in American homes when families discovered that they, too, could have these "moving" decorations in their homes. A wide selection of moving fixtures, ranging from complete vignettes to licensed collections to talking animals found enormous growth in this decade. In 1982, one million dollars worth of such figures were sold. By 1986 over ten million dollars was spent by Americans who purchased such items for prices reaching to $199. Companies who retailed such items included James A. Cole, Bronner's of Frankenmuth, Michigan, R-K International, and David Hamberger of New York. One of the hottest sellers was Mrs. Santa Claus mixing a bowl of cookie batter while a group of "elfettes" help her bake pies and cakes. Animated figures became increasingly sophisticated with computer-controlled movement.

In 1989, animated figures were especially strong sellers on the West Coast. Rennoc Corporation was one of key players in this segment of the market with such strong sellers as Mr. and Mrs. Santa, boy and girl figures dressed in elaborate red, green, and tartan plaid-trim, angels, and Dickensian carolers. Rennoc bought all of the trademarks and design copyrights when Display Arts filed for bankruptcy in 1989. Rennoc offered eighty-one animated pieces for Christmas that year. Prices at the end of this decade ranged from a low of $33 for a simple, smaller animated figure to over $220 for elaborate settings.

Santa cookie jar. Marked by owner "Christmas 1983." $20-25.

Santa planter. Marked "Japan" with paper sticker. $7-10.

Santa teapot. Notice tiny cup at end of hand which acts as spout. $35-40.

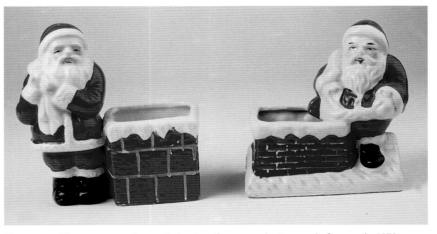

Two types of Japanese-manufactured planters. Common planters made from early 1970s through early 1980s. $15-18 each.

Japanese planter imported by Enesco. $10-15.

Santa cookie plate which doubled as a wall decoration. Japan. Mid-1970s to early 1980s. $10-15.

Santa ashtray. Paper label identifying it as "Japan." $7-9.

Unmarked flower vase. Found in 1980s collection of ceramic items at a Christmas estate sale. $7-10.

American Influences on Glass Ornaments

Hallmark Ornaments

One of the most familiar names, due to their greeting card history, continued to gain new respectability in the decorations market. They continued to provide an entire new dimension to Christmas with a line of limited edition ornaments. As early as the late 1970s, Hallmark produced ornaments for our trees; but, the 1980s witnessed a mania as collectors' clubs were born and a huge market created for limited edition decorations and lights.

In 1980 Hallmark introduced seventy-six new designs, eighteen more than they offered in 1979. Seven commemorative ball ornaments were inaugurated: Son, Daughter, Grandparents, Dad, Mother, Mother and Dad, Grandfather, and Baby's First Christmas for a black child. Pastel colored, unbreakable "cameo" designs were introduced. Made of acrylic, they featured delicate, milk-white "cameo" reliefs on soft pastel backgrounds. By 1980, collectors adding to their collection purchased fifty-five percent of their ornaments.

In 1982, Hallmark celebrated its tenth issue year by introducing three new series of collectible ornaments: Holiday Wildlife series, the Tin Locomotive series, and the Clothespin series. That year, for the first time, Hallmark stamped their ornaments with an identifying Christmas tree symbol or the words "first in a series." An edition number was also printed in the tree symbol to mark the ornament's Issue date. In 1983, they added porcelain ornaments.

In 1984 Hallmark introduced Holiday Magic Lighted Ornaments as a natural extension of the tradition of decorating the tree with electric lights. Hallmark designers and technicians had a four-fold goal in mind during this developmental stage. The ornaments were to be beautiful, unique, easy to use, and safe. Packaged with complete instructions, the ornaments were fashioned to fit easily onto midget light strings. The first year's lights included a village church, sugarplum cottage, city light, Santa's workshop, Santa's arrival, nativity, stained glass, Christmas in the Forest, Brass Carousel, and All are Precious.

In the last half of this decade numerous new looks were added in an attempt to meet customer's requests for ornaments that looked homemade and fashioned of natural materials such as wood and fabric. Due to their immediate success, lighted ornaments were available in many more varieties in each successive year of production. In recent years, Hallmark has continued to provide new creative ornaments, lights, and decorations for our trees and homes.

Edward Philip Franke, Jr., one of the pioneers of the trim-a-tree industry, died late November 1981. The retired chief executive of George Franke & Sons had become president in 1951, taking over from his father. Franke's grandfather founded the firm in 1868. At its peak, the firm produced more than forty million Christmas decorations a year. Frank was president until 1969. When the company was sold to Marathon Manufacturing Co., he became chief executive officer.

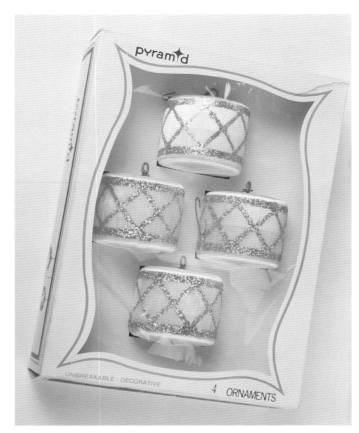

Set of Pyramid drums. Satin over Styrofoam. $3-5 for boxed set.

Hallmark commemorative ornaments. $3-5 each.

Examples of Corning Glass Works with shrink wrapped sleeves around the glass with different commemorative scenes. $7-10 each.

European Influences on Glass Ornaments

Italy

Italian figurals gained great popularity due to their quality, subject material, and availability in the 1980s. Centered on the Lake Como region in Italy, these ornaments continue to be blown in a number of small factories which have banded together to form a loose association. Some factories disappeared in this decade. Darlo Moranduzzo, once a large producer of glass ornaments, changed to primarily an import business which wholesales nativity sets, garlands, and trees. Galvas, once also a family involved in manufacturing glass ornaments, switched to producing plastic tree decorations for the European market. Still another, the Bizzocchi family, closed its business in the late 1980s. But a solid core of four factories continued to thrive and produce countless figural ornaments for the American public. The Brambilla family (known as SAVA), the Terruzzi family (known as Soffieria De Carlini S.A.S.), the Mortelman brothers (known as Mortelmans S.N.C.), and Enrico Scaletti (known as LAVED) are the four producers of Italian glass figural ornaments. The majority of these are located in Bellagio with De Carlini being located in Macherio.

In this decade Soffieria De Carlini S.N.C. was the principal producer of glass figural ornaments for the American market. Other companies were involved, but they did not match the quantity and variety of figural ornaments that came out of this factory, located near Milan. This business was (and continues to be) operated by Rosa (daughter of the original De Carlini family), her husband Guilio Terruzzi, and their son Luca. Together these three family members, with their employees, carefully design, plan, and create hand-crafted glass ornaments of high quality. This workshop was founded in 1947, with the inspiration of Enrico DeCarlini. Enrico was a gifted man with a great sense of inventiveness and fantasy. Enrico's father studied at the famous Brera Academy in Milan, so he developed a strong background in sculpture. Enrico was assisted by his daughters, Rosa and Maria Luisa, and by his wife, Elisa. Rosa became involved in the business as a very young girl by helping paint and hand-decorate the glass figural ornaments. Her interest continued to grow and grow as she developed a true love for producing these glass tree ornaments. Maria Luisa was extremely artistic and is known for her fabulous hand-painted balls and pear-shaped ornaments. It is Maria Luisa's artistic skill which attracted the attention of Wally Bronner, who observed these ornaments displayed by the De Carlini family at the Toy Fair in Milan in the early 1980s.

Wally Bronner wanted to buy these religious-themed painted ornaments and thus become the first American customer of this factory. Bronner then became fascinated with the free-blown figural ornaments produced by this family and he began to import both the hand-painted ornaments of Maria Luisa and the figural ornaments and sold them in his Michigan-based store. There is no doubt that Bronner's promotion of these Italian glass figural ornaments helped to spark the interest that promoted a huge growth in the manufacturing of such glass figural ornaments in Italy.

Their son Luca also became involved at a very early age by helping with blowing ornaments during his summer vacations from school, boxing ornaments, and helping in any manner he could. His love for producing ornaments led to his joining the family business in partnership with his parents in 1985. All their ornaments are hand-blown in the old manner, meaning, shaped by paddles as the glass bubble is slowly blown. Trained glass-blowers (many of whom are young) carefully heat the tube of glass, blow, shape, and create the many different figurals. It must be noted that the creation of these glass figurals is indeed an artistic achievement since these figurals are not blown from a mold. The process is somewhat similar to the process used by German glass blowers.

However, it does differ in that hands, feet, and other appendages are formed by heating a tiny tube of glass and then that tube is annealed onto the basic figure. Once completed, these are put to the side to be decorated by other individuals. The next step includes dipping the ornament into a pearl lacquer to give it a soft shine. Currently, most of the De Carlini ornaments are dipped in this pearl lacquer and not silvered inside as done in previous decades. Once dry, they are hand-painted. Clothing, ribbon, and even hair are added to these glass figurals. Thus, each one of these ornaments is handled by different artisans who all have their area of expertise in preparing some very unique and creative figurals for the American market.

The manufacturing of Christmas ornaments in Italy also differed from other European countries in that each family had its own factory for the production of their Christmas ornaments. All of the work was done in the factory, unlike in Germany where much of it was still done in individual homes. Each Italian factory averaged about forty employees, of which there were from ten to fifteen blowers in every large factory, each with their own specialty. In addition, approximately ten artists were responsible for the individual painting and the addition of fabric and other trims. The painting was done by skilled artisans, carefully trained and cultivated. The resulting Italian ornaments were becoming increasingly collectible due to their individual artistic detail and creativity. Phantom of the Opera, Christopher Columbus, Smurfs, and countless other personalities were blown each year, adding to the already numerous items being produced.

These Italian ornaments reflected our culture in the 1980s, as German ornaments reflected our culture before World War II. These ornaments became extremely popular and their price did not dampen the spirits of Americans. In 1984, $25 Italian figural ornaments were almost entirely sold out in the United States, sending importers scrambling to assemble a line of ornaments for the succeeding year.

1980s Italian blown figural ornaments. Top to bottom, left to right: Mother Goose, $45-55; football player, $40-50; Raggedy Ann, $50-60; Mrs. Santa Claus, $35-45; Raggedy Andy, $50-60; Christmas mouse, $40-50.

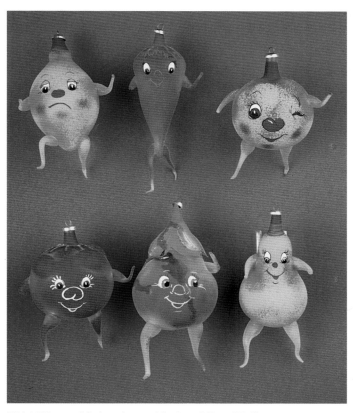

Mid-1980s set of fruit and vegetable shaped figural Italian ornaments including lemon, carrot, orange, tomato, grape, and pear. $45 each. $300-350 for complete set.

Mid-1980s Italian ornaments manufactured in area of Bellagio. Left to right, top to bottom: Pig with red bandanna, $35-45; Seated bear, $45-55; Mouse with annealed tail, $55-65; Little kitten with whiskers, $40-50; Dancing pig, $50-60; Seated kitten, $40-50.

Mid-1980s elaborately trimmed Italian ornaments from the De Carlini factory near Milan. Left to right, top to bottom: Colonial man with hair, $40-45; sea horse, $40-50; Colonial lady, $40-45; Daisy headed boy, $55-65; Daisy headed girl, $55-65; Daisy skirted girl, $60-70.

Late 1970s into mid-1980s Italian ornaments attributed to LAVED. Left to right, top to bottom: Elephant Uncle Sam, $80-90; Santa bell with clapper, $70-80; Dolphin, $65-75; Pinocchio, $60-70; Clown with flask, $65-75; Clown with yellow necktie and cardboard hat, $70-80.

Mid-1980s Italian ornaments attributed to LAVED in Bellagio. Left to right, top to bottom: Bear with heart, $35-45; Lobster, $85-95; Monkey with fabric bow, $40-50; Dinosaur (red), $50-60; Dinosaur (green), $65-75.

Late 1980s Snow White and Seven Dwarfs set. Blown by De Carlini family. $380-425 for set.

Stylish late-1980s Italian blown ornaments. Attributed to De Carlini family. Left to right, top to bottom: Blue flapper girl in swimsuit, $65-75; Harlequin figure in red, $60-70; Flapper girl in black suit, $65-75; Harlequin figure in blue, $60-70; Girl dressed in winter finery, $60-70; Elegant Lady of the Night, $85-95.

Mid-1980s Italian ornaments. Left to right, top to bottom: Papa bear, $60-70; Alice in Wonderland, $60-70, Mama bear, $60-70; Little kitten with hair, $40-50; Goldilocks (original version to go with illustrated three bears), $75-85; Baby bear, $65-75.

Statue of Liberty. Original 1986 commissioned ornament by Bronner's to commemorate the Statue of Liberty's 100th birthday. $95-105.

Germany

While companies in West Germany flourished and grew in size, the state-owned VEG in East Germany in the area of Lauscha struggled with its existence. While it continued to formulate one huge cooperative, the production itself still was subject to huge tariffs and its reputation was yet to be established as a quality line. In 1984, the VEB finally concluded its formation of a cooperative by connecting itself to the companies in Lauscha and Steinheid. Finally in 1983, the VEB had its own booth at the Nuremberg Toy Fair, which allowed East Germany to promote and market their goods. Their wares were quickly purchased and orders for many more thousands of ornaments were taken. Thus, finally there was a start to success.

Heinz Matthai K.G. of Coburg was one of Germany's largest exporters of glass ornaments in this decade. Like so many other young men, Heinz Matthai was a soldier while his father, Louis, conducted the family ornament business, which had been founded by his father, Bernhard, in Steinach. Heinz Matthai was the third generation of this family to continue in the glass ornament business. Their firm of collector-owners of molds was established in 1873 at Steinach near Lauscha in the Thuringian Wald. Heinz died in 1985, and currently the business is being run by Michael Matthai. At the end of this decade, they had over 580 molds in their possession. The firm produced figural ornaments as well as balls, bells, treetops, teardrops, reflectors, and ovals. These were all mouth blown and then hand-formed using special tools to shape the glass into many patterns.

The glass blower-family Eichhorn, which comes from Lauscha in the Thuringian Forest, produced mouth-blown glass and Christmas tree decorations in the fourth generation. In the beginning of the twentieth century, Klara Eichhorn, the grandmother of the present proprietor Erwin Eichhorn, Jr., made up the decorated iridescent glass creations. This tradition was carried on by her son, Erwin Eichhorn, Sr. After the division of Germany, the Eichhorn family moved to the Federal Republic of Germany and established itself in Neustadt bei Coburg. This business was consequently managed by Erwin Eichhorn, Jr. and his wife Walburga. They supervised the production of more than 2,000 different types of balls, hearts, stars, discs, teardrops, cones, treetops, and molds in the old German style. Their daughter Birgit assisted them in making creations of her own and keeping up the traditions as the fourth generation. Birgit and her family were especially proud of their very large ornaments such as a 12-inch full figure Santa, their 10-inch

Santa head, and their 12-inch nutcracker. In March 1993, Eichhorn was purchased by Inge-Glas. Much of their production was combined into one giant operation. However, large mouth-blown figurals continued to be produced under the "Eichhorn" name. These exquisite, huge, detailed figurals were considered to be some of the most lavish and ornate figurals produced in Germany in the 1980s.

The company, Käthe Wohlfahrt GmbH & Co. K.G., in Rothenburg ob der Tauber, offered the most extensive inventory of traditional German Christmas decorations anywhere in the world. The handmade decorations are sold mainly in year-round Christmas specialty stores.

Harald Wohlfahrt pioneered the first year-round Christmas store when he envisioned the design in 1979. Käthe Wohlfahrt reached international recognition in 1981, when the "Weihnachtsdorf, or Christmas Village, opened on Herrngasse in Rothenburg ob der Tauber. Wohlfahrt states, "Our 'Weihnachtsdorf' is a unique retail store that attracts people from near and far. Hometown folk, tourists from all over the world, and leading national and international retailers come to visit our stunning store in the small romantic city of Rothenburg above the Tauber River. Our customers become so enchanted with the store's warm atmosphere, the dazzling displays, and the superbly crafted merchandise that they often pay return visits for the sheer pleasure of it."

As Käthe Wohlfahrt Christmas stores grew in popularity, Wilhelm's involvement with the business also grew, leading to his decision to focus his energies exclusively on the company. At this point, it was determined that a larger showroom and more retail space were a must. The search for store property outside of Herrenberg brought Wilhelm moments of frustration and extreme disappointment. What seemed to be tragic developments for the company initially were followed by opportunities, however, that led to the establishment of a Christkindlmarkt in Rothenburg ob der Tauber and the further growth of the Käthe Wohlfahrt Company. The new Christkindlmarkt opened in 1977 as the first year-round Christmas specialty store in Europe. Contrary to prevailing opinion in the town, the business' growth was unstoppable.

From its inception, Käthe Wohlfahrt was a family business that involved every member. Wilhelm and Käthe, of course, were in charge of overall operations and sales at the weekend bazaars. Grandpa Willi became a specialist in packing and loading, and in repairing broken items, as well as serving customers in Herrenberg. Grandma Johanne looked after the children and helped Grandpa with customer service. The children took the responsibility of loading and unloading goods, packing and unpacking, sorting and labelling.

As the business grew and as family members matured, responsibilities changed. Wilhelm and Käthe eventually concentrated much of their attention on purchasing merchandise. Warehousing and logistics also demanded their focus. Birgitt helped her father with the bookkeeping and Carmen with sales. While a university student, Harald, devoted time to setting up a marketing structure and taking care of the strategic organization of the company. At this stage of the company's development, Harald became its creative force, and persistently worked on its image. He held internal courses for sales people, trained personnel on decorating and merchandise presentation, and developed a dress code for his store personnel. He envisioned and created the unique Käthe Wohlfahrt stores that we know and love today and the internationally famous "Weihnachtsdorf," the Christmas Village.

A master glassblower training youth in producing Thuringer tree ornaments at VEB Glasschmuck in Lauscha, East Germany, 1983.

An East German machine designed to mass produce ornaments. More common shapes were produced this way such as the pine cones illustrated.

Glassblower shown blowing large glass ball "at the lamp" in his own cottage. Lauscha, East Germany. 1982.

Finishers decorating ornaments at VEB Glasschmuck, Lauscha, a state-owned company. East Germany.

Artist finishing a fancy tree top at VEB Glasschmuck in Lauscha, East Germany.

Color catalogue page from mid-1970s East German VEB government co-operative factory.

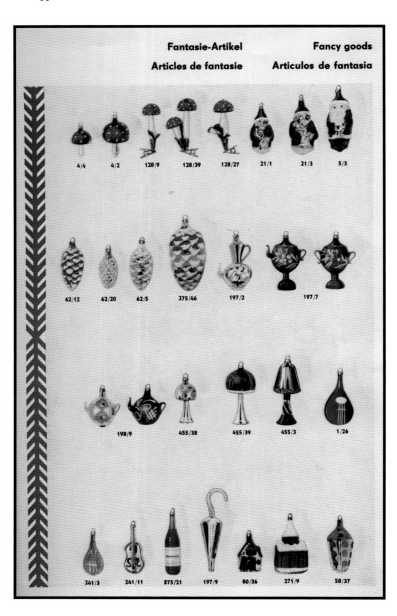

Krebs & Sohn of Rosenheim, West Germany. Catalogue page from early 1980s illustrating figural ornaments still being produced in Germany from old moulds.

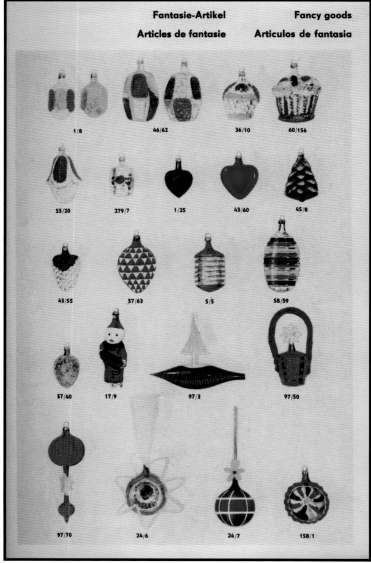

Krebs & Sohn of Rosenheim, West Germany. Catalogue page from early 1980s illustrating wire-wrapped (with gold wire) ornaments still being produced in Germany from old moulds.

It's beginning to look like Christmas

398 Sears ALL

Celebrating the 50th Edition of our Holiday Wish Book "Wrap up a beautiful Christmas at Sears"

West German blown ornaments with plastic tops indicating origin. All blown in original pre-World War II moulds. Mushroom, $3-5; Indian head, $6-8; squirrel with nut, $2-4.

Early 1980s East German ornaments, but sold as West German due to the high tariffs imposed on Eastern European items. Bird with spun glass tail on clip, $10-12; little boy in gold suit, $10-15; large elaborate pine cone, $5-8; clown, $7-9.

Mid-1980s West German ornaments. Left to right, top to bottom: Zeppelin, $10-15; Acorn, $3-5; Man in the moon, $15-20; Polar bear, $25-30; Teddy bear, $12-15.

Fruit and vegetable ornaments from various glass blowers, all in the West Germany region. $6-9 each.

American Importers and Manufacturers of the Decade

Christopher Radko

Christopher Radko had his start in a most unfortunate way when one Christmas, in the early 1980s, his family's tree fell and a good portion of the Radko's antique family ornament collection was destroyed. After searching for a period of time, he realized that he could not find people who created "these terrific large glass Christmas ornaments anymore." On a trip to Poland after that, he accidentally located an artisan who agreed to re-create the ornaments Radko knew as a child if he could describe exactly what he wanted. Radko grabbed a pencil and started to sketch, a sketch that launched him into an ornament business.

When Radko decorated his tree with these newly created treasures, people wanted to know where he purchased such beautiful ornaments. "The results were breathtaking." After a few years of weeding out suppliers, Radko settled on a team of Polish glass workers because of the quality they had provided. "As a consumer, I had seen too many sloppy paint jobs and flimsy thin ornaments offered in stores. I insisted on using durable glass and having the painted details accurate and consistent." His first catalog was produced in 1989 and included only ornaments created in Poland.

Array of West German ornaments of this decade, illustrating the many different figurals once again blown from old almost-forgotten moulds. Note the large amount of silver showing which is indicative of this 1980s period. $4-15 each.

Some of the late 1980s ornaments produced in Poland and marketed by Christopher Radko. Left to right, top to bottom: Smitty, $45-55; Cat rattle, $60-70; Little girl with rabbit, $65-75; Horn with large face, $65-80; Cowboy Santa, $65-75; Santa in long underwear, $75-85; elf, $50-60; Santa on pear shaped ornament, $55-65; Patrick with bunny, $75-85.

Right:
Some of Christopher's early ornaments blown in Poland. Left to right, top to bottom: Green frog, $45-55; Einstein Kite, $85-90; Peacock on purple ball, $75-85; Madonna and child, $45-55; Santa with tree, $35-45; Lion head, $75-85; Aztec bird, $85-95; Tiger head, $65-75; Purse, $65-75.

Old World Christmas

Many American companies quickly turned to Germany for old-fashioned tree ornaments like those made before World War II. Old World Christmas was founded in 1981 when the owners, Tim and Beth Merck, realized a void in the market for high quality, collectible Christmas ornaments and decorations. When Old World Christmas first introduced its ornaments to the market, glass ornaments from Europe were of very inferior quality and offered no collectible value. Old World Christmas believed that collectors would actively seek exceptional Christmas ornaments and in 1984 the German family workshop of IngeGlas was commissioned to produce the Mercks' design concepts for importation to the United States. These items proved to be extremely popular and the original line of glass ornaments was expanded to include additional Christmas collectibles and giftware.

The Muller-Blech of Inge-Glas was a natural choice for Old World Christmas as the Muller's founded Lauscha in 1597 where the art of German glassblowing originated. Further contributing to the history of glass ornaments in the 1800s, the Muller-Blech family invented the metal cap for glass ornaments. This metal cap is still being used today. The glass ornaments that Inge-Glas produces today exclusively for Old World Christmas are created in the same centuries-old art that has been passed down through the ages by their ancestors.

In 1985 Old World Christmas and Inge-Glas developed the first ever non-round suspension ring hanger (ornament cap) to distinguish their ornaments in the marketplace. The exclusive star-shaped hanger that proudly topped each ornament was an Old World/Inge Glass registered trademark that guaranteed fine craftsmanship, original design, and collectibility. The "star cap" became the symbol collectors seek when acquiring Old World Christmas heirlooms.

Old World Christmas also claimed an industry first in 1984 with the introduction of slip-on glass light covers. The light covers were fashioned after turn-of-the-century Christmas lights and were designed to slip-on over mini-lights. They were produced both in molded glass and bisque porcelain featuring fine detailing and hand-painting. The production of these light covers was recently moved from Taiwan to the Inge-Glas factory in Germany.

Old World Christmas, founded by Tim and Beth Merck in 1980, became a dominant force in the recreation of German glass ornaments in this country. The majority of their 5,000 plus ornaments were made from antique molds smuggled from East Germany into West Germany by Klaus Mueller-Blech's elderly grandmother. She was allowed to cross the border between East and West Germany due to her age. Each time she crossed the border, she would carry half of several molds. If she were stopped, she would tell the border guards that she was taking the molds for her grandchildren to play with in the sand. Since half molds had no value, they let her pass.

Inge Muller-Blech, painting old world moulded ornaments in early years of their business at Inge-Glas, West Germany.

Some of the earlier Inge-Glas blown by Klaus Muller Blech and his father and mother, Heinz and Inge, in Coburg, Germany. Note the ornaments with the familiar star-shaped hook later adopted as the trademark of Old World Christmas. $5-25 each.

Heinz Muller-Blech, blowing glass ornaments in the early years of his business at Inge-Glas, West Germany.

Old World Christmas ornaments from mid-1980s. Germany. $15-20 each.

Variety of Santa shaped figural ornaments from Old World Christmas, the rarer being the Santa on horse clip-on and the Santa airplane ornament. $10-45 each.

Inge-Glas Santa tree top from the late 1980s. $25-30.

D. Blumchen & Company

Importing some very interesting high-quality European Christmas decorations as well as reproducing some in this country, D. Blumchen & Company, Inc., a mail order house started for the express purpose of reproducing antique Christmas decorations, was incorporated in 1985. Deborah L. Boyce (daughter) was President, Diane S. Boyce (daughter), Vice-president, and Beatrice Blum Boyce (mother) was the Secretary-treasurer. The name "Blumchen," loosely translated, means "little flowers." All three were holiday collectors, especially of Christmas. But price, poor condition, and scarcity combined to render their efforts difficult. In the early 1980s, better department stores and carriage trade shops, which had handled traditional Christmas items, were not carrying them; often times these stores were taken over by disinterested conglomerates. Although they were not pleased with what they were able to buy, they did not realize why the beautiful blown glass, colorful Santas, delightful paper items, and old-fashioned tinsels, which had previously been imported from Europe, weren't available any longer.

Their first catalog featured their own line of custom-crafted antique reproductions. When they decided to expand by directly importing from Europe, they assumed almost everything they wanted to sell would be readily available. On their first buying trip in 1985, they were surprised to find that these items were not easy to find. Indeed, most seemed to have disappeared off the face of the earth. This lack of pre-made products wasn't too great a problem because Blumchen was still small, and they just needed a few interesting things to expand their line. But, as years went by and their company grew, they became increasingly alarmed at the rate old-style European and American decorations were disappearing under the onslaught of more inexpensive decorations imported from Asia.

As Christmas collectors and enthusiasts, they decided they should try to do something to stem the tide. This led to their greatest challenge, perhaps one could even call it Blumchen's "raison d'être:" preservation, re-introduction, and re-creation of the fine quality, old-style, traditional products that did really represent "The Best of Christmas Past." This proved to be a more difficult task than imagined. The attitude of manufactur-

Right:
Assortment of ornaments imported, trimmed, and prepared for the American market by Blumchen's in 1986. Glass, cotton, paper, chenille, and cardboard were represented in this selection.

ers in Germany was "we used to but we don't any more." "We can't any more." "We won't any more." This was followed by "Why don't you buy these nice, modern style products?" They were quite amused that Beatrice and her daughters wanted reproductions of old ornaments. "Don't you know that isn't modish (fashionable) anymore?" Many Europeans seemed to be unaware of their history and the fabulous creations they exported to the rest of the world.

Partly to augment the pictures of antique ornaments they had always taken with them on buying trips to the Nuremberg Spielwarenmesse, and partly to overcome the language barrier, they prepared their "bag of tricks." They bought antique ornaments and removed the old crinkly wire, and bought traditional pieces of "bouillon and kontille." When they arrived at stands of manufacturers who had previously told them it was too much trouble and that no one knew the skills anymore, they finally agreed to make one piece or another. Beatrice explains best in her own words: "In some instances, when we couldn't get anyone to reproduce old style ornaments, particularly our Victorian Whimsey tinseled ornaments, we collected authentic old, and authentic new supplies and had the reproductions made in house. We would then bring this example to Germany. We would then tell how them the Victorian Whimseys were presented in our catalog. When they thought some other European company had made it, all of a sudden they were able to do the same type of ornament for us." The company that currently makes their Whimseys had no knowledge of how to use tinsel wire anymore, so they had to bring in an elderly crafter to teach them how to wrap the blown glass ornaments in tinsel wire. Because of their expertise in doing design work and in-house crafting, Blumchens was able to give the glass blowers in Germany tips on how to use bouillon. Thus, Blumchens began to be known for their authentic "one of a kind" wire-wrapped ornaments.

1989 Victorian Whimsey Collection by Blumchen's. Each German ornament was hand wrapped in real silver Eisdraht and Leonic crinkle wire, then finished with silk flowers and Dresden scraps. $35-45 each.

1989 "Prince of Peace" tree top from Blumchen's of their own design; the German wax baby is nestled into a bed of golden tinsel and surrounded by a spray of silk flowers accented with Dresden scraps. 10", $75-95.

Gerlach's of Lecha

Another retail business was Gerlach's of Lecha in Emmaus, Pennsylvania, basically a mail-order business dealing in Christmas items from Germany. Bob and Sylvia Gerlach had a deep interest in glass for many years which led to their business of the direct importation of Christmas ornaments.

Unlike any other retail Christmas-oriented business in this country, the Gerlachs of Lecha had its roots solely in the "Christmas industry." Gerlach's had its beginnings in 1968 when Bob and Sylvia saw some stained glass pieces to be hung in the window. Like so many of their German ancestors, they decided to learn how to create these items themselves. From their research into German stained glass, they learned much about early Pennsylvanian Christmas ornament designs. The results of this early research were compiled in *Christmas in Scherenschnitte* by Sylvia Gerlach. Roberta, a daughter in the armed forces, sent home some German ornaments while she was stationed in Germany. This piqued their interest in European decorations. Their first importation of the hand blown glass Christmas ornaments occurred in 1982 when the Gerlachs attended the International Toy Show in Nuremberg, Germany, and were introduced to these glassblowers. They obtained their first European crafting supplies at this fair as well.

Over the course of the next several years, the Gerlach family personally traveled yearly to Germany and developed a friendly rapport with their mentor, the late Heinz Matthai, owner of Heinz Matthai KG in Coburg, Germany. He personally rebuilt his family's business after World War II and was known for his benevolence toward his employees. After Matthai's death in 1985, the Gerlachs moved on to carry other ornaments made by Inge KG.

These glass artisans still used the plaster of Paris molds, complete with wire bands used to clamp the mold's sections into position and to help to reinforce the molds. The mouth-blown process of producing ornaments had not changed to a very large extent, with an experienced blower producing 500 and 600 ornaments a day (many more if the mold is smaller and simpler). One difference did occur in the silvering of ornaments since in the 1980s they were immersed into a vat of electrically heated warm water and shaken until the heat of the water acted as a catalyst to create the chemical action which made the silver adhere to the glass. Gentle shaking was very necessary so that even silvering would be the final outcome.

Throughout the course of their business in the 1980s, they offered a vast array of crafted blown glass figurals, including such things as a Keystone cop, belsnickel (stern-faced Father Christmas figure), pipe-smoking Indian, various angels, snowmen, pickles, and a sailor at the helm. Hand-twisted glass icicles produced in clear, blue, green, red, or yellow, figural light covers for midget lights, and countless other ornaments for the tree were offered.

But ornaments were not the only items sold by Gerlach's. Upon publication of *Pennsylvania German Folk Art Christmas Tree*, written by Sylvia Gerlach in 1983, the family concentrated a portion of their efforts on the made-at-home decorations. With the emphasis on the do-it-yourself Christmas, the Gerlachs soon imported many of the hard to find crafting supplies such as Dresden trims, metallic trims, and chromolithographs. They were located in Emmaus, Pennsylvania, which was open by appointment. They opened a second store in a recently renovated factory-turned-shopping-mall which was open year round. The Gerlachs continued to maintain a high standard of quality in all of their items. Unfortunately, Gerlach's went out of business in the early part of the next decade. Robert became quite ill and Roberta closed out the business. In 1993, there was no longer a catalog and they were closed.

Five examples of the type of ornaments imported and marketed by Gerlach's in 1986.

Santa's Choice

Originally begun in 1945 as a nursery and garden center, this business gradually expanded to include holiday items. This family owned and operated business was started by Thomas Strickfaden, who conceived of the idea for a year-'round Christmas shop in 1975 and imported a large number of German mouth-blown ornaments every year; among the ornaments imported were the "Inge Glass Collection" from Klaus Muller-Blech. An early 1980s catalog lists such items as the musical clown with drum, a heart, lantern, automobile, turkey, and various lamps. When Strickfaden encountered an allergic reaction to plants, he needed to find a new line of work. With a marketing minor, opening a full-time Christmas business was only natural. His father Joseph heartily approved and the business was launched in 1975.

In 1981, full figured elephants, mushrooms, lamps, teddy bears, ladybugs, doll's heads, fish, owls, ducks, a turkey in front of a house, and other such ornaments were featured. One of the first catalogs, just a line sketch of ornaments, featured such ornaments as the Santa in basket, a clip-on candle, clip-on drum and Santa, teddy bear with heart on chest, a glockenspiel, Christ in the hay, and a Santa in the chimney.

Santa's Choice, Inc. was started as a new wholesale division of Strickfaden's in 1982. This line was made available to larger department stores as well as to local independents. Showrooms were set up in Columbus, Dallas, Atlanta, New York, and Chicago. A 1983 color brochure lists such ornaments as the gnome in tree trunk, the musical clown with accordion, a locomotive, Indian in canoe, a genie, and Santa in auto. Santa's Choice was a central figure in the continued importation of German figurals as well as Polish glass ornaments. In 1983, over twenty-five percent of Strickfaden's Christmas business was in glass figural ornaments from Germany.

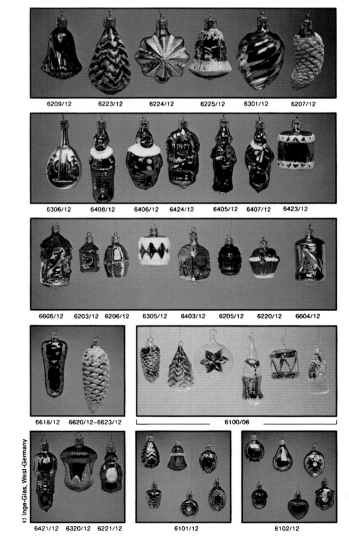

Ornaments marketed by Santa's Choice and made by Inge-Glas, West Germany.

Stahl Imports

Started in 1950, Stahl Imports began its decorations business, but not until ten years later did this company begin to seriously import tree decorations and toys. They import items from Europe and several Asian countries. The current president is Philip Stahl, who operates this import business in Pelham, New York. Nutcrackers, glass figurals, wooden tree ornaments, plastic novelties, and miniature Christmas toys were their most featured items in a 1989 catalog.

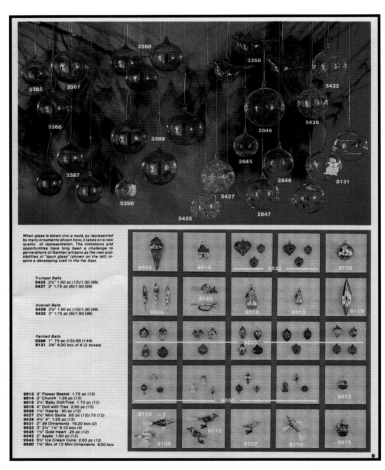

Assortment of clear glass and figural ornaments imported by Stahl Imports in 1986.

Evergreen Press

Another company specializing in Christmas items, especially those fashioned from paper, was "The Evergreen Press, Inc." of Pleasant Hill, California. Reproductions of antique Christmas cards, children's Christmas books, and Christmas postcards comprised the majority of their line. The ornaments they sold were manufactured in the United States using artwork they had previously published for one purpose or another. Needlepoint ornaments using Santa Claus designs were made in the Peoples Republic of China. Many of the items were reproduced or adapted from collections of major museums throughout the United States. In particular, some of the Thomas Nast's illustrations were from the Strong Museum in Rochester, New York, and the Denver Art Museum in Denver, Colorado. Other museums whose products they have reproduced include the Henry Ford Museum in Dearborn, Michigan; County Heritage Society in Dallas, Texas; and the Plumas County Museum in Quincy, California. Established in 1968 in Nevada City, California, Evergreen Press was moved to the San Francisco Bay area in 1975.

Bradford Novelty Company

Bradford Novelty Company, Inc. of New York continued its leadership in the importation of Christmas items into this country, becoming one of the largest importers of Christmas decorations in this decade. In its early years, under the direction of founder Jack Burnbaum, its focus was plastic injection molded ornaments to replace European glass ornaments. Current president, Arnold Frank, bought into the business in 1953, having worked for Irwin Corporation. In the 1950s the company expanded its line to include tree toppers, a continued specialty over the decades. In the 1970s, Bradford Novelty was the first Christmas firm to manufacture glass ornaments in Mexico.

Bradford's multi-color lighted tree toppers were a year-round hit with college students who used them as strobe lights in their dorm rooms in the 1960s. Glass, ceramic, vinyl, paper, cardboard, wooden, and metal decorations were imported from Hong Kong, Taiwan, Korea, Thailand, and mainland China. These items were supplied to retailers through various channels of distribution (mass merchandising, warehouse clubs, garden centers, specialty shops, mail order houses, etc.) According to Arnold Frank, more and more countries were added to the list of countries supplying ornaments. Exporting and importing ornaments became a major trend toward the end of this decade. As trade barriers were broken down, new business prospects were sought in Mexico as well as South and Central America.

Bronson Imports

Bronson Imports of New York City was started in 1967 by Lawrence Bronson. In their earlier years, they imported glass ornaments from Germany as well as lights, tinsel garland, and nativity sets from Italy. In the mid-1970s they phased out European imports due to their rising costs and turned to the Far East and South America. At Bronson's death in 1982, the Bronson Company was bought by Birchwood Sales Corp. and Birchwood sold The Bronson Company in 1983 to Poolmaster, Inc. of Sacramento, California. Bronson Imports has showrooms in all major markets and currently imports glass ornaments from Europe and lights, trees, and ornaments from the Far East.

West German Steinbach created wooden ornaments. $4-7 each.

East German manufactured ornaments. Smuggled into West Germany, they were then imported into the United States, avoiding high tariff on East European goods. Detail is amazingly intricate. $5-10 each.

Late 1980s West German manufactured wooden ornaments purchased in Frankfurt. $3-5 each.

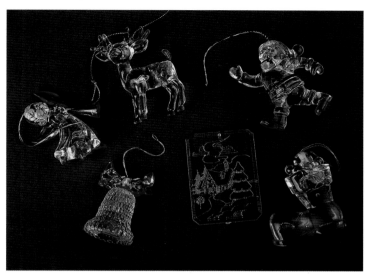

Plastic molded ornaments from mid- to late 1980s. $.50-1.

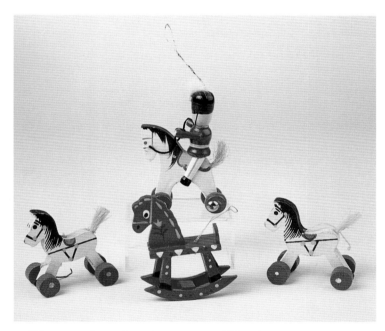

Taiwan manufactured wooden ornaments. $1-2 each.

Train set made in Taiwan for use on Christmas tree branches or as table decoration. $3-5.

Silvestri Art Manufacturing Company

Silvestri of Chicago, Illinois, started as a high-fashion display company in the 1940s. George Silvestri and Bernard J. German formed Silvestri Art Manufacturing Company in 1940 when they bought out Silvestri's uncle. The two had worked for the company as salesmen, and "sought control when they failed to convince the uncle that he should diversify out of his original business of making plaster vases, plaques, statues, pedestals, and similar articles." Operating from an old seven-story plant on Chicago's northwest side, Silvestri soon became one of the nation's top designers and manufacturers of Christmas displays.

In 1965, two years before he died, George Silvestri sold the business to Eckmar Corporation. Three members of the present executive management purchased the business on December 31, 1968. Jim Peltz, who specialized in sales, Richard Feldstein, who operated the business's finances, and Steve Berkowitz, who dealt in the marketing and sales end of the business, are the present owners.

Silvestri was responsible for the original impetus in importing midget lights from Italy. Spurred on by this initial success, Silvestri began importing items from Mexico, Italy, and Japan. Once these goods became a bit pricey, Silvestri began to import items from Hong Kong and Taiwan. In this decade they were importing items from the Philippines, Thailand, India, and the mainland China in an attempt to provide a variety of holiday items for sale.

Silvestri's product lines consisted of over 6,000 consumer-orientated products. Of these, only the midget Christmas tree lights remained from the George Silvestri days. On November 30, 1987, Silvestri acquired a majority interest of Confections, Incorporated. Silvestri Corporation was acquired by Alco Standard, and became an operating company of Alco Gift and Glassware. In April 1989, the warehouse operations previously located on Paulina Street moved to Bedford Park, Illinois, and the Confections operations moved to the Paulina Street headquarters in Chicago.

Christmasphiles—Paper and Tinsel Decorations

One company known for their American-production of "old-fashioned trimmings" created with European materials was Christmasphiles of Watertown, New York. This company was begun in 1983 with only two products—a sixteen-page booklet, "Victorian Christmas Tree Ornaments," and a set of pattern sheets for making Victorian paper cutouts called "Christmas Cutouts for the Victorian Tree." In 1984 Laura Lynn Scharer, owner, added her first kit, "Victorian Christmas Cutouts," which contained patterns for making the paper cutouts they had given patterns for in the previous booklet. In 1985, they added two new kits, "Reflectors" and "Victorian Star," and two new booklets. One of these booklets was a cookbook which included several tree ornaments made from foodstuffs. Other subsequent kits were added throughout the decade. The main emphasis of Christmas was authenticity, each item carefully researched and featuring material as close to the Victorian originals as possible.

Tin Originals

A company dealing in European, Asian, and American made decorations is Tin Originals, started in 1987 under the leadership of Mildred Starling. A number of different Christmas items were featured in these catalogs, including feather trees ranging in size from 13-inches to 37-inches. Papier-mâché Santas were fashioned in the style of the early celluloid Irwin Santas which always carried a basket of fruit in the left hand and a sack (over the shoulder and revealing dolls in the back) in the right hand. Candy containers were made in shapes of Santas in net bags, standing by houses, and on bells resembling those manufactured in Japan in the 1930s. German-appearing Santas sitting on logs, like those fashioned in Germany in the 1920s, were featured in several different styles.

Counterbalance candleholders with Santa, snowmen, and bear weights realistically painted were interesting variations on an old theme. Also included were wax, tin, glass, and wooden ornaments reminiscent of the types used in years past. But the majority of ornaments sold by Tin Originals in this decade were of the small to miniature size for feather trees.

313	Medium Red & Green Fence	812	Tin Mistletoe Holder Ornament (holds 4
317	Small Double Cherry on Jute		candles, not included)
575-R	Red Wooden Candle	823	Small Rocking Horse Counterbalance (candles
702	Santa Candy Basket		not included)
703	Santa Candy Container w/Sack of Toys	824	Small Rocking Horse Ornament
705	Small Primitive Santa Candy Container		
787	Medium Bird in Nest (assorted 6 colors)		
811	Tin Kissing Ball Ornament (holds 4 candles, not included)		

A 1989 catalog page from Tin Originals illustrating the country craft and old world look for which they were so famous.

Kurt S. Adler

In the 1980s, Kurt S. Adler introduced the world-renowned Louis Nichole Heirloom Collection, one of the most elegant ornament lines ever produced. Designed by famed designer Louis Nichole, the group featured Victorian styled doll ornaments dressed in elaborate fabric and lace costumes with stunning colors—some of which were included in the prestigious White House Collection. In the mid-1980s, the Smithsonian Carousel Series was unveiled and included ornament replicas of antique carousel animal figures found on merry-go-rounds in the Smithsonian Museum Archives. These reproductions featured hand-painted designs and the exact detailing of original, turn-of-the-century carousel animal figures. Each year they retired and introduced two new figures.

Bronner's

Bronner's of Frankenmuth, Michigan, continued to expand its offerings in a decade which quickly began to return to the traditional tree decorations of times past. Their store stocked over 30,000 different items with over 3,000 ornaments produced in Germany, Austria, Poland, Italy, and Czechoslovakia. They also displayed and sold over 500 different crèche scenes. Bronner's produced huge displays for chain stores and

department stores as well. Wally and Irene Bronner were the main tourist attraction in Michigan, gaining publicity across the United States. Thousands upon thousands of visitors descended upon this tiny town to visit Bronner's. It is also important to note that Bronner's enterprise really was the impetus for so many individuals to open a year-around Christmas store. It could be said that Frankenmuth, Michigan, is the birthplace of the "Year-around Christmas Store."

Whitehurst Imports Company

In 1982, Mary Lou Armstrong, along with four other partners, purchased this company from the Whitehursts. The Whitehursts were in their 70s with no children, and Morris had Parkinson's disease, so Olga opted to retire in order to take care of him. Armstrong became this company's president as well in 1982. With a bachelor of arts degree in theater and English, Armstrong was lured to the Christmas industry. With Armstrong at the helm, this company grew tremendously in size, dealing strictly in European imports. Armstrong is quoted as saying, "We've found that things should come from where they're born. Anything else is a copy."

A Closer Look at Tree Decorations of This Decade

Cotton Ornaments

This decade witnessed the return of countless variations of cotton ornaments like those produced in the late 1890s and early 1900s. Snowmen, Santas, and snowballs with added decorations once again appeared for sale. Fruit and vegetables likewise were commercially produced again, especially lemons and oranges in the larger sizes, and plums, apples, oranges, and simple round shapes in the smaller sizes. Often they were sold with an attached velvet-finished leaf. Icicles and pinecone shaped cottons were made in the Scandinavian countries and are easily identified since they are usually hollow and dent easily.

However, people figural-shaped cotton ornaments were the mainstay of the decade. Artists explored different holidays and created patriotic and Halloween-themed cotton people. All of them were extremely detailed and just as elegant as those made in the past in Germany. They just need time to develop the patina of old age. Numerous artists began producing cotton ornaments. One such artist was Janet Combs, who used organic cotton batting and dyed it as needed for her ornaments. Among her figural shapes were Santa Claus, an Indian chief, plum pudding, and even an ice cream cone.

Other well-known artists included Jerry and Carol Smith and Cynthia Jones. All of these Ohio artists are well recognized for their detail in paint, trim, and clothing for their human cotton ornaments. They produced countless angels, Santa figures, and children in perfect detail, attracting collectors who could not afford the price of the older cotton ornaments. Plus, many collectors were unable to locate any for sale. Thus, these artisans revived the creating of cotton ornaments in the United States.

Paper and Cardboard Ornaments

Elegant Victorian paper ornaments like those handcrafted almost a century ago were manufactured by Bruce Catt of New York City. He graduated from the University of Iowa with a BFA in theater and once served on the wardrobe staff of *Saturday Night Live*. Catt has numerous movie credits to his name for costume designs include *Godfather 3*, *Garbo Talks*, and *Power*. His endeavors in ornaments grew out of a hobby. Bruce grew up in a house where nothing was ever thrown away. Scraps of decorative papers and trims were all over. When he initially started, there was very little documentation on Victorian paper ornaments. So, he decided to create ornaments based on authentic Victorian shapes.

Each of his designs was extraordinary in that each was assembled from beautiful imported papers, scraps (such as angels, flowers, etc.), delicate gold foil Dresden trims, gold braid and ribbons, and even tiny silk flower buds. No glue gun was employed. Special glue was meticulously applied with toothpicks. Catt produced flats, three-dimensional designs, and tree toppers in an infinite variety of designs. Countless whimsical designs were created by Catt in this decade.

Metal Ornaments

William and Janet Rigby of Cooperstown, New York, started working out of their home in 1986 making reproductions of antique tin ornaments using actual molds dating back to 1880. Their very first pieces made for collectors were made by melting tin in a pot on their own kitchen stove and dipping the antique molds into the liquid. Due to an almost instant demand on the part of collectors, the Rigbys quickly created a full workshop in their basement. Each ornament came with a small card giving instructions on caring for the ornament and a brief history. The inside of their card read, "The ornament you hold in your hand was made on one of those ornament molds used by Gustav A. Mayer over 100 years ago. He probably brought the molds with him from his homeland of Germany. In his time, he was most famous for his dessert wafers created for the New York hotel trade. The ornaments were a sideline along with a number of other unlikely business ventures. His ornaments were sold world-wide and many still remain in private homes and private collections. We have worked hard to copy Mr. Mayer's production techniques and colorings to give you authentic sparkles for your holiday tree."

William and Janet used pure tin, which was much safer than the original antique formula mix of tin, lead, and antimony. Their styles include stars, snowflakes, animals, and parrots. These tin ornaments were a shiny, bright silver on the front (with lacquered coloring) and the back.

Also regaining popularity were Zinnefiguren or "Tin figures" which were a product dating back to eighteenth century Europe. Mostly fashioned in Germany and in Austria, these tin and lead alloy figures were used under Christmas trees in Putz scenes, on mantles, on tables, and in a variety of other ways at Christmas. It had always been the custom to make badges for the military, then gradually little toys were made for children. Eventually these toys began to double as Christmas display figures. The figure was rough cast, then die-cut. A long-standing shop in Nuremberg, Germany, not only displayed the old figures, but sold painted and unpainted versions to holiday enthusiasts.

Gurley choir boy candles from early 1980s. $3-4 each.

A 1988 animal assortment of tin and lead alloy ornaments made by Wm. J. Rigby Co. of New York.

Lead Tinsel Icicles and Tinsel Garlands

While the traditional gold and silver tinsel garlands were the mainstay of this decade, some interesting colors emerged. Rainbow colors of red, green, blue, and purple abounded as American's decorating trends changed. Another trend was to add lights to the garland which Americans found fascinating; therefore, the sales of such tinsel garlands rose dramatically. Manufacturers included National Tinsel, General Foam Plastics, Union Wadding, and Holiday Originals.

In 1984, National Tinsel Mfg. Co. introduced a series of garlands specifically designed for soft needle artificial and live trees. This new garland featured a light, airy construction which rested gently on tree branches and complemented the delicate open construction of those natural appearing trees.

General Foam offered over twenty varieties of garlands, with the 4-inch and 5-inch ply being the most popular. Generally these garlands were sold in 30-foot lengths.

Plastic Decorations

Green Plastics' American Holiday Division introduced three new bead garlands, in six new colors including mauve, gold, silver, and three aurora borealis colors, all made from plastic. Each garland was fifteen feet in length. Plastic ornaments continued to be produced, but most Americans were much more intrigued with the European-style figural ornaments.

Wax Ornaments

In the previous decade, Asian imports began to seriously threaten the domestic production of figural wax candles. In the early 1980s, Gurley Candle Company ceased production but attempted to remain in business by manufacturing specialty items for Avon and other similar companies. In 1992, the company closed permanently.

Large Gurley Christmas tree candle. 7", $4-8 (in good condition).

Pine cone based-candle, $4-5. Poinsettia wax candle, $5-7. All late Gurley products.

Gurley assortment of angel wax candles. All from 1970s into early 1980s. $2-5 each.

Home-crafted lace doily ornaments. All made by hand according to provided instructions. $3-4 each.

Wooden hand-painted ornaments. All made from kits which contained cut-out patterns, paints, and brushes. $.50-1 each.

Typical electrified tree top of this decade employing midget lights. $3-5 with box.

German blown tree top from Coburg, Germany. $5-7.

Under Our Trees

Snow Baby Figures

Snow baby figures were extremely popular in the period before World War II. While they continued to be produced after the war, they lost most of their charm for families seeking new decorating trends and themes. However, in the 1980s with the revival of tradition, snow baby figures were avidly collected by Christmas enthusiasts. Department 56 conceived the idea of recreating these figures, but in larger sizes. Department 56's interest in snow babies became a reality when they opened a factory in Taiwan that was able to produce porcelain items with hand-applied crystals. These crystals were characteristic of the older snow baby figures produced in Germany and Japan in earlier decades. The original figures ranged from one-inch to about three-inches in height. Their "snow babies" ranged in height from four-inches to six-inches. Their adorable, bright, blue-eyed, and snow suit-covered kids who made snowballs, rode polar bears, and frolicked with their friends soon became a hit with collectors. First introduced in 1986, a variety of over ninety different bisque figures, porcelain snow babies, water globes, ornaments, and music boxes were produced in the 1980s. In 1989, responding to the requests of collectors of miniatures, they began to offer a line of pewter snow babies, much the same size of the original figures.

Department 56 Village Scenes

Using Putz scenes as a focus of Christmas decorating, along with the traditional tree, became extremely popular once again in this decade. Several companies specialized in providing such materials for Americans who wished to place such a scene under their tree, on a table, or even in the corner of their living rooms. One of these companies was Department 56 of Minneapolis, Minnesota. Before Department 56 became an independent corporation, it was part of a large parent company that used a numbering system to identify each of its departments. Department 21 was administration, Department 54 was the gift warehouse, and "Department 56" was the wholesale gift imports area. Department 56, Inc., headed by Edward R. Bazinet, originally began by importing fine Italian basketry and German pottery; however, a new product line introduced in 1977 paved the way for the "The Original Snow Village," a series of lighted buildings continuing the age-old tradition of Putz scenes under the tree.

The idea for these buildings grew out of a holiday meal Bazinet shared with friends in Stillwater, Minnesota, a small town on the St. Croix River not far from Minneapolis. It was a very dark evening with snow in the air, white puffs of smoke curling out of the chimines of old historic homes, and Christmas lights glowed from windows and trees. Everyone in attendance agreed on the beauty of this scene and how it reminded them of their childhood Christmas celebrations. That setting and nostalgia inspired The Original Snow Village pieces—four house and two churches—each lit from within so that they appeared somewhat like the scene that evening in Stillwater.

Bazinet left the parent company, formed an independent corporation, and with a team dedicated to this new idea, began designing and creating these miniature porcelain villages. In 1979, Department 56 made an important operational decision; in order to keep "The Original Snow Village" at a reasonable size, buildings would have to be retired from production each year to make room for new designs. Since its beginning, in 1977, over 136 lighted designs were produced in this decade.

In 1979, the first Snow Village accessory pieces were introduced—"Carolers," a set of three pieces. This grew out of requests from collectors who had begun to group these houses to create tableaus, but no people or figures were available to place outside the houses in these settings. Then they began to produce sleighs, snowmen, children at play, street signs, and even cars. Judith Price was with this design team from the very beginning and has done so very much to ensure their authenticity and design. As Price explained, these accessories "are a natural extension to the villages."

In 1984, they commenced "The Heritage Village Collection," with "The Dickens Village." Neilan Lund, a master architect, approached Department 56 with the idea of creating a village based on Victorian England. The pieces in this category were an inch or two smaller than those in the Original Snow Village, and had a matte, rather than a glazed finish. The Dickens set recreates Victorian England and the times in which Charles Dickens created his famous works. *A Christmas Carol, Oliver Twist, Great Expectations* are but a few of the inspirations for buildings and accessory pieces which include characters from Dickens' novels.

This was followed by the "The New England Village" in 1986 as part of The Heritage Village Collection. Neilan Lund was also the chief architect for this series. This series is characteristic of the northeastern part of the United States, with its white clapboard churches, town halls, and general stores.

"The Alpine Village" was also introduced in 1986. The Alpine Village pieces have German names such as "Bessor Bierkeller,' "Gasthof Eisl," "E. Straub Backer," "Apotheke," and "Milch-Kase." These were the first pieces in the series in 1986. These buildings are reminiscent of the architecture found in European mountain villages and towns. "The Alpine Village" grouping recreates the charm of a quaint mountain town, where glistening snow and clear lakes fed by icy streams dot the landscape.

"The Christmas in the City" followed in 1987. Christmas in the City is reminiscent of large cities with tall buildings and lots of bustling crowds. There are brownstones, spire cathedrals, decorative and elegant theaters, corner newsstands, and multi-storied buildings featuring shops on ground floors and apartments on the upper levels. The "Christmas in the City" scene evokes memories of busy sidewalks, street corner Santas, friendly traffic cops, and bustling crowds amid cheery shops, townhouses, and theaters.

Also introduced in 1987 was "The Little Town of Bethlehem." This series is unique in that it is sold in a set of twelve and has never been expanded. There are three lighted buildings and nine accessories. The buildings are authentic in that they are reminiscent of the shapes and style of the buildings that existed in Israel at the time of Christ's birth.

Hard plastic bank with plastic screw-out in bottom for emptying piggy bank. $5-7.

Roly Poly musical Santa. Made in Hong Kong from which bells jingle when he is moved. $7-10.

Rubber Sani-toy which was a squeaker. Often times these were taken into bathtubs to get children to take baths. The squeaking sound and the floating Santa helped to allay fear of water (and being washed). $4-6.

Hong Kong walking Santa toy from the mid-1980s. $5-7.

Interesting home-crafted decoration. Plastic Santa and sleigh glued onto varnished wooden platform which was trimmed with pine cones to serve as trees and a cardboard church. Early 1980s. $10-15.

Santa friction toy. Riding tree, Santa glides across floor when lever is activated. $10-15.

Made in Hong Kong, soft plastic Santa, sleigh, and reindeer set, heavily embellished with silver glitter. $5-8.

Variety of hard and soft plastic reindeer still produced in Japan in the early 1980s. $1-3 each.

Indoor Electric Lighting of Our Trees

In 1980 the Consumer Product Safety Commission (CPSC) moved into step one of its field program to monitor Christmas lights safety standards. This program included viewing samples in wholesaler's showrooms and purchasing lights from distributors and retail outlets. In 1981 the CPSC's once voluntary standards became effective and mandatory, forcing manufacturers to meet increased safety standards. Traditional lights made a come-back in this decade. NOMA bubble lights doubled in sales annually in the early 1980s with GE's lighted ice and twinkle sets also experiencing significant increases in sales. Along with the increase in old-fashioned decorative ornaments came this interest in traditional tree lights. General Electric successfully test-marketed a new line of domestically produced miniature light sets in 1981. GE tested two basic styles in its Super-Set line—a basic midget design and a more traditional styling with a plastic cap over the bulb to resemble a standard bulb.

Another phenomenon hit the tree when NOMA released "Ornamotion." The ornamotion motor was plugged into any 35, 50, or 100 set to rotate any ornament on the tree. Sold in packs of three, Americans turned to these with glee, for now they could have revolving ornaments on the tree. That special Hallmark ornament, or another figural ornament for that matter, would revolve to the delight and glee of both children and adults. Musical Mini-Lites also appeared in this decade. Light sets played eighteen popular songs, and lites danced with or without music. Chiming Christmas brass bells that played ten popular Christmas songs were also the perfect choice for the tree, mantle, or even wreath.

In 1981 NOMA created midget light sets that connected end to end, therefore ending the never-ending maze of extension cords and different arrangements needed to decorate a large Christmas tree. Illuminated water globes also were a hit when NOMA marketed a set of four decorated illuminated water globes with snow falling continuously, and moving figures inside. Each globe had a hook to enable it to be hung on the tree. The box was marketed under the label, "Let It Snow." In 1987, NOMA also introduced "Marquee" chasing lights and heavy-duty lights in its premier light line.

Novelty midgets, like tiny candles and tinsel bursts were extremely popular with Americans. While Italian midget lights were the most creative and innovative, their higher price soon led to a decline in sales. Japanese-manufactured midget lights were so much less expensive that Americans quickly purchased any figural midget lights on the shelves, including miniature bubble lights, starbursts, and even miniature Japanese houses with miniature lights inside them. The bulk of sales were in the 35-light midgets since the 75 and 100 light sets had high defective rates. String-to-string miniatures which lent themselves very well to outdoor decorating also were the light sets of choice in the early 1980s. Clear miniature lights continued to gain in popularity, contributing to almost sixty percent of the miniature light sales in 1982. Manufacturers and retailers attributed this to the outdoor trees and Christmas displays in cities and suburban malls that employed clear lights. Americans merely imitated this trend. Twenty percent of total light sales were in fancies, midgets, and standards combined. Single colored light sets in other colors—red, green, and blue, most commonly, generally garnered only about fifteen percent of light sales.

Christmas 1984 was one of the brightest ones on record, with sales of lights up about twenty-five percent according to the National Ornament & Electric Lights Christmas Association (NOEL). The demand for miniature lights had far exceeded the supply because manufacturers had underestimated demand; shipments from the Far East had been delayed, and there was a frantic last moment effort to fill orders.

Flexible string-to-string sets, introduced in the early 1980s, continued to gain a larger share of the market in 1986—about sixty percent according to some suppliers. Longer light sets with 50 to 100 lights as opposed to 20 or 35 also continued to gain momentum.

Christmas 1987 was a rough year in that large quantities of lights arrived late from the Orient. There was a tremendous shortage. Lights sets booked early in 1987 were often not shipped because of the lower prices at that time. As the American dollar fell, so did shipments, unless reps were willing to rebook at higher prices. Manufacturers and importers worried about the changing Taiwanese economy, a move to a more middle class structure that made factory jobs less appealing. Therefore, lighting companies knew they had to concentrate on new resources in other countries. The shift from Taiwan to The People's Republic of China was one fundamental change. Mainland China became an important producer, not only of lights, but other Christmas goods as well. Malaysia and Thailand also produced lights for the American market.

In 1989, C-7 (CANDELABRA) and C-9 (INTERMEDIATE) sets were the largest sellers for NOMA, who quickly noticed the renewed interest in Americans of that traditional look which employed these larger sized bulbs.

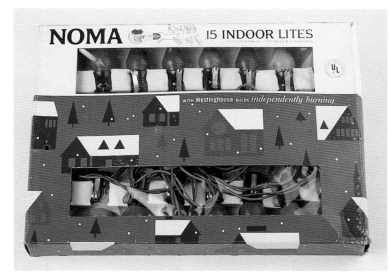

NOMA candelabra base bulbs. While many Americans turned to midget lights, traditionalists continued to use these 15-light sets. $5-7 boxed set.

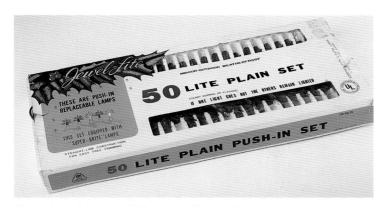

Clear midget light set in 50-light set which quickly became the number one best seller of this decade. $3-5 for boxed set.

Multi-colored counterpart of the 50-midget light set. $4-5 for boxed set.

A bit more expensive, GE marketed their 35-midget light set as being safer than any other set on the market. $5-7 for boxed set.

More expensive Tiara midget light set. With tiny plastic points, they emitted tiny sparks of light when lit on the tree. $10-12 for boxed set.

Double blinker midget light set intended for indoor use. This was one of the more popular styles of the decade. $5-7 for boxed set.

Outdoor Electric Lighting

A resurgence of outdoor decorating helped propel sales figures for miniature lights to new heights as Americans tried to outdo their neighbors in outdoor light displays. Even C-7 (CANDELABRA) and C-9 (INTERMEDIATE) bulbs sets increased significantly in 1980.

Miniature Lights gained in popularity, edging out the larger style bulbs formerly employed for outdoor displays. Most popular were clear miniature lights. NOMA marketed light shapes which transformed a plan C-9 (INTERMEDIATE) light set into a decorative wonderland by snapping on stars, spheres, and bells. Being white, they glowed in the color of the bulb to which they were snapped. They were weather resistant, used on eaves, gutters, and trees for a novel effect.

Outdoor lighting became more and more popular with each passing year of this decade. As Americans forgot about the energy crunch and lighting restrictions of the 1970s, they turned to getting out those lights not used for several years. Then they quickly discovered that, in order to really have an effective light display, they needed to purchase new lights as well. This helped to create a demand for more lights year after year. By the end of the decade, Americans were lighting large trees on their front lawns, placing lights along roof lines, and floodlighting architectural elements of their homes with abounding energy.

General Foam Plastics noticed a large increase in sales of outdoor decorations during the later part of this decade. Four-foot Santa figures, Santa in sleigh, and three-piece nativities were among their largest sellers. Business was up sixty percent for PSI, according to David Nesbit, national sales manager. The company produced ninety-five new items for 1989. Bronners' of Frankenmuth, Michigan, also reported an upsurge in sales in the late 1980s. Their life-size seventeen-piece fiberglass nativity set was a large commercial success. Other good sellers in fiberglass were carolers and Santa with his sleigh and reindeer.

Indoor-outdoor approved midget light set with "Add-a-Set" feature. $3-5 for boxed set.

New straight line construction making for easier trimming of those outdoor bushes and house lines. $5-7 for boxed set.

End of the decade 100 midget light set with five-way flasher which led the way for Americans to add more motion than ever to their outdoor displays. Motion was the novelty of the later part of this decade. $6-8 for boxed set.

The 1990s—The Designers Influence Our Christmas Decorating

Historical Perspective—Designers and Their European Designs

With the explosion of the World Wide Web, literally thousands of sites devoted to Christmas became instantly accessible to all who had Internet access. Pages were devoted to Christmas trees, Christmas holiday celebrations and customs, recipes and songs, Christmas related charities, Santa Claus himself, and even pages where celebrants could explore classic Christmas literature or chuckle over Yuletide humor.

Technology hit Christmas with both a vengeance and a loving touch in the 1990s. While the notion of writing a letter to Santa is old-fashioned, the methods employed to write Santa toward the end of the 1990s were most interesting. With the advent of both personal computers and the Internet, it became even easier for children to connect with the North Pole. Via the Internet, youngsters could directly send a message to Santa, Rudolph the Red-Nosed Reindeer, or to one of Santa's elves. Seconds after the letter was sent via email, an interactive message arrived from the North Pole. Also available was much information regarding weather conditions at the North Pole and an email address to send a gift list directly to Santa. For a nominal price, kids could order a button saying they emailed Santa.

Specialty companies introduced an innovative idea that captured immediate attention, the decoration of high-rise office buildings for the holidays. One such company, Panache Productions, Inc., a suburban Atlanta design firm, was founded by Pam Anderson. Granted, the work is concentrated in a six to twelve week cycle around the Christmas holidays, but many of the props were so elaborate that it took over a year to make them. One of her firm's more unusual projects included a five-level tower of steel and light reaching up amid the huge chandeliers of a seven-story atrium. Another used 25,000 lights to make a clock tower look like a 50-foot high Christmas tree. Anderson's firm grew to the point that her company handled fifty to eighty large projects each Christmas season.

In this decade, more than any other to date, Santa took on a multi-cultural, multi-ethnic look. African-American, Asian, and Hispanic Santas sat on Winter Wonderland thrones in shopping malls across America, listening to the whispered requests of youngsters. "We have African-Americans who play the role of Santa, we have females who play the role of Santa, we have Santas who sign for the deaf, singing Santas, Hispanic Santas," said Sandra Majestic whose Majestic Photo firm coordinated the Santa program for shopping centers coast to coast. In 1998, Majestic's firm provided twenty-five Santas and fifty-two elves to staff three full-time thrones at Marshall Field's flagship store in Chicago. Over 3,000 children a day visited Santa that year.

Holly Valant and her husband continued to operate the Charles W. Howard Santa Claus School in Midland, Michigan, originally founded in 1937 by Howard, the First Macy's Thanksgiving Day Parade Santa. The grooming, costuming, and behavior of Santas who made public appearances were continually monitored by this school and other Santa specialists. Santa Plus, a St. Louis firm, was also involved in providing well-trained Santas. This company published a thirteen-page manual covering everything from jewelry and deodorant to not using a public restroom while in costume.

While African-Americans made up roughly eleven percent of the U.S. population, the Christmas industry, like many other retail marketers, had long neglected the needs of this group of consumers. Kurt Adler, Silvestri, Midwest Importers, Possible Dreams, and Enesco all introduced figurines, ornaments, snow globes, and tree toppers with African-American characters. Even Kwanzaa cards were printed in larger supplies to meet the demands of Kwanzaa, an African holiday celebrated by an increasingly large number of black Americans. This holiday falls around the same time as Christmas. Hispanic Americans were also a large group of consumers somewhat ignored by the Christmas industry until more attention was paid to Nativity items, so very much a part of Hispanic culture. TV commercials, magazine advertisements, and newspaper promotions were conducted in Spanish to help attract this segment of the market.

Holiday decoration wasn't just for Christmas. In this decade, more than ever, Americans began to decorate for Chanukah and Kwanzaa. A collection of tabletop and accent pieces was designed for Kwanzaa in 1996. The best selling Kwanzaa ornaments incorporated phrases pertaining to hope, peace, and related principles behind the observance. Companies such as Enesco Corporation, Pacific Rim Corporation, and Kurt S. Adler reported heightened interest in both these holidays not only because of consumers' desires to set as festive a mood as their neighbors, but because these families wished to protect their children from feeling envious of friends whose homes featured lavish Christmas decorations.

The newest Christmas retailer became television. Television home shopping was a rage in the early to middle part of this decade. QVC and the Home Shopping Network reached a total of sixty million households and chalked up more than two billion dollars in sales in 1993. Some of the first companies to sell on television were Capricorn Electronics, Mr. Christmas, and Telco Creations. In the later part of this decade, television faced still another opponent in its efforts to attract buyers: the Internet. The Internet continues to attract thousands upon thousands of buyers every single day. Many predict that the Internet will dominate the retailing market. Time will tell.

In the 1990s, mainland China and Thailand were natural heirs to Taiwan's throne of dominance. Both countries benefited from U.S. laws giving financial benefits to developing countries. Because of its economic success, Taiwan no longer received such consideration. Many American manufacturers set up plants in mainland China, particularly along the coast where shipping was facilitated. Some Taiwanese business people were also dealing with mainland China, acting as brokers, but they were hampered by political restrictions, requiring them to work through neutral areas such as Hong Kong. The shift from Taiwan to The People's Republic of China mirrored the same shift from Japan to Taiwan that occurred fifteen to twenty years ago. Workers had to be trained to produce quality goods at low prices and plants had to be assembled to assure availability. All of this took time. But a trend was started and only the future years hold the answer to the probability of Taiwan losing its place in the manufacturing of Christmas items for the American market. The North American Free Trade Agreement (NAFTA), by which the United States, Mexico, and Canada provided preferential rates of duties to each other's goods, resulted in renewed interest in importing and exporting Christmas decorations and ornaments. The gradual elimination of tariffs with other countries, including Chili, Columbia, Argentina, Guatemala, and Ecuador, also helped to promote this increased trade. More and more South American buyers attended the Toy Fair in New York City rather than dealing exclusively with exporters in Texas or Florida. The Uruguay Round Rules of Origin Agreement called for a three-year study aimed at developing uniform rules for determining the country of origin of goods moving in international trade.

Surveys of the mid-1990s pointed to a most interesting trend. When collectors were surveyed about their favorite theme of collecting, more collectors named Christmas than any other theme. There were an estimated 10.1 million adults Christmas collectors who spent as much as $1.1 billion on Christmas collectibles in 1997. The largest share of sales in Christmas collectibles, or thirty-six percent, was attributed to collectible ornaments. Christmas-themed figurines and nativity related items accounted for just less than one-third of category sales. Christmas-themed villages accounted for the remaining share of sales. Much of this can be attributed to limited editions, organized collectors clubs, special club member discounts and exclusives, annual or continuing series programs, and licensed or artist positioning.

The market leader in ornaments in the 1990s continued to be Hallmark's Keepsake Ornaments, which accounted for seventy-five percent of the collectors. Keepsake boasted of one of the fastest growing collectors organization in the country.

Christmas Day, 1990 with Kristin, Amy, and Jill VanBerkel in Darboy, Wisconsin.

Linda, Mark, and Karen Giebel on Christmas Eve in the early 1990s when they hadn't quite finished decorating their Christmas tree for Santa Claus. $Priceless.

Alan VanGrisvin watching big brother, Michael, trim the family Christmas tree in 1990.

Aaron, Adam, and Anna Baltz telling Santa that they've been good and what they would like as rewards for Christmas. $Priceless.

Julie, Janet, Kevin, and Mike Brenner opening presents Santa had just delivered in the mid-1990s.

Jenny, Andy, and Billy Brenner showing off their favorite
presents received from Santa Claus on Christmas Eve, 1998.

Bob and Sharon Brenner in front of their Christmas tree
after they and the elves decorated their house for Christmas
in 1999.

Chad and Justin Balthazor filled with excitement as
they open presents on Christmas morning. $Priceless.

Our Trees

More than ninety-eight percent of Christmas trees were plantation grown, not plucked from their forest homes. Trees are harvested every ten years, with ninety percent of the trees remaining on the plantation to ensure continued production. Those who favored real trees pointed to the fact that one acre of Christmas trees provided enough oxygen for eighteen people while at the same time taking carbon dioxide out of the atmosphere, counteracting some of the effects of fossil fuels. They further recognized the fact that most municipalities had a special pick-up for trees, which they then used for mulch, firewood, or donations to local nurseries. Most importantly, many Americans felt that a real tree offered a more "homey" and "traditional" atmosphere at Christmas.

In 1993, 41.4 million artificial trees versus 34.8 million live trees decorated American households. For the fourth year in a row, artificial trees outnumbered live trees. Nine to twelve-foot trees became more and more available due to the large number of homes being constructed which provided high-ceiling living rooms and family areas.

In 1995, 37.1 million trees were sold with a retail cost ranging from $3.10 to $5.65 per foot. Those figures did slightly decline in 1997 with total sales around $33 million while maintaining the same cost per foot.

Artificial trees ranged from discount-store specials at $14.97 to trees costing hundreds and even thousands of dollars. However, the lure of a fresh scented tree from outdoors continued to attract countless Americans who valued the look of an imperfect tree, one grown by Mother Nature and one that did not have the perfect shape and perfect sized branches of the artificial variety. Proponents of artificial trees condemned the killing of oxygen-producing live trees. Proponents of live trees condemned the pollution caused by the manufacturing of artificial trees.

National Tree Company received the 1998 Product of the Year Award from NOEL (The Christmas Decoration Association) for its fiber optic tree. Changing colors from red to green to blue to gold, these trees were reminiscent of the color wheel floodlight concept used to light those aluminum trees of decades past. Fiber-optic strands were inserted into the needles of the tree, and a color wheel and a halogen light in the base of the tree to provide this ever-changing color pattern. In 1999, millennium colors: green, red, purple, silver, and a very hot pink were used on one model. In 1999, the bottle brush tree was revived by National Tree in a softer PVC for a retro look. Pre-lit trees also gained in popularity toward the end of the decade. Completely outfitted with miniature lights, it was simple to decorate a tree since it already had its lights.

Feather trees enjoyed renewed interest in this decade as Americans rediscovered the beauty of antique ornaments on these sparsely branched trees. With the increased demand for these trees, collectors simply could not find enough of the older trees or found their prices out of reach. As a result, numerous craftsmen founded companies devoted to the manufacturing of new feather trees. Sandy Elliot's Christmas Bazaar made kits available for people who wish to create such a tree by themselves at home. But for those who wish to purchase a tree already assembled, there were many companies from which to choose.

One such individual was Nancy Messinger of Cedarburg, Wisconsin, who founded her company, *Primitive Trees*, back in the mid-1980s. With her partner, Sandy Pape, they first researched trees, contacted other collectors, and even took a trip to a feather warehouse in Chicago. Their trees ranged in size from six-inches to six-feet. These trees have also been widely recognized for their individual characteristics since they appeal to many interested in "the country look."

Another well-established company was The Feather Tree Company, founded by Rob and Dianna Carlson. Originally started in Marion, Ohio, their beginning was rooted in their Christmas traditions with Sunday School pageants, family gatherings, and visions of sugarplums. Their trees duplicated the German goose-feather tree of decades past. After finding a feather tree at a country auction, the couple became intrigued with these trees. After locating a source of goose feathers and other raw materials, the couple began the creation and marketing of these trees in their home. Since that beginning in 1988, the company has grown to include a small group of workers, mostly stay-at-home mothers and retirees, who wrap branches and assemble trees.

Feathers are shipped to the Carlson's in bulk. When the feathers are received, they are cleaned with a mild bleach solution and spread out on large towels to dry. Then these clean feathers are immersed in a vat of colorfast dye. The dyeing time varies greatly depending upon the color dye and the individual feather thickness. Then individual goose feathers are wrapped around stiff wire to create braches. One feather typically wraps one to one and a half inches of branch, with thousands of feathers required for a seven to eight-foot tree. The feathers are wrapped and attached one by one in succession with a very fine steel gray color pliable wire. The center rod, or "trunk," is hand-wrapped with brown tissue to simulate bark. Each tree is shipped fully assembled, with branches folded upward, which makes it convenient to store.

They make trees in sizes of ten-inches to ten-feet, and in a variety of colors. Table-top trees are the most popular; such three-foot trees take about six hours to craft. Although the company moved in 1998 from their living room to a historic building, it continues to be a family affair with the couple's children, Erin and Ryan, helping with the mailing and the packaging. Located in Sun Prairie, Wisconsin, their popularity has become well-established as the producers of trees with very heavy branches which don't bend easily with a large number of glass ornaments placed on the branches. In addition, the proportion of the trees as well as the quality of the feathers have gone far to make it sometimes difficult for the Carlson's to keep up with supply and demand for these home-crafted feather trees. The Carlson's produce feather trees that replicate, but don't duplicate, the feather trees which first came to America in the earlier decades of the twentieth century.

The Twins Feather Trees, Inc. of Cincinnati, Ohio, was another major producer of feather trees in this decade. Karen and Sharen Bauer's father, Louis Bauer, was born in Germany and constantly recounted his memories of a six-foot feather tree his parents decorated with old-fashioned ornaments and candles. His dad had made fence to surround the tree and a small Nativity set was placed inside the fence. This German family with eight children, not wealthy by any means, lived in an 1850s stone house with only four rooms. They decorated their feather tree each year and standing by with buckets of water, lit the candles on Christmas Eve. Karen and Sharen Bauer stated, "Feather trees, we realized, were too special to be forgotten. So we decided to make a whole new generation of them ourselves." It was in 1984 that these twin sisters took their first handmade feather tree to a craft show. However, there was little interest in such trees, and the twins thought they were almost "publicly scorned." Their first few years were somewhat uneventful, with time spent educating the public about feather trees. They found people were interested in the historical aspects of the trees but had little desire to own one. They continued to do a few shows a year and the feather tree grew in popularity. They started making white trees in 1985 and a faded wintergreen tree in 1986. The year 1989 was a year of major additions and changes. They introduce the pastel pink and yellow trees for Spring, the patriotic blue tree, and the black tree for Halloween.

By the early 1990s, they could barely keep up with their orders. Their father is really the brain behind the scenes—designing the bases for the trees, doing all of the woodworking, and painting the bases so the finish is clear and smooth.

Some of their trees are dark green, others blue-green, and still others white. They further experimented with that blue feather tree for the 4th of July and the black-dyed feather tree for Halloween. In 1996, they decided to take the blue patriotic tree and the black Halloween tree one step farther. They added orange feather tips to the Halloween tree and incorporated a red/white/blue feather mix to the patriotic tree. These trees were an instant hit, making it almost impossible to keep up with the high demand. In 1999, they reintroduced the music tree box as a fifteenth anniversary special edition. Their dad once again designed and turned a gorgeous base that would house a small music box. The base was painted antique gold and played "O Christmas Tree."

The third major player in the production of feather trees was a couple from Bellevue, Ohio, Dennis and Joyce Bauer. Their rich German heritage also led to their production of these feather trees. Dennis learned how to make feather trees from Crispin Treadway in 1983 at a workshop held in Bethlehem, Pennsylvania, at Gerlachs. As a result, he started his own business in the mid-1990s, specializing in the production of trees in dark green, snow white, off white (ecru), black, and orange. Their 18-inch trees use a round base painted white. The bases for the other sizes are box shaped, painted white with a gold Dresden band.

Rob and Dianna Carlson pictured with one of their white feather trees they manufactured at end of 1990s. *Photograph by Gregg Schieve.*

Variety of feather trees produced by the Carlson family during this decade.

Karen and Sharen, who own The Twins Feather Trees, Inc. of Cincinnati, Ohio, and produced countless feather trees during this decade.

Dennis and Joyce Bauer of Bellvue, Ohio, also provided many feather trees such as these pictured during this decade for Americans.

Patriotic tree, white tree, and tiny miniature feather tree on music box stand, all produced by The Twins Feather Trees, Inc.

Dennis Bauer working with dyed feathers in his home, 1999.

Joyce Bauer hanging ornaments on one of the old-fashioned feather trees they decorate each year, this tree being the inspiration for their newly produced trees.

TABLE TREES

NORTHERN FOREST

21340.2 4' Balsam Fir; see pg. 3
For Fashion Table Trees; see pg. 13.

Aspen Pine
20020.8 2'
20140.1 4'
(left)

Elegant Spruce
28230.7 3' (left)
28240.4 4'

Noble Green Spruce
24230.5 3'
24240.2 4'

Noble Blue Spruce
25230.8 3'

Winter White
Iridescent
30020.5 2'
30230.0 3' (right)
30240.7 4'

Northeastern
Blue Fir
27230.4 3'
(above)

Canadian Pine
22020.4 2' (above)
22130.0 3'
22140.7 4'

Northeastern Green Fir
26230.1 3'

Douglas Fir
23020.7 2' (above)

Although tabletop trees are illustrated, this 1993 catalog page from Northern Forest illustrates the many popular styles and types of artificial trees of this decade.

How We Decorated Our Homes and Trees

Licensing continued to be a viable market as Americans more and more turned to "names" they recognized to be used as decorations for their trees and their homes. Coca-Cola Polar Bears, Barbie, Lucy and Desi, the Flintstones, Little Orphan Annie, countless Disney and Warner Brothers cartoon characters, and others appeared on our trees, regardless of the fact that the prices for many of these ornaments were especially high. Families were willing to purchase a few licensed pieces rather than many "generic" decorations. The median age of the American population increased from twenty-eight in 1970 to thirty-six in 1998. The baby boomers were the most influential consumer group. Boomer nostalgia drove the 1999 licensed products line. Properties such as *I Love Lucy*, *Howdy Doody*, and *Casablanca* appealed to the fond memories found in television and at the movie theaters. Adler acquired industry licenses for James Dean, *Phantom of the Opera*, and the television show *Wheel of Fortune*. Others included Chiquita Banana, Cracker Jack, Smokey the Bear, and Texaco. Telco Creations, Inc. acquired the Disney Classics license for Snow White, Cinderella, Pinocchio, Peter Pan, Bambi, Dumbo, and Alice in Wonderland. Midwest of Cannon Falls had licenses including Swanson Frozen Diners, Tabasco, Miller Lite, Kellogg's Cornflakes, Rice Krispies, LifeSavers, and even Spam. Christopher Radko's studio collection included *The Three Stooges*, Irving Berlin's "White Christmas," and Yoda, a character in *Star Wars*.

"Limited Editions" was a term which took over the Christmas market, becoming a windfall category for Christmas retailers. Department 56, with their line of various under the tree village houses, figures, and scenery, soon became the fad of this decade. Also, designers such as Christopher Radko, Larry Fraga, Patricia Breen, and Glenn Lewis became familiar names in the homes of collectors who cherished these limited edition ornaments for their trees and for house decorations as well.

Tree décor became something of a fine art, requiring shopping for ornaments, garlands, tree toppers, and house decorations which were more subdued, with a quieter, richer, and deeper look. Deep reds, green, and plums replaced the jewel-tone purple so popular in years past. The look was akin to what we would associate with European antiquity. Demographers recorded the fact that Americans stayed home more and attempted to make their homes as attractive and comfortable as possible for themselves, family, and friends. This trend resulted in boosting sales in the broad trim-a-home classification. Christmas textiles experienced a fifty percent increase from 1994 to 1995 as Americans decorated with needlepoint pillows, throws for their chairs and sofas, and wall hangings, all embellished with various Christmas themes.

Our Cards

Christmas history will continue to be made. From cards to telegraph to phones to computers, all took their recorded spots as our lives evolve. One new novelty implemented was the computer, which allowed many card manufacturers – including Hallmark – to help customers personalize their greetings in the store and obtain a truly personal card for someone they loved. The plunge into Internet communications in the mid-1990s allowed Americans to e-mail their greetings as well as to choose cards from the Internet and electronically send them instantaneously. So, many people took to the idea, either going onto an Internet site to send an already produced electronic Christmas card, or they produced their own card, employing digital images which they downloaded or took with a digital camera.

For many, the choice still remained to send a Christmas card through the mail. The National Stationery Show held in the Jacob Javits Center, New York, from May 15-18, 1993, in its show catalog, listed no less than 160 companies involved in the manufacturing, distribution, and selling of greeting cards. Hundreds of styles were available. Many of our new cards depicted designs and replicated artistic cards from the past. Among current popular items were twentieth century designs by artists Ellen Clapsaddle, John Winsch, and Ernest Nister, priced from fifty cents to a dollar. More elaborate die-cut cards reproduced from nineteenth century cards range in price from $1.50 to $5.00. The custom of sending Christmas cards was still firmly established in this country, in spite of a rapidly advancing technological society.

Array of greeting cards from the 1990s. $1.00-1.50 each.

Table and House Decorations—
Papier-Mâché

Christopher Radko captured the eyes of Americans with the re-introduction of papier-mâché Santas like those manufactured before World War II. While the production of these items had never ceased, they were not widely known outside of Germany. Radko changed that with figures made by the Schaller family in the Neustadt area of Germany. Carl Schaller, Thomas's grandfather, created the original molds used by Thomas Schaller in this decade. Great-grandfather Carl Schaller exported his Santas and other holiday decorations at the turn of the twentieth century. In the 1890s, Neustadt was the center of paper holiday articles, including flocked and pressed cardboard items as well as papier-mâché items. Carl learned the trade of "brossiere," the person who modeled these forms by hand. This was the most crucial and creative part of the manufacturing process. At this time, there were only five mold makers compared to twenty-five families who poured the papier-mâché and formed the figures, and around one hundred families that painted the dried articles.

Carl Schaller was one of six children born to farmer parents. Since the youngest and the oldest would inherit the farm, Carl had to find his own way – which happened to be through the creation of Christmas articles. After apprenticing with an old model maker, Carl started his own business in 1894. His business was successful for almost five decades; by his retirement, he had created molds for over forty Santa figures and over 180 other papier-mâché figures. The process stayed somewhat the same over the decades.

Liquefied paper pulp, clay, glue, and other mineral ingredients were combined. Then the mixture was blended into smooth consistency and poured in a two-part plaster mold. The plaster mold drew out excessive water, producing a thin shell. The excessive liquid was poured out and the shell dried gradually in a specially heated room.

The dried forms were dipped in liquid plaster, which gave each a thin whiteskin that was easily painted. Layers of background lacquer, paint, fine details, and a fine glaze were added and allowed to dry. Final details, such as chenille, pearls, and mica, were added in the last step to produce a final figure.

Carl's son, Ino Schaller, continued his father's craft after the war; but, by the 1940s, papier-mâché was somewhat abandoned as its popularity waned. Ino shifted production into pressed cardboard items, and then, in 1961, to plastic. Ino's son, Dieter, also made cardboard toys and figures, including Santas. In the early 1950s, they were decorated with real rabbit fur and wood felt; but, by the late 1950s, only fake plush was used. In the mid-1980s, Thomas, representing the newest generation of the Schaller family, uncovered his great-grandfather's molds in his attic. Fascinated by their artistry and variety, Thomas was inspired to learn the craft of mold casting and pouring papier-mâché. Thomas's sister, Kristina, oversaw the painting of these intricate figures, painting many of the faces herself. Thomas's mom cut fabrics from trimmings and took care of the administrative work. Their company was living proof that a cottage industry like those prior to World War II could survive and be quite feasible.

Thomas Schaller's papier-mâché Santa candy containers as illustrated in 1993 catalog of Christopher Radko.

Ino Schaller papier-mâché candy containers pictured in the Coburg museum. Produced just after World War II.

Ino Schaller papier-mâché candy containers made in late 1950s into the 1960s. Coburg, Germany, museum.

Linda Baldwin

Artist Linda Lindquist Baldwin purchased a book filled with images of old-world Belsnickle figures for a nickel. According to the book, original Belsnickles were selling for thousands of dollars. Being a single mother, she knew they were far beyond her reach. Although she had never attended an art class or even dabbled in arts or crafts, she mixed toilet paper with glue and water to form miniature Belsnickles. Crude as they were, she sold them for six dollars each at a craft fair. Good fortune was on her side at her next craft sale. *Better Homes and Gardens* spied her papier-mâché Belsnickles and told her that they were of museum quality. She was referred to the Smithsonian Institution and the Museum of American Folk Art in New York City. Her Belsnickles were featured in a museum exhibit, causing an unbelievable demand for her figures. Since she could only produce eight to ten originals in a year, she signed a contract with Schmid in 1992; but, the company filed for bankruptcy in 1995. Enesco Corporation offered her a contract on January 1, 1996, and she continued the fine tradition of producing these figures, releasing from six to eight new figures each year, with many copies of each figure available.

D. Blumchen & Company

With Deborah L. Boyce (daughter) as President, Diane S. Boyce (daughter), Vice-president, and Beatrice Blum Boyce (mother) as Secretary-treasurer, D. Blumchen & Company continued their business with gusto. Building upon their tradition of fabricating original ornaments from materials they purchased in Germany, every year new and delightful designs were quickly snapped up by eager collectors, whose demand for these whimsical designs often exceeded the numbers available.

Almost every item in their catalog had Blumchen input. All three owners have put a lot of time and energy into research and development. To ensure quality and authenticity, for which they were so well known, they assembled their own reference "library," encompassing books, magazines, newspaper clippings, old post cards, photos, and actual antiques – from glass ornaments to Santas to packaging. Sketches were constantly rendered after visiting doll and toy museums throughout Europe.

They have continued their buying trips to Europe. Their increased creativity and ingenuity ensure their top place in years to come when it comes to European-style home-crafted ornaments and decorations.

1992 Blumchen wire-wrapped fancy ornaments. Left to right: parasols, $25-35; violet umbrella, $23-27; Santa in airplane, $55-65; Angel's flight, $40-45.

1993 Blumchen Victorian Whimsey collection. Left to right: First frost clean-up, $40-45; Dutch love, $40-45; Victorian Easter basket, $45-60; Wine-taster Gnome, $35-45; Spirit of St. Nicholas (plane), $75-90; Evening Cathedral, $50-60.

Array of ornaments marketed by Blumchen's in 1990 including two-sided Dresden paper ornaments, $12-15 each; wire-wrapped boats and baskets, $35-45; cotton figural ornaments, $35-55; and glass angel and candle clip-on ornaments, $25-35.

Spun glass ornaments fashioned by Blumchen's in 1994. $10-15 each.

Unusual spun glass ornaments fashioned by Blumchen's in 1994. $12-17 each.

Blumchen's "Town of Bethlehem" Nativity Tableau marketed in 1995and all manufactured by Marolin in Steinach, Germany.

Blumchen's 1998 offerings. Cotton figures, $65-75; Angels sitting on ornate wire-wrapped ornaments, $50-60; Comets and stars, $15-20 each; Other wire-wraps, $35-45 each.

Debbie Thibault American Collectibles

Debbie Thibault was another American who created ornaments for our trees. Her style was reminiscent of American folk art. Since 1985 she had been producing folk art figurines. In 1995, she decided to establish her own manufacturing facilities through the help of two investors, Sandy Stevenson and Pat Berco, friends who also become actively involved in this business. Gradually, they invented a paper composition casting material which combines resin and papers to closely resemble antique toy material. The colors are muted and soft. In 1997, Debbie Thibault introduced her very first ornaments, limited to an edition of 2,500 or less.

Born and raised in Orange County, California, Thibault was an extremely creative child. At the age of four, she was designing paper doll outfits and Halloween costumes. In 1984, while on a maternity leave from Lasting Endearments, a Christmas decoration manufacturer, Thibault created an antique-style Santa, based upon her personal antique holiday collecting and library research. The body of her first Old Country Santa was created from a mixture of glues, newspaper, and starches which she formed onto a wooden dowel armature. Santa's clothing was sewn from linens and old worn dishrags. She traded this first Santa for an old quilt. In her second attempt, she included a commercially available paper pulp. Thus more durable and moldable, she was on her way to creating some fanciful Santa figures.

By the end of the decade, Thibault, her two partners, and nine employees offered over seventy-seven different figures. Each design continues to be handmade in this country from a papier-mâché and resin composition and each was numbered. Thibault's ornaments were made at her studio in California, truly creating American-crafted holiday decorations.

Tenna Flanner

Also working with papier-mâché was Tenna Flanner of Wisconsin. Teena became an expert on papier-mâché quite by chance. As an elementary school teacher raising a family of three children, she discovered a nineteenth century Santa mold in an area antiques shop. She was drawn to the design, but surprised at the $100 asking price. She purchased the mold because she realized she could use that mold to create a Santa figure and sell them. Teena's aim had been to pursue this as a hobby. But, with her marriage over, she turned to this as a business venture in 1991. Armed with a load of Santa figures and snowmen she hit the wholesale show circuit, but met with resistance.

At first, retail buyers were not interested in the glitter she applied to each piece. But it did not take long, and people were quickly attracted to these papier-mâché, glitter encrusted pieces, which mirror creativity and whimsical ideas.

Flanner developed her own formula for papier-mâché, which she forces into the molds. She dries, or bakes, each piece, hand-paints it, antiques it to look old, then adds her trademark touch of glitter. Flanner's jolly Santa Claus in the style of that created by nineteenth century cartoonist Thomas Nast is her most popular model. However, dozens of different styles of Santas have been created, including different styles of St. Nicholas and Belsnickle Santas that carry switches, have pointed hats, and black shoes.

Teena Flanner's Christmas figures, for which she is well known.

American Influences on Glass Ornaments and Tree Decorations

Victor

While the majority of glass ornaments were imported from Europe during this decade, there were some very elegant ornaments being manufactured in the United States by Victor, who began his career in 1975 blowing "intricate scientific apparatus for the medical, environmental, and research industries." Gradually, he considered creating some artistic work and developed his own line of ornaments after studying Venetian glass blowing with Lino Tagliapietra in Italy. Thus, his use of color and silver to shape his very abstract ornaments appealed to countless tree decorators who sought the unusual. Some of his most unusual were Cratered Moon, Cyber Galaxy, and Saturn Ring.

Mountain Lake Glassworks

A husband and wife team, Ed and Sally Russell, also created some very unique American-made ornaments in this decade. They did not start out as glass blowers. However, a set of circumstances led to Ed learning the art of the glass blowing business by taking courses part-time at the California College of Arts and Crafts. Eventually, they located their business at the former site of Camp Mountain Lake in Tracy City, Tennessee.

Using only recycled glass, they drew a ball of clear molten glass from the furnace onto the end of a five-foot stainless steel blowpipe. Since the temperature of the glass drops to 900 degrees in just three minutes, they had to keep re-heating the glass. If a base color was to be added, the form was rolled in a pulverized colored glass powder. Finally, the ornament was rolled in large shards of colored glass and reheated to fuse the powder and shards into a single piece of glass. Once the ornament reached its desired shape, it was slowly cooled for ten to twelve hours. Each is unique since each is individually made. Each is etched by the artists with CML (Camp Mountain Lake) and dated.

Memories in Glass

Cathy Warren, Mary Jane Sparkman, and Anita Swearengin formed "Memories in Glass" in 1995, which was headquartered in Tulsa, Oklahoma. These women created all of their designs using favorite "Depression Glass" patterns and colors shaped into Christmas ornaments. Cathy Warren holds a degree in Management and collected Christmas ornaments for years. Mary Jane Sparkman had extensive experience in Finance and also had a love for collecting glass ornaments. Anita Swearengin held a degree in Marketing and her passion was collecting Depression Glass.

These three friends combined their talents and headed to Fenton Art Glass with their new product. They design the ornament, they own the molds, the copyrights, and the distribution rights. Fenton Art Glass hand-crafted the designs in the United States. In 1997, they produced an angel entitled "Kelly Angel," made in the Depression Glass Roses and Butterflies pattern in Burmese glass. These ornaments appealed to Fenton Art Glass and Depression Glass followers.

Mary Jane Sparkman and Cathy Warren then became co-owners of "Memories in Glass." Each of their ornaments is reminiscent of Depression Glass designs, completed in an ornament style by Fenton Glass. Each is limited from a low edition of 216 to a maximum of 1,000 pieces. They could double as sun catchers in a window.

Mary Jane and Cathy obtained permission from the Fenton family to use Burmese glass, a glass mixed with gold and Uranium to give it a solid yellowish beige color instead of clear. Where heat was applied to the mold, a pink tint appeared on the edges. Flat shapes included angels, snowmen, houses, bells, nuts, and even bears. Each of their ornaments was lovingly named in honor of their family and friends.

William Sparkman Designs

An entirely new look appeared in 1998 with "Earthenware" ornaments introduced by Bill Sparkman, who was married to Mary Jane Sparkman of "Memories in Glass." Produced in Oklahoma, each design was limited to 2,500 pieces. Each was designed by Bill himself, but all the sculpting and painting was left to artisans. Produced from earthenware, they were much sturdier than glass. Made from this substance, many of them had attachments such as Santa holding out a candle or an angel holding out a star.

European Influences on Glass Ornaments and Tree Decorations

Germany

Due to the Cold War, the training of glass blowers in technical schools was abandoned. Before this, the blowers were once trained by masters who had vast experience in blowing glass ornaments. Training took as long as one year to become proficient at blowing a simple glass sphere, and several subsequent years to create a craftsman to master the art of blowing intricate and fanciful ornaments. Usually three years of school were required to get a certificate, then eight to ten years of on-the-job training to learn the art, and then three more years of schooling to gain an advanced "masters" degree which allowed the glass blower to then teach others this skill. Therefore, older glass blowers were highly coveted employees because very few young people were able to learn the skill while on the job.

However, since the early 1990s, the German glass artisans school has been in operation, and in 1997, they finally saw their first graduates of the "masters" class. Only five students were qualified to graduate, and only three of those were able to produce the required "masterpiece" to receive their master craftsman certificate. Three of those first graduates work at the Inge Glass Company. Erwin Eichhorn, who attended the school before the Cold War, was one of the first to re-enroll when the school re-opened. His masterpiece, "Santa on Bell," was over 15" tall and featured a blown Santa robed in red with white glitter placed on top of an extremely large free blown red bell.

Rene Moller, also employed by Inge Glass, was one of the first younger men to achieve this status with "Santa Reflector Tree Top," which featured a mold blown Santa in a dark matte red with gold glitter trim placed on top of a free blown six pointed star with deep indents and glass glitter accents.

The tradition of creating glass tree ornaments continued in its birthplace, Lauscha. As of 1999, there were eleven different family workshops listed as being involved in the manufacturing of ornaments. These names include Helmut Bohm, Peter Bohm, Helmut Greiner-Lar, GmbH Greiner-Lar, Michael Haberland, Walter Hahnlein, Marlene Hellbach, Heldun Hertzsch, Mike Lerch, Heinz Robner, and Rolf Stadter. All of them either provided ornaments for larger companies or wholesaled their designs to American importers through various toy and ornament fairs.

Erwin Eichhorn blown ornament completed as a special commemorative ornament for the "Golden Glow of Christmas Past" convention in 1995. $Priceless.

Lauscha in summer of 1993, renewed in the ornament tradition after the reunification of Germany.

Klaus Hertzsch of Lauscha showing a mold which has been in his family for decades.

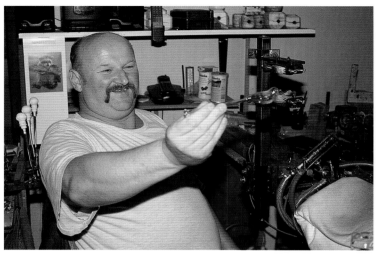

Klaus Hertzsch showing ornament just released from mold.

Klaus Hertzsch at work in his home in an attached workshop in Lauscha blowing ornaments as he has for decades.

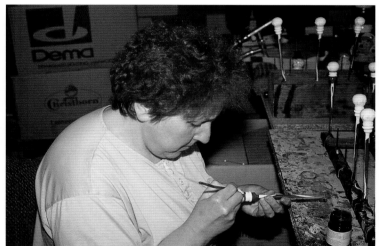

Heindrun Hertzsch, wife of Klaus, painting ornaments as she does every day in their attached workshop.

Heindrun Hertzsch in the back of their home in a tiny showroom they have which illustrates ornaments they have created as well as a storage area for boxes of ornaments waiting to go to the American market.

Krebs & Sohn

This decade witnessed a huge growth in the Krebs & Sohn glass ornament manufacturing business in Germany. Immediately after the reunification of East and West Germany in 1991, Helmut Krebs purchased the business from the former East German government. He privatized this business and combined it with his business in Rosenheim and Roswell, New Mexico. Since Lauscha was the birthplace of the glass Christmas tree ornament industry, he found it perfect for this expansion. Steeped in the history of these hills, Krebs created ornaments like those created generations before. A large, newly constructed factory at the edge of Lauscha creates thousands of ornaments for the American market.

Wolfgang was in charge of operating the business in Rosenheim, Germany. Helmut and third son, Michael, established a large, newly constructed ornament factory in Lauscha. This factory was established immediately after the reunification of East and West Germany. Helmut Krebs found this area to be the perfect spot to expand their business, considering that Lauscha is the birthplace of the Christmas ornament business. On November 20, 1998, Wilma died, leaving a void in this family-run business. Helmut retired in the late 1990s to Rosenheim. In charge of production was Gerd Ross, who was an original sales promoter for the VEB in East German times. Over the years, Ross became an expert who was widely recognized as such by the East German government. Ross is a valuable source of information for what occurred in the Christmas ornament business in East Germany before its reunification with Germany. Before the reunification of Germany, Ross would often visit with Helmut Krebs at the Nuremberg Fair. Over the years, they became very close. In 1991, there were 150 employees with over twenty million Deutsch marks invested in the business. In 1991, over one-third of the sales were to the Soviet Union. However, their economic difficulties caused them to cut orders. Thus, the state-owned cooperative was divided into three companies.

Some of the most encouraging news was that Germany, in the late 1990s, recognized glass blowing as a trade and will continue to teach it to the young. Young apprentices came to Krebs with skills that continue to be perfected with each year of blowing glass figurals. Individually blown, silvered, painted, and then packed into boxes for importation to different parts of the world, the ornaments were just like those earlier produced in Lauscha. Currently Krebs ships ornaments to Mexico, Canada, South America, England, France, other European countries, and the Army f-system, as well as selling them in the United States.

Helmut and Wilma Krebs in their Lauscha showroom in 1993 among the thousands of moulds in their company's possession.

Wilma Krebs in the Lauscha showroom in 1993 among their thousands of models of moulds.

Lauscha Glas Creation owned by Krebs family in Lauscha. Newly constructed building to help consolidate manufacturing of glass ornaments. Finished in 1995.

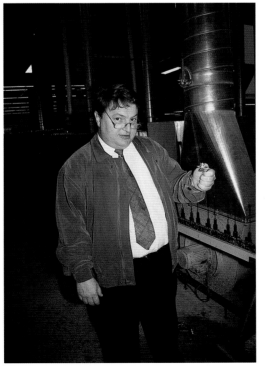

Gerd Ross, in charge of production at Krebs— also very involved in the early years of VEB.

In Rosenheim, 1994. Left to right: Wolfgang Krebs, Pete Peterson (sales manager of Krebs USA), and Eberhard Krebs.

Table of moulds and stylus types used for the creation of elaborate reflector ornaments, all owned by Krebs in Lauscha.

Glass blowers at work in what was an old VEB co-operative factory, creating heavy glass kugels in the old traditional manner.

Glass blower blows tree top with careful attentive detail which results in some of the elaborate examples facing him at his work table at Krebs.

Case of newly created kugels (heavy glass ornaments with tin tops) from Krebs in Lauscha.

Close-up of glass blower heating glass to anneal glass to the basic shape.

Filling the glass ornaments with the silvering solution to give them that mirror-like appearance.

Placing the ornaments over "nails" to run them through a heated tunnel to quickly prepare the ornaments for the next step.

Submerging the ornaments in hot sudsy water to act as a catalyst to coat the silver nitrate mixture to the inside walls of the ornaments.

Painting the ornaments one by one is the next step in the process of creating ornaments for our trees.

The final step includes scoring the pike, breaking it off, placing a spring cap into the ornament for hanging on the tree, and then placing the finished ornaments in boxes ready to be packed to come to America.

Tree top from Krebs "Lauscha Glas Creation" in 1993. Hand-painted by Helmut Krebs. $Priceless.

Helena Horn and her assistant, Frau Schmidt, in the Glas Keramik museum in Lauscha dedicated to the history of the rich tradition of blowing glass in this area.

One view of recreated glass blower's cottage in Lauscha museum. The museum's restoration and renewed dedication to Christmas glass ornament history is due completely to the ingenuity, creativeness, and dedication of Helena Horn.

Close-up of glass blower's work table, Lauscha museum.

120

Close-up of silvered ornaments on nails pushed through a wooden plank. Ornaments were put in rafters to dry before being hand-painted.

Close-up showing boxes of ornaments resting on a light wooden plank. The boxed ornaments were carried down the steep hills of Lauscha to the train station.

Side view of glass blower's cottage illustrating paints off to right and bird cage on wall which served as a carbon monoxide detector in the winter when the windows were tight and the glass blower was at work.

Lauscha train station, where ornaments were delivered to be taken by train to the seacoast where they were packed into the holds of ships destined for our Christmas trees.

Käthe Wohlfahrt

Harald Wohlfahrt eventually set up an internationally oriented public relations and advertising department, and conducted a successful campaign, promoting the German Christmas in foreign tourism markets. During his tenure, several new Käthe Wohlfahrt stores have been established in Germany.

In 1983 Harald opened a wholesale and customer service office in the USA. And in 1988 he partnered with a Japanese businessman to open the first Käthe Wohlfahrt store in Japan. Each store is a unique creation, unlike any other, and yet each maintains the Käthe Wohlfahrt trademark look that ties it to the entire family of Käthe Wohlfahrt stores.

In the 1990s, Wohlfahrt added another store in Rothenburg, one in Riquewihr, France, and one in Kamakura, a historic Japanese city. By 1999, Harold Wohlfahrt, their son, was the Company CEO of an enterprise, which employed over one hundred people and sold over 70,000 different Christmas items.

Among Käthe Wohlfahrt's selections are Erzgebirge nutcrackers, smokers, candle-powered rotating Christmas pyramids, and music boxes; hand-painted wax angels; hand-carved Nativity scenes from the Tyrolean Alps; stuffed toy animals from Steiff; and wood, glass, straw, and pewter tree ornaments. The emphasis at Wohlfahrts is on traditional, German-style decorations and ornaments. Most of the customers are German until the summer months, when Americans and Japanese tourists account for the largest percentage of off-season customers—about twenty percent each.

On September 29, 2000, a long awaited dream came true for Harald Wohlfahrt. Together with over one hundred invited guests and the help of Santa Claus and "angels," who travelled a long way just to get there, the first permanent exhibition showing the historical development of German Christmas traditions opened to the public. Over 2,950 square feet on the second floor of the "Weihnachtsdorf," the Christmas Village, provides the visitors a view of extraordinary exhibits in forty-two glass cabinets and displays how Christmas was celebrated by our forefathers.

The opening of the German Christmas Museum in Rothenburg ob der Tauber fulfilled a wish for Harald Wohlfahrt. He had first conceived of the Museum eighteen years earlier when he purchased the first exhibit in Leipzig for his future collection. He has actively worked on the fulfilment of this project since that time. Many thanks go to the moral support of collectors like Adolf Heidenreich and Elfriede Kreuzberger, who supplied their valuable nutcrackers and tree ornaments on a permanent lease basis. Considerable work was necessary to construct the museum inside this historic building. A total of over DM 2.5 million was invested for the interior reconstruction with the safety of all the visitors in mind.re:

Three rooms display decorated trees ranging from the Biedermeier era to 1945. Unique exhibits of the following categories are on display in glass cabinets:

• Early Heavy Glass Kugels and Glass Fruit from Lauscha, lead finished;
• Formed Glass Kugels: Heads, Fruit, Santas, Flowers, Animals, Figures with Legs;
• Tragacanth;
• Wax and Stencils;
• Wire-Wrapped Ornaments;
• Cotton Ornaments/Russian Cotton Ornaments;
• Pewter Ornaments/Tinsel Ornaments with/without Scraps;
• Early Gablonz Ornaments;
• Cotillion Medals – Candy Containers;
• Yarn-Wrapped Frame Ornaments/Stars;
• Embossed Ornaments/Russian Paper Ornaments;
• Bohemian Cardboard Ornaments;
• Art Deco Ornaments, Icicles, Glass Bead Strands, Reflectors and Stamps;
• Imperial Period Ornaments/First World War;
• Wax Angels/Tree Toppers;
• Candleholders/Oil Lamps/Electrical String Lights;
• Advent Tree Ornaments;
• Edible Tree Decorations;
• Miniature Christmas Trees for Doll Houses/Christmas Tins.

A look inside Kathe Wohlfahrt's in Rothenburg ob der Tauber, Germany.

A view of the newly created Christmas museum in Kathe Wohlfahrt's in Rothenburg ob der Tauber, Germany.

Oberfrankische Glas

In 1990, after Germany reunified Oberfränkische Glas established a mechanized production near Lauscha and employed many glass blowers in the area. After the opening of East European markets, Oberfrandische Glas entered a joint venture with a Polish company and began production in Greece as well.

Italy Gains New Prominence in Manufacturing Glass Ornaments

LAVED

In this decade, LAVED continued to be one of the major producers of Italian glass ornaments. Purchased in the late 1980s by Enrico Scaletti from the Lemmi glass blowing family, LAVED moved into its new factory in 1995. While the figural ornaments are all created in Bellagio on Lake Como, about two hours from Milan, the company opened a subsidiary in Romania to provide small molded indents and balls. There are two small factories in southern Italy which also help to provide simple shapes to LAVED to design and paint in their Bellagio factory. Thirty percent of its production generally went to Christopher Radko ornaments while another fifty percent went to other major lines including the Gifford Line of Delavan, Wisconsin. However, in the mid- to late 1990s, LAVED began marketing a large number of elaborate figural ornaments under its own label through various department stores and its own web site which illustrated the ornaments. Their own personal line included more than sixty figural ornaments each year. Twenty were added and twenty removed each year. Eventually they plan on including a line of one hundred ornaments.

Interestingly enough, there is no apprenticeship program or school to train Italian glassblowers. They are trained on the job with not even an apprenticeship program in place. However, through their training by master craftsmen, Italian glass blowers continue to create the most delicate and intricate of free-blown figurals in the world.

The process starts with a very complicated glass cutting machine which turns six-foot long glass rods into shorter segments about six-inches to twelve-inches in length. Then this piece is enlarged in one portion (to allow for faster softening in the flame), creating a "blank." Now the "blank" is ready for the glass blower. The blanks are placed on baskets that sit on the floor at the feet of each glass blower.

The blower sits at a table, fitted with a gas torch used to heat the glass as the blower blows it. The blower picks up the blank, heats the enlarged middle portion of the tube into which he intends to blow, and begins to fill the heating glass with air from his lungs. As the glass softens, the blower shapes the main body and pulls various appendages out of the piece. Some of the appendages are created by heating another tube of glass, and then welding it to the main body. Each glass blower works with a particular shape, lending expertise to each ornament. The glass blowing process is extremely complicated and glass blowers gradually move from the simple shapes to those as elaborate as crabs and other figures with multiple appendages.

The next step is the silvering of the ornament. The dark appearing silver mixture is placed in each ornament. Each ornament is shaken until the solution turns a bright silver right in front of the eye of the viewer, coating the entire interior surface.

Then each ornament is allowed to dry and is then taken to the painting and decorating part of the factory. Here, artisans apply bright colors with amazing precision that leaves no spots, streaks, or accidentally unpainted areas. German lacquers are used for paint. Still attached to their long stems, each ornament is scored with a sharp knife, and a metal cap is inserted into the open neck. The process ends when the ornaments are individually packaged, boxed, and shipped to various destinations around the world.

One portion of this factory contains a host of tall, deep metal cabinets filled with large shallow drawers. In each of the drawers are the current LAVED samples which can be viewed by prospective customers. This showroom displays myriad colors and designs, with decorated trees and hundreds of ornaments hung on the walls. A retail store in Bellagio illustrates the glass blowing process through various exhibits and offers for sale many of the original designs created by LAVED. Future plans include a museum which would highlight all the various designs created by LAVED going back to its original owner, Ilia Lemmi.

Many of these very creative designs are the inspiration of Luca Ferraresi, who will personally execute the decoration of the first several pieces to help the various artists who are completing the decorating process. Interestingly enough, there is a reason given for many of the free-blown figural ornaments. Molds can be copyrighted, but actual free blown shapes don't really belong to any one person. But their knowledge of production has been passed down from generation to generation. For the Christmas of 1999, LAVED began an exclusive designer line of ornaments which bears the LAVED tag and cap. Luca's designs run the gambit from Christmas themes such as Santa Claus and reindeer to fanciful designs like Aladdin on a flying carpet.

Enrico Scaletti, owner of LAVED, showing off an angel mould and ornament created from that mold. In addition to free blown ornaments, his company does work with molds in the German-style.

Luca Ferraresi, the artistic side of LAVED, holding one of the metal moulds, the positive figure of which he sculpted and designed.

Enrico Scaletti, owner of LAVED, in 1998 illustrating one of the ornaments created for Christopher Radko.

Close-up of some of the mid-1990s angels produced by LAVED.

Box of ornaments produced in an earlier decade by LAVED, before it was owned by Enrico Scaletti.

De Carlini Soffieria, SNC

Located near Milan, another Italian factory continued to be a prominent player in the production of figural ornaments in this decade. The Terruzzi family owns the DeCarlini ornament workshop which is widely recognized for its hand-painted and decorated ornaments. This decoration, which includes ribbon, fabrics, felt, and yarns, is what sets aside their ornaments. Giulio Terruzzi, his wife Rosa, and their son Luca continue to operate this factory, which is about thirty minutes from Milan. Currently his four-year old daughter, Alice, also helps with the family business in many different ways, indicating a true interest as a fourth generation family member in this business. Her artistic curiosity and creativity is already evident in designs she creates for her school art projects.

The DeCarlini Family outside their factory in Macherio, Italy. Left to right: Rosa, Alice, Luca, Sabrina, and Giulio Terruzzi. Their newly constructed addition was completed in Fall, 2000.

There are only two actual pieces of machinery used in producing their ornaments. The first was a glass-cutting machine. The long narrow pieces of glass are heated and cut by this machine to produce workable sized blanks. These blanks resemble a rolling pin in shape, narrow at each end with an elongated bubble in the center. The other machine used in this business actually shakes the ornaments after they are filled with the silvering solution. This coats the inside in an even manner, a difficult task when one considers all the appendages of these free-blown creations. Gino, their master glass blower, began in 1947 at the age of thirteen and worked at the

DeCarlini factory his entire life. In the early 1990s, he started to help develop new designs for the business. In 1993, he traveled to the United States with Giulio and Rosa to Frankenmuth, Michigan, to demonstrate the Italian glass blowing process to countless Americans who made special travel arrangements to personally view this complicated, artistic process. His most important role at the present time is to personally train all new glass blowers since no formal schooling is available to learn this art. His skilled craftsmanship skills have been imparted to many different employees of the DeCarlini business over the decades.

Rosa is the master creator of the decorating area, where she supervises the dressing of all the glass ornaments produced there. The finest fabrics and ribbons of brocade satin and soft velvet are combined with yarn hair and many other decorations to create ornaments of great value and creativity. Through a complicated, orchestrated process, each ornament is passed from artisan to artisan. Each artist has developed a particular skill, be it applying a wig of hair, ribbons for skirts, or tiny starts on magic wands. This decoration portion of the factory contains table upon table of glass figural ornaments, all being dressed and decorated in sequential steps until they are ready to be finally inspected, packaged, boxed, and stored in the warehouse awaiting shipment to the United States.

Their business space has tripled in size with the addition of factory production space, a newly enlarged warehouse, and a lavishly designed display room which highlights all the fanciful figural ornaments produced by this family. Finished in early 2000, this expansion allows them the possibilities of providing even more ornaments for the American market.

After being blown, the ornaments are dipped by colored lacquers by Giulio.

Enrico DeCarlini, originator of the company. Enrico was assisted by his daughters, Rosa and Maria Luisa, and by his wife, Elisa. Rosa became involved in the business as a very young girl by helping paint and hand-decorate the glass figural ornaments.

Gino, their master glass blower, at work blowing ornaments from a single tube of glass. He began in 1947 at the age of thirteen and worked at the DeCarlini factory his entire life.

Ornaments are finished one by one. Ornament details include hand-tied bows in hair, skirts, and even braided hair, all hot-glued to glass ornaments.

Cinderella's coach is waiting for gold foil details after the wheels and basic trims have been included.

Moulds used by Enrico DeCarlini in his factory's early history. Their first ornaments were made from these moulds in the traditional style and then gradually the Italians developed their own free-blown style for which they are known today.

Close-up of street car mould with glass silvered ornament inside which was produced from this very early mould.

Rosa cutting bolts of ribbon which will become skirts for little ornament girls. The entire family works in the factory each and every day along side their employees to provide the elaborate finishing details, for which the DeCarlini family is so famous.

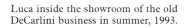

Luca inside the showroom of the old DeCarlini business in summer, 1993.

Mortelmans, S.N.C.

Mortelemans S.N.C., owned and operated by Fausto and Fiorenzo Di Gilardoni, emerged as a major producer of glass figural ornaments. Originally started in early 1979, this firm produced metal caps for ornament tops and metal clips for birds. Owned by Ilia Lemni, this portion of her entire company only produced these parts. In 1985, when Mrs. Lemni sold out her companies as she went into retirement, Fausto and Fiorenzo purchased this company. They supplied these caps and clips to all major producers of glass ornaments.

Their entrance into the production of glass ornaments was quite interesting. Their sister Rita had worked from the early 1960s for Mrs. Lemni and then worked for LAVED when it was purchased by Enrico Scaletti. Initially, Rita helped her brothers get started in the business. Their first venture were glass candles in metal clips because they felt these figurals were unique. In 1984-85, they started producing spheres and other glass figurals.

In 1996, they expanded their business with the addition of a new factory on the outskirts of Bellagio which serves as space for decorating ornaments as well as a warehouse and showcase room which displays every single one of the figural ornaments they produce. They no longer produce metal caps, obtaining them from Germany. But they do produce metal clips for birds and clips for candles. They have six to seven glassblowers on the premises blowing figural ornaments in the free-blown Italian style. Over thirty people are employed in various capacities, eight to ten of these who are the artists who all hand paint every single ornament.

Their long glass tubes are purchased from Schott, a German company. They then have machines to soften and extend the middle of each glass tube to help the glassblowers when they start the glass blowing process. High quality German lacquers are used to paint their ornaments.

Currently Iris, the wife of Fausto, works in the factory every day as a decorator. Along with the other artists, they carefully detail every ornament with loving care. While each ornament is different, each is exact in detail and carefully color coordinated to produce some very elegant pieces. Fiorenzo's wife is also involved in the daily running of the business as an office worker. Therefore, Mortleman's is truly a family business.

They do designs for larger importers, but do much of their own designing for their individual lines. They have done work for the Waterford Crystal Company for four years, currently being the only Italian factory to be so commissioned by Waterford Crystal.

Experienced glass blower at work creating ornaments for Mortelemans S.N.C.

Iris, the wife of Fausto, at work painting individual details one by one on these intricate glass ornaments.

Bellagio, Italy. Home to LAVED and Mortelemans S.N.C.

Mortelemans S.N.C. with an experienced painter adding those final details to glass ornaments destined for shipment to the United States.

Left:
Fiorenzo and Fausto Di Gilardoni inside their business, Mortelemans S.N.C.

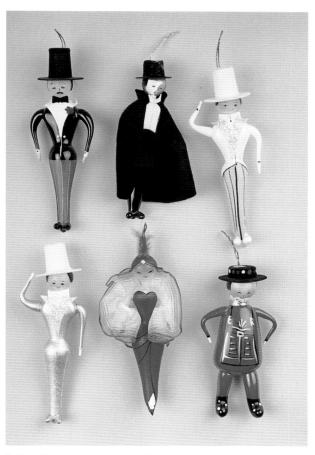

Italian blown ornaments from the early 1990s. Left to right, top to bottom: Gentleman with black cardboard top hat, $25-35; Phantom of the Opera (original piece), $45-55; Gentleman with white cardboard top hat, $45-45; Man with white cardboard top hat in silver suit, $45-55; Elegant lady in red, $45-55; and British military man with glass hat, $35-45.

Mid-1990s Italian figural ornaments, mostly attributed to De Carlini near Milan. Left to right, top to bottom: Rabbit from Alice in Wonderland, $45-50; Angel with blue glittered wings, $40-50; Uncle Sam, $50-55; Clown on top of children's block, $40-50; Cinderella's wicked stepsisters, $40-50; Elegant Arabian lady, $50-60.

1996 set of Louisa May Alcott's Little Women. $120-140 for boxed set.

Astronaut on the Moon, 1990s remake of earlier version. DeCarlini produced. $75-85.

Italian figural ornaments, all blown by LAVED in Bellagio. Late 1990s. Musical pig, $50-55; Oriental man, $45-55; German opera singer, $45-50; Lady with metal skis on snowball, $50-55; Comic character, $55-60.

Grasshopper with top hat. Designed and commissioned by Kristmas Kringle of Fond du Lac, Wisconsin. Morteleman produced. $75-80.

Set of bugs ornaments, all produced by the De Carlini family in 1999-2000. $30-35 each.

Czechoslovakia

Manually blown and painted Christmas decorations have been produced in Czechoslovakia for many years. In order to understand the current make-up of their production for the Christmas market, it is necessary to look into the past. The economic depression of the 1930s caused the fall of the market demand for the decorative blown hollow beads produced in huge quantities by the Czechoslovakians. For that reason the manufacturers in Bohemia looked for other possibilities of applying their acquired skill. In this way, a glass-making co-operative was founded at Zdobin, near Dvui Kralove, in 1931, and gradually the production of glass decorations was extended to other regions all over the country.

The manufacturers in Dvur Kralove, Horni Bradio, Cadca, Opava, and Prague have not been able to cope with the well-proven articles, which at Christmas time have brought pleasure to people all over the world for many years. Every year they offer about seventy new sorts of Christmas decorations to accompany new waves of fashion. The exporting of Christmas decorations today is a monopoly of the Foreign Trade Corpora-

tion of JABLONEX formed in 1952, which has its domicile in the town of Jablonec nad Nisou. Besides exporting ornaments to the USA, Jablonex exports decorations to the Soviet Union, Great Britain, France, Italy, Sweden, and Holland.

A number of companies specialized in glass bead Christmas tree ornaments: IRIS (Zasada), ASTIR (Jablonec n.N. production in Lucany), CESKE PERLICKY- Bohemia Beads (Zasada), and GOJA (Jablonec n.N.) who produced primarily the larger shapes. NEOBANE (Jablonec n.N.) made tree ornaments from various materials, including glass beads.

JABLONEX

JABLONEX, with its headquarters in Jablonec nad Nisou, is one of the best-known exporters of Czech ornaments. These Christmas decorations are under the commercial section DECORA (Christmas Tree Ornaments and Flower Decorations). Mirek Vesely spent over twenty-eight years in both costume jewelry as well as in the Christmas ornament exportation. To be promptly connected with their business partners all over the world, Jablonex makes use of their wide network of affiliated companies and agencies in France, Germany, Italy, the United States, Mexico, Poland, Spain, Great Britain, Canada, Brazil, Singapore, and Russia.

Every August and September, there is an exhibition termed "CHRISTMAS BY JABLONEX" in the company's showroom, which is a sought after event of the season according to Filip Brogowski, the Decora division manager. He goes on to state, "Foreign customers can see what Jablonex has prepared for the next Christmas season and choose the appropriate goods." In January and February, the company starts preparing their collection for the following year. They cooperate with approximately 210 private producers of Christmas decorations from the Czech Republic and Slovakia. The selection comprises hand blown, painted glass decorations of different shapes that follow the latest trends in color and theme. Their painting is very important since it is carried out by hand. In their decorating, painters employ materials such as powdered glass, plastics, and aluminum. Some ornamentation is sprayed directly by hand or by using various stencils. The relatively demanding technique of silk-screening is even used to place intricate motifs on the ornaments. In the mid-1990s, ornaments were made by "fusing," a process which sealed together several layers of multi-colored glass into a certain motif. In the early 1990s, their style changed considerably, through the creation of their own designing department creating roughly ninety percent of their own original designs. Jablonex, Co. Ltd. regularly presents part of their Christmas collection at the Spielwaren Messe fair in Nuremberg in February.

Working with the silvering of glass ornaments in the traditional fashion at Jablonec.

Applying glue and then glitter as a final touch to ornaments produced at Jablonec for exportation to the United States.

Painting glass ornaments at Jablonec in a small workshop located in the Czech Republic.

Jablonex assortment of ornaments produced in the 1990s.

Czechoslovakian ornaments from the early 1990s, all part of Christopher Radko's line. $35-45 each.

Poland Gains Prominence in the Creation of Glass Ornaments

In Grebynice, Poland, Ewa Calik, the president of the glass ornament factory that she and her husband Grzegorz, founded in 1882 in the basement of their farmhouse about twenty-five miles from Krakow, related their early start in the business. In 1994, the Calik factory completed over 600,000 glass ornaments ranging from Father Christmas figures to turtle doves to parrots and piglets. Most of the Calik's ornaments were sold to Christopher Radko, who started his Christmas ornament import business ten years after the Caliks. Radko discovered the Caliks when he came to Poland in search of replacements for some ornaments handed down from his German, Czech, and Polish relatives.

When discovered by Radko, Ewa and Grzegorz had a little gas burner and bottles of paint. They first blew their ornaments while they grew tomatoes and roses in their greenhouse for extra income. In those early years, the Caliks produced only round shaped ornaments. The Caliks found an artist who modeled Radko's designs in clay. From the designs, a metal mold was made. In the mid-1990s, the painters—who earned an average Polish wage of $250 a month—decorated the ornaments with techniques similar to those used by painters of fine porcelain. Slightly over 300 people were employed by the Caliks in the manufacturing of their glass ornaments. More than 100 painters were employed by the Caliks. One such artist was Marzena Mazurek, a twenty-one-year-old art student, who worked at benches in well-lit rooms at the farmhouse and two other plants nearby. After painting, drying, and inspection for quality, the ornaments were wrapped in special paper and sent by truck from the Polish countryside to ships or, in the days before Christmas, by airfreight to New York. In 1994, they provided over 200 designs for Christopher Radko.

According to Ewa Calik, about seventy percent of the materials used in the ornaments, including the hard glass and base varnishes, were Polish. The glossy acrylic paints and the fine gold and silver glitter were imported from the United States. "Polish acrylic paint is of poor quality and the glitter is too coarse," Calik explained. Eighty percent of their ornaments went to the United States with the remainder being marketed in Western Europe.

Gedania

The industrial co-operative GEDANIA is a well-equipped modern manufacturer employing close to 750 people, eighty-five percent being women. Its daily output includes about 30,000 glass ornaments, two-thirds of which are hand-painted by women. Gedania got its start in 1950 as a cooperative company who exported ornaments through Varimex, and later through Coopexim. In 1953, only fifty to sixty companies were allowed by the government to export goods to other nations. In 1983, they obtained their own license for export. And, in 1985, they exported two to three thousand dollars worth of Christmas ornaments. In 1986, they exported 65,000 dollars of merchandise and by 1995, they were exporting two million dollars worth of ornaments. The mid-1980s were lean years for Gedania, which was tied to the economic situation in Poland. Poland lost UN- most favorite nation status. This resulted in a sixty-five percent duty for goods sent to the United States. This all but shut them out of the market due to the high cost of their goods. There was very limited exportation.

In 1987 changes occurred and the most favored nation status clause was once again adopted. Polish ornaments were competitive once again. This caused Gedania to exhibit their wares at the Nuremburg Toy Fair. This exhibition helped them to quickly build their business once the duty was gone and the western world got to see the excellent quality of mold and paint detailing.

Most of their ideas for ornaments come from the employees themselves. There is an annual contest among employees with a cash prize being awarded to the winners of the chosen designs. There are also lots of brainstorming sessions where management creates different designs for the market. The production manager for Gedania is Mrs. Ciumajcis, who manages pretty well the entire glass ornaments production line. They produce over two million ornaments a year, with about seventy percent of their export sales being to the United States.

Marek Pawlowski started to work for Gedania in the export department in 1986. His supervisor at that time was Mr. Kaminski. In 1988 Kaminiski left to work in Libia, with Pawlowski taking over his position as export manager. From 1988 to 1993, Gedania's export sales increased about 165%. In 1994, Marek Pawlowski was elected to be a member of the board of directors and became a Commercial Manager of the whole cooperative.

Assortment of ornaments produced in the Calik factory and purchased in Crakow, Poland, in the mid-1990s. Left to right: Santa football player, $35-40; fish, $20-25 each.

Pope John Paul ornament produced in the Calik factory and purchased in Crakow, Poland, in 2000. $75-85.

Marek Pawlowski, Commercial Manager of the cooperative, showing some of the finished ornaments.

Silvering in Gedania, accomplished through means of a Polish invented machine which allowed for the silvering of up to twenty-four ornaments at one time.

Eyes and intricate facial details being added by a Polish artist in Gedania.

Painting details on glass ornaments in Gedania, the bright colors of which distinguish the Polish ornaments from other European ornaments.

Two Polish artists at work in Gedania with a table of ornaments and Polish-manufactured lacquers adding details one by one to ornaments.

Scoring and packing ornaments in Gedania in preparation for their exportation to the United States.

American Importers and Manufacturers of Tree Ornaments

Old World Christmas

New designs, advanced technology, exclusive contracts with German manufacturers, national recognition for design excellence, and the introduction of a Collectors' Club set Old World Christmas into high gear with record sales and product development. Old World Christmas established long-term contractual agreements with Inge-Glas of Neustadt b. Coburg, Germany, for sole distribution of their glass ornaments. The smokers and nutcrackers in the line were supplied exclusively in North America to Old World Christmas by K.W.O. of Olberhau, Germany. With the support of these two fine companies, who were known for their traditional designs and quality products, Old World Christmas was able to overcome the stereotype of mass-produced products by offering pieces that receive generous amounts of time and attention to detail that result in very collectible heirlooms.

E.M. Merck, premier designer for Old World Christmas, possesses a strong background in German language, culture, and art history and holds a degree in fine arts. In 1992, E.M. Merck created a special glass nutcracker ornament to commemorate the 100th anniversary of Tchaikovsky's ballet the "Nutcracker." This piece was successfully produced in a new mold which was created through a process that was "lost" in East Germany for many years. Old World Christmas now has the ability to use either new molds or original antique molds. Old World Christmas has access, through Inge-Glas, to the largest collection of antique glass ornament molds in the world. With access to the best of both new and old molds, the possibilities are endless for wonderful new creations from Old World Christmas.

E.M. Merck was nominated for a total of three "1993 Collector Edition Awards of Excellence" in two separate categories. Two of the artist's glass ornaments, Large Cornucopia and Santa in Chimney, are nominees in the "Ornaments" category. The Fuessen Father Christmas Nutcracker received its nomination in the "All Other Collectibles" category.

Due to an overwhelming demand from retail customers, Old World Christmas founded a collectors' club in August 1992 to bring together the group of collectors and Christmas enthusiasts that are dedicated to the enchantment and the collectible value of Old World Christmas collectibles. As the supplier who has pioneered the concept of presenting only the highest quality in Old World holiday collectibles and decorations, it is only fitting that Old World Christmas should present the industry with a collectors' club dedicated to traditional, hand-made holiday products of skilled European artisans. The Old World Christmas Collectors' Club became a tremendous success. Yearly membership entitled members to purchase exclusive collectibles limited to club members only and to receive the quarterly club newsletter, *The Old World Christmas Star Gazette*, which contained up-to-date information regarding new designs, retired items, and general information on the history and traditions of Old World Christmas collectibles.

Over the past two decades, Old World Christmas became a leader in the Christmas decorations industry. The firm has brought to the industry an unsurpassed level of performance by focusing on exclusive quality products, outstanding service, and strong retail sales support. These are the commitments to excellence upon which the company was built, commitments the company continues to uphold today to take its rightful place as a significant supplier of holiday collectibles and decorations.

Old World Christmas continued to expand to a very large extent in this decade. While most of their designs were from old molds, Beth Merck delighted in creating ornaments for the 1990s. Some very marvelous examples were a cowboy boot with stitching to resemble a Christmas tree; a Burgermeister who looked like the head of the McDonald's cartoon figure, Mayor McCheese; a cigar ornament complete with gold seal; an ice skate with gold glittered laces; and even a life sized peanut with a dusting of glitter, helping it to resemble a nut freshly pulled from the earth.

In 1996, they introduced ornaments designed by Birgit Muller-Blech, wife of Klaus, the president of Inge-Glas. Each sculptured mold was a limited edition, encased in its own gift box with a certificate and story telling about the piece, and was produced in a limited edition of no more than 1,800 pieces. They continued the importation of their glass ornaments from Germany into the United States until the turn of this century.

However, in the year 2000, Old World Christmas severed its contacts with Inge-Glas and began importing ornaments from China. Their entire line of glass ornaments was then exported from China, leaving behind their German ties.

More elaborate array of Old World Christmas ornaments. Germany. $15-45 each.

Fruit and vegetable ornaments imported by Old World Christmas from the mid-1980s into the early 1990s. Germany. $15-55.

Childhood Memories

"Childhood Memories" items from Birgit's Christmas Collection for Old World Christmas 1996. Left to right: "That's Mine," $45-60; "Noah's Ark, $60-75; "My Little Darling," $50-65.

Inge's Christmas Heirlooms

Toward the end of this decade, Klaus Muller-Blech made the decision to start his own distribution company in the United States with the founding of *U.S.A.:inge-glas U.S.A.,LP.* Being the fourteenth- generation descendent of a glass-blowing tradition, Klaus and his wife Birgit (also a descendent of a rich glass-blowing tradition) both spent countless hours of their youth in the glass workshops of their grandparents and parents in Neustadt, Germany. In 1992, the Golden Glow of Christmas Past (a collector's group dedicated to the preservation of old Christmas) met in Reading, Pennsylvania. Klaus and Birgit had made arrangements to attend the convention to search for ornaments of their families' past. Through their activities there, they went home with more than the antique treasures they expected. These two individuals met for the first time in the United States and as a result, they were married. The families joined forces and combined their tradition and skills at the Inge-glas workshops in Germany. Together their collection includes more than 6,000 antique glass blower molds dating from the 1850s. In addition, they created new designs each year. Inge's Christmas Heirlooms is named for Klaus Muller-Blech's late mother.

Germany's first Christmas museum was in the planning stages at the end of this decade with completion of this museum being summer, 2001. Klaus and Birgit felt that Germany needed to preserve as well as display to the world its rich heritage of providing Christmas items for the world. Thus, over 20,000 holiday artifacts from the nineteenth and twentieth centuries will serve as the foundation for this museum in Neustadt near Coburg. The museum will cover an unbelievable span of history, featuring dollhouses, ornaments, lights, and life-sized Santas of papier-mâché. Tree decorations made from cotton, paper, cardboard, glass, and wood will be featured. In addition, glassblower workshops will be in operation, demonstrating the process of creating glass ornaments. Also included will be a collector's literature shop, a gift shop, and a teddy bear museum as well. This will be the largest permanent display of Christmas history in the world.

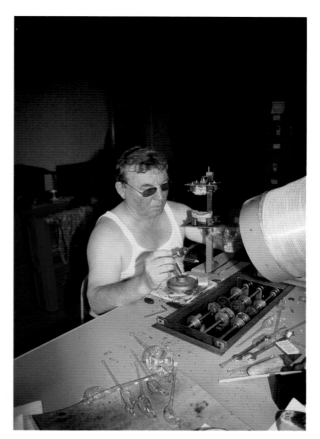

Heinz Muller-Blech blowing glass ornaments in the Inge-Glas factory which were sold in the United States by "Old World Christmas" in 1993.

Klaus Muller-Blech holding one of the beautifully painted finished ornaments made at Inge-Glas in 1993.

134

Painting purple coat details on Father Christmas ornaments one by one at Inge-Glas in 1993.

Adding small details such as eyes is a delicate job at Inge-Glas in their well (naturally) lighted design area.

Assortment of the first "Inge's Christmas Heirlooms" from Inge-Glas in Coburg, Germany.

Hallmark Ornaments

Hallmark introduced glass ornaments into their line in 1998 with "Crown Reflections, Keepsake Ornaments." Indents, the "Gifts of a King," "Frankincense," and "Murray Fire Truck" were among those released. Designers included Tammy Haddix, Tracy Larson, Sue Tague, and Kristina Kline.

BRONNER'S Christmas Wonderland—

Christmas Decorations

Bronner's is considered to be the world's largest retail and wholesale Christmas decorations company. When tourists and Christmas enthusiasts venture into Bronner's in Frankenmuth, Michigan, eighty miles north of Detroit, they find over 30,000 decorations for trees and homes. It was in 1986 that they received the first "Golden Santa Claus Award" at the Nuremberg, West Germany, International Toy Fair, for their constant attention to providing new and unique Christmas items. Bronner's Christmas Decorations have the largest display of Christmas decorations in the country; their store is roughly the size of eight football fields.

Wally Bronner is known all over Europe as America's ambassador of "Christmas Cheer" and "Good Spirits." Wally and his artistic team of designers and buyers make numerous trips to Europe each year to seek out the finest products for inclusion into their Christmas line. In 1997, Wally delivered a speech of tribute to glass artisans in Lauscha, Germany, on the 150th anniversary of the tree ornament production that originated in the Thuringer Forest in Germany in the same time that glass ornaments emerged from Bohemia.

Doris Reda designed the majority of the ornaments for production in Europe, and retired from the business in the late 1990s. Most of Bronner's ornaments continued to be designed and sketched by Connie Larson. The artwork is sent overseas to be produced by the glass artisans of Germany, Austria, Italy, and Hungary. Bronner's was, and continues to be, the largest importer of Italian glass ornaments.

Wally and Irene's family members all play an active role in the management of this business, along with their grandchildren. Daughter Carla, and her husband Bob Splesser, Maria, and her husband Chris Sutorik, and son Wayne, and wife Laurene, are all actively involved every day in the running of this business. Their business motto is, "Enjoy CHRISTmas, It's His Birthday; Enjoy Life, It's His Way." The Bronner family intentionally capitalizes the word Christ in CHRISTmas and Bronner says, "We're really in the business of supplying decorations for a birthday observance. Christmas is the birthday of Jesus Christ. Jesus is the reason for the season."

In 1991, Bronner's opened a 100,000 square foot addition, doubling its size and bring the shop's total building footage to nearly five acres for four football fields. In 1992, as an expression of gratitude to God, Wally and Irene Bronner erected (with permission) a replica of the Oberndorf/Salzburg Silent Night Memorial Chapel. The chapel replica is located on the south end of the Bronner property and celebrates the world's favorite Christmas carol with a posting of one verse of the carol in over 300 languages. In 1993 and 1999, Wally spoke at the Stille Nacht Symposiums at the University of Salzburg and the Joseph Mohr School in Wagrain.

An ever-increasing number of visitors grew in the mid-part of this decade to over two million visitors a year and 2,000 motor coaches annually. A brand new snack area, "Seasons Eatings," the World of Bronner's digital (DVD) video presentation, and the recreation of the Silent Night Memorial Chapel, and Bronner's stunning showroom featuring over 50,000 gifts and trims make the world's largest Christmas store a "must visit" for countless Americans as well as foreigners.

In recent years, Bronner's has brought glass blowers from Italy and Germany to illustrate for their visitors the complex and artistic process employed to produce glass ornaments. Today Bronner's imports mouth-blown ornaments from Germany, Austria, Italy, Poland, the Czech and Slovak Republics, the Ukraine, Romania, Columbia, Mexico, and Asia.

When Bronner's buyers first visited the European glass producers, most artisans had their workshops in their homes. In the last quarter of the 1900s, ornaments started to be produced primarily in factory buildings with ideal working conditions and space that accommodates machinery that is needed in many phases of the trade. Through the years, Bronner's has enjoyed a personal, friendly relationship with numerous glass craftspeople, which translates into exquisite decorations for American trees in homes, churches, stores, and businesses.

Most recently, Bronner's has become a source where movie studios select and purchase decor for Christmas-themed movies. In September of 1999, a 39,000 square-foot shipping expansion was opened to accommodate the packing and shipping of a growing number of salesroom, catalog, and web site orders.

In 1998, Wally Bronner and his wife Irene transferred their leadership of the business to three of their children. Wayne serves as president and chief executive officer. Daughters Carla and Maria are company vice-presidents. Son-in-law Bob Spletzer (Carla) serves as the human resources manager and building coordinator, and son-in law Christopher Sutorik (Maria) is the visual/internet merchandising manager. Daughter-in-law Lorene Bronner (Wayne) serves as the firm's sales room manager. Son Randy resides in Arizona. Wally and Irene continue on the board of directors with Wally serving as a chairman. Wally still refers to the business as his hobby. "My hobby of signs and displays developed into a full-time business, and I never went to work," Wally said. "Since I never went to work, I don't have to think of retirement, and I'll continue the hobby, God-willing, but only on days that end in 'y'."

"Golden Santa" Award, February 1994. Left to right: Herr Kijewski, Varstadt; Kathy Stacey, GB; Herr Bergmann, Frau Hermann "Ka DeWe Bererlier; Wilma and Helmut Krebs; Wally Bronner, Bronner's Christmas Wonderland USA; Frau and Herr Wohlfahrt of Kathe Wohlfahrt, Rotenburg.

Wally and Irene Bronner, founders of Bronner's in Frankenmuth, Michigan. 1994.

Entire family of Wally Bronner, all of which play an important role in the importation and merchandising of Christmas decorations into the United States. Front row (left to right): Carla (Bronner) Spletzer, Paul Speltzer, Wally Bronner, Irene Bronner, Ryan Spletzer, Greg Spletzer, and Bob Spletzer. Back Row (left to right): Chris Sutorik, Maria (Bronner) Sutorik, Randy Bronner, Garrett Bronner, Dietrich Bronner, Lorene Bronner, and Wayne Bronner.

Whitehurst Imports

In 1998, Whitehurst Imports introduced a new Polish line, "Czestovkowa Gallery Collection," produced in the medieval city of Czestochowa, Poland, home of the revered Marian Miracle shrine of the Black Madonna and scene of the first Papal mass in Poland. Each ornament came individually boxed with a story enclosure. The large five new pieces introduced in 1999 included Basket of Flowers, Nutcracker Dreams, Bring in the Clowns, Proud Papa Penguin, and I Can't Ski Penguin; all retailed between $18 and $25.

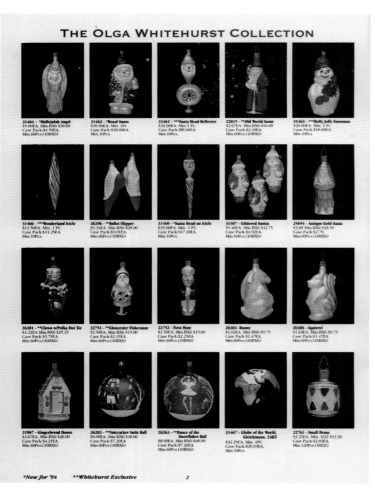

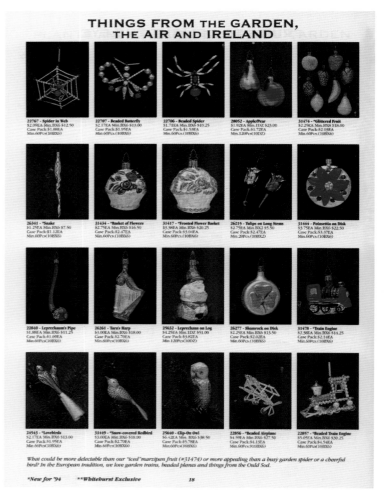

Representative examples from the The Olga Whitehurst Collection of 1994.

"Garden, Air, and Ireland" from the The Olga Whitehurst Collection of 1994.

ENESCO

Eugene Freedman started Enesco Co. as a giftware import company in 1958. Very quickly Freedman recognized the potential in the Christmas market, and in 1970, they offered a fifteen-page Christmas catalog. One of their most profitable ventures was the development of the Precious Moments collections. During a stop in California on one of his annual trips to the Orient, Bucher discovered the inspirational artist Sam Butcher's drawings of teardrop-eyed children on greeting cards and posters. Freedman took a chance and transformed these images into three-dimensional figures. In 1978, their first twenty-one Precious Moments figures were introduced. The rest is history. When the Precious Moments Collectors Club was launched in 1981, just fewer than 70,000 members joined in the first year. Also, a recent development is its Treasury of Christmas Ornaments line, for which a collectors' club was launched in 1993.

Adrian Taron & Sons

Adrian Taron & Sons is a family business which has its roots back to 1949; however, they first began importing ornaments in the 1970s. They offered fruits, vegetables, snowmen, angels, and owls, all imported from Germany. All figures were produced from antique molds like those previous to World War II. But, in 1997, they began to create ornaments produced from original molds created from their own designs. These ornaments were the original artwork of Susan Rosas and each one was initiated by the artist who painted the actual piece. These ornaments were produced in Poland. Thus, "Humpty Dumpty" and "Buster and Belle" were among the first of their original designs.

YCG Enterprises

In 1993, Yolanda Czyzewski started her own company importing glass Polish ornaments, having actually lived in Poland for three years. In 1995, she formed "YCG ENTERPRISES" with Claire Griffith, an acquaintance of twenty-five years. These two women imported decorations from eight different countries, with five countries supplying glass ornaments. Some of their more distinctive pieces were manufactured in the Czech Republic.

The Giffard Collection

Based in Wisconsin, this company started the ornament portion of their business in 1996. Long time Christmas ornament collectors, they worked with companies in Germany, Italy, Romania, the Czech Republic, and Poland to produce ornaments for the American market.

Dick and Joan Gifford began establishing their own holiday traditions by seeking out unique ornaments for their family tree. One year, Dick accompanied Joan to the gift shows in Chicago where she was selecting merchandise for a gift shop as well as her own antiques shop. Dick set the goal of finding some blown glass Disney ornaments for their tree. Unable to find even one ornament, Dick knew he had discovered a void in the marketplace. Therefore, his goal was to produce a Mickey Mouse® ornament from blown glass. Partnering with a Mexican company and two German ornament production firms, his first ornament was produced. The Gifford's also produced an ornament of Sleepy® and a disc design depicting Mickey and Minnie® skating. In 1997, with contacts established and extensive research under their belts, they traveled to Poland, Italy, and Germany. In 1998, they launched their first collection of eighty ornaments. The Gifford's contracted with ornament blowers from Germany, Italy, Poland, Romania, and the Czech Republic. Their son, Dick, is involved in the family business. In 2000, they expanded their collection to over 220 ornament designs. Within the collection, individual production numbers range from as few as 100 to as many as 2,500. Currently represented in nearly one hundred retail locations, they worked hard to blend the look of the traditional old European designs with the whimsy of new designs.

Vaillancourt Folk Art

Their studio is located in Sutton, Massachusetts. Located in an 1840s antique-style house, Gary and Judi Vaillancourt have carved their niche into the Christmas market. Gary and Judy Vaillancourt debuted their glass ornaments in 1998 at the Atlanta Gift market. Preceding this, Vaillancourt Folk Art chalkware figures, produced by Judy and Gary, were made using antique chocolate and ice cream molds, circa 1830 to 1950.

When Gary Villancourt gave his wife, Judi, a gift of three antique chocolate molds in 1984, neither of them knew it would change their lives forever. Their passion included the collection of antique confectionery molds.

Fascinated by the exquisite detail of her molds, Judi, an artist by training, filled them with plaster, and hand-painted the resulting "chalkware." While the chocolate makers palette had been limited to chocolate brown, Judi's colors gave these figurines the look, feel, and faces of a bygone era. Vaillancourt Folk Art maintained one of the largest collection of antique molds (both chocolate and ice cream), many of them made by Anton Reiche (1860-1930) of Dresden, Germany. Their molds also include whimsical Santa molds from the 1930s, 1940s, and 1950s. Judi meticulously researched the history of each piece, and a staff of thirty artists worked year-round to produce these figures. In the latter part of the decade, they were releasing some 300 different versions of Santa Claus and Father Christmas each year.

In 1997, the Vaillancourts started a collection of exquisite German hand-blown glass ornaments, based on their popular chalkware designs. They worked diligently with German mold makers to create the minutest details of the original confection molds. Once completed, their challenge was to duplicate this artwork on glass. Thus their unique ornaments were quite different from any others produced during this decade. All of their ornaments are produced in the village of Lauscha, Germany, the birthplace of the Christmas ornament. The master craftsmen of Lauscha re-sculpt their historic designs into plaster, create a metal mold, and then blow glass into the molds to shape the ornaments.

All are replicas of antique Villancourt chalkware figures including Santa Clauses, snowmen, and angels. Each is painted with a matte or unglazed finish, not with the familiar bright silvery finish. The first eight Villancourt glass ornaments were introduced in 1997, with twenty-one additional patterns added in 1998. Each piece is limited to a production of 3,000.

Every one of their folk art ornaments is labeled in an inconspicuous space. Take, for example, VFA 9899: the first two digits represent the year the ornament was introduced—in this case 1998; the second two digits represent the year the piece was actually produced—1999. If ORMD appears in the ornament number, the corresponding chalkware figure is only available from a master dealer.

Three Santa themed ornaments from Villancourt—late 1990s.

Various artistic renditions of snowmen and Father Christmas as created by Villancourt for the American market in the late 1990s.

Villancourt chalkware figures, for which Villancourt first gained much fame. Note the intricate details and elegant styling.

Christmas Reproductions

Christmas Reproductions is headed by Don Warning, who started his own sales representative company in New York called Christmas Eve, Inc. Don Warning was born and raised in Dayton, Ohio, as a member of a family who considered Christmas not to be a day, but an entire season, starting at Thanksgiving and not officially ending until January 6th. A long-time collector of old Christmas artifacts, he displayed his collection of sixty-five antique chocolate molds, mostly Santas, in his office. By arranging the Santas in order from early to later molds, he conceived the idea of the "Memories of Santa Collection," telling the Santa Claus story chronologically. Warning could not find a manufacturer or importer he thought would understand or undertake the project; as a result, he decided to start a new company to manufacture his Santas, "Christmas Reproductions." The research and designing for the first pieces was done in 1982, with the first Santas being introduced to the trade in 1983. Each year the collection consists of twenty-four hand-painted earthenware Santas representing different countries at various periods of time. Each year, four new Santas are added to the line and four Santas are retired. Since 1983, Christmas Reproductions, Inc. has designed and produced forty-four Santas.

According to Warning and Christmas decorations producers, the 1980s was the decade of trends such as French Country, Southwestern, and other styles. Don Warning was responsible for much of the development and thought behind these different trends. It was he who would coordinate tree skirts, ornaments, lights, and even bows to create a complete effect. Close to ninety-five percent of the work was designed in the United States and taken to different countries to obtain the necessary decorative items.

In 1991, Christmas was affected for the first time by the recession. The mass-market style previously used was no longer affected. Themed trees and decorative effects sales slowed up considerably. It was then that Warning and, of course, many others capitalized upon the "collectibles" market. This means that consumers were no longer interested in purchasing ornaments in large quantities. Purchasing a single, or even a few ornaments, which could be collectibles in years to come was intriguing. Thus the Christmas market took a new turn as countless high-quality ornaments and decorations were created, many of which are destined to be family heirlooms in years to come.

In March 1992, Christmas Reproductions started a collectors' club after conducting a survey of people who purchased their Santas. Membership benefits include "Members Only" items, "Memories of Santa," a quarterly newsletter, and other benefits including attendance at their national convention devoted to Santa collecting. Christmas Reproductions continued its rich heritage of producing Santas throughout this decade.

9053	8070	8075	8074	8072	8067	8073	9052

"Memories of Santa Collection" Woodtex Collection for 1993, all made of resin composition.

Kurt S. Adler

Kurt S. Adler's vast line of the 1990s included ornaments, snow globes, nutcrackers, musicals, candles and candleholders, dolls, figurines, houses and villages, miniatures, nativities, religious collectibles, smokers, stockings, and tree toppers. Snowtown, Angel Heights, Coca-Cola™ Christmas Village, Gingerbread Junction, and Spring Town (for Easter) are the village series and houses created by Michael Stoebner, a veteran sculptor, painter, and illustrator who created holiday designs with a "handmade look that brings a feeling of warmth and meaning back into Christmas." In the Snowtown series, each of the buildings included a cleverly placed heart logo.

Their Polonaise™ Collection won the Collector's Choice Award for four years in a row with its spectacular array of glass ornaments handcrafted in Poland in the age-old tradition of European master glassblowers. The hand-workmanship is very involved—creating forms and fashioning shapes by hand-blowing glass—then silver coating, lacquering, and decorating the ornaments—all done by Europe's most highly skilled and well-trained artisans. Kurt Stefan, a designer for KSA, began a personal signing tour in 1997. His artistic talent was revealed at an early age, and at seven he won his first scholarship to attend Saturday morning art classes. He attended the Columbus College of Art and Design, and continued his education at the Kansas City Art Institute and at the London Poly-tech Institute. In 1988, after working for Hallmark Cards, Inc., he joined KSA as a product designer.

Co-president Clifford Adler attributed much of the success of the company over the decades to his father. "He has superb taste," said Clifford. "My father brought a

European flavor to the American Christmas industry." Clifford and his brother Howard act as co-presidents while their father currently serves as Chairman of the Board.

Their Disney collectibles accessories are divided into two major groups: *Mickey and Friends*, which features traditional characters such as Donald Duck®, Pluto®, and Goofy® and *Disney film characters*, such as Ariel® of *The Little Mermaid* and Jasmine® from *Aladdin*. Their Disney characters are produced from Fabriche™ ornaments and figurines based on the old concept of papier-mâché combined with modern methods and materials. Thus Mickey Mouse® and Goofy® are featured as Santa Claus figurines while Minnie Mouse® and Donald Duck® were designed as carolers. Other series include the Seven Dwarves® and Snow White®, 101 Dalmatians®, Jiminy Cricket®, and Gepetto®. Even Belle®, The Beast®, Cogsworth®, Lumiere®, and Mrs. Potts® were produced as ornaments following the release of *Beauty and The Beast*.

Even McDonalds was represented in this decade, when, in 1997, McMemories, Inc., the only McDonald's authorized collectibles company marketed Ronald McDonald® and a Large Fries ornament, both made in Poland.

After so many years of "Christmas every day," Kurt Adler and his family might understandably become jaded about their close relationship with Santa Claus. Yet Mr. Adler insists that he loves every piece in his line, and never tires of his holiday focus. He does take one yearly reprieve from his ornaments, however. "Christmas Eve I put them away and go to Florida," he admits with a wink and a smile worthy of old St. Nick himself.

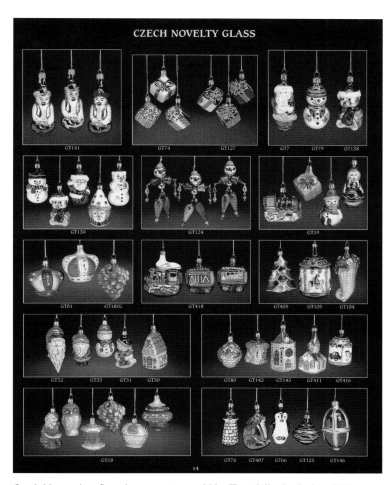

Czech blown glass figural ornaments as sold by Kurt Adler in the late 1990s.

German and Polish blown glass figural ornaments as sold by Kurt Adler in the late 1990s.

"Little Mermaid" from the Polonaise™ Collection. $125-135

"Wizard of Oz" from the Polonaise™ Collection. $145-165.

"Coca Cola™" from the Polonaise™ Collection. $85-105.

Polonaise™ Collection ornaments imported by Kurt Adler. Cowboy, $45-55; Seven days of Christmas, $45-65; Betty Boop, $60-75; Seven days of Christmas, $45-65.

Early set of Egyptian themed ornaments sold through the Museum Company stores in the early to mid-1990s. Originally sold individually and packaged singly in white cardboard boxes. $50-65 each.

Phantom of the Opera from the Polonaise™ Collection marketed by Kurt Adler. $60-65.

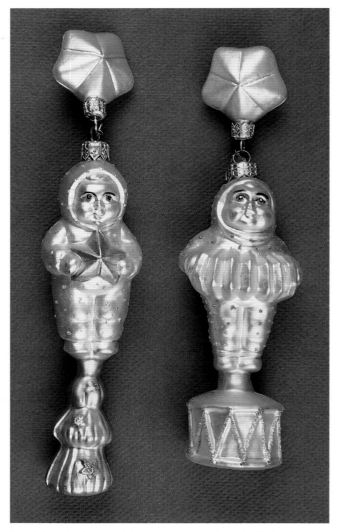

Early set of Roman themed ornaments sold through Museum Company stores in the early to mid-1990s. Originally sold individually and packaged singly in white cardboard boxes. Made in Poland. $45-75 each.

"Made in Poland" snow baby ornaments marketed in Hallmark stores in the late 1990s through the Snow Baby collection of Department 56. $45-55 each.

Midwest Importers

Midwest Importers of Cannon Falls, Inc., was founded by Kenneth W. Althoffas as a retail gift shop in 1953. Product emphasis was based on imported handcrafted articles from Europe and an extensive line of religious goods which were wholesaled to denominational publishing houses and religious bookstores.

The retail store was closed in 1963 and the business moved to a larger headquarters in downtown Cannon Falls, Minnesota. A permanent showroom was established in 1964 at the Minneapolis Gift Mart and the line was shown at many shows across the country in temporary spaces. In 1974, Heinz Paternoster established the European office.

Midwest Importers currently wholesales its seasonal giftware line at permanent showrooms in all the major U.S. giftware markets including Atlanta, Bedford, Charlotte, Chicago, Columbus, Dallas, Denver, Kansas City, Los Angeles, Minneapolis, New York, Northville, Phoenix, Reston, San Francisco, and Seattle. Kathy Brekken, daughter of Ken Althoff, became president and its chief executive officer in 1985. Brekken continues to be very excited about the company's future, with the production of more everyday products, such as home décor and gift accessories.

While Midwest Importers did not handle a lot of glass ornaments, their emphasis lay in wooden ornaments, nutcrackers, and wooden toys. Their main suppliers were Ulbricht and Steinbach, both from Germany. They also imported wooden ornaments from northern Italy and Taiwan.

The Erzgebirge region continues to be the source of some of the most beautiful wooden articles in the world. Their natural resources, potential labor skills, rich cultural past, and economic factors combine to create a perfect manufacturing environment. Located in a tow mountain range in the Province of Saxony, the area lies just north of the Czechoslovakian border, extending a total of ninety miles. It rises from the Elbe River to the highest altitude of 4,000 feet. The word "Erz" means "ore" and "Berg" is translated as "mountains." Thus the word "Erzgebirge" can be translated as "ore mountains." An abundance of wood and continuous water power makes it possible to use the force of water for turning saws and lathes.

The monumental change in Germany in 1992 had a tremendous effect upon wooden ornaments, for some of the finest were designed and created in what was the German Democratic Republic or East Germany. With the elimination of borders and cultural barriers, these wooden ornaments began to flood our American markets. While still quite expensive, they found, and continue to find, collectors who cherish wooden ornaments as perfectly crafted and detailed as those fabricated before World War II.

In recent years other countries have commenced the production of wooden ornaments including Japan, China, Taiwan, and even Spain. But none of these wooden ornaments can match the German craftsmanship so evident when looking at their proportion, detail, and painting.

By the mid-1980s and continuing into the present, many miniature wooden ornaments made solely for the tree have been manufactured by such companies as Steinbach and Zurnber. Fashioned after the smokers, miniature 5" nutcrackers (in name and form representing the fact that they had "to crack a tough nut"—a German expression referring to someone who has big problems) have tiny metal screws imbedded in the heads for hanging. Nutcracker kings, policemen, soldiers, and other military figures have been very popular because woodcarvers enjoyed having these figures of authority "crack their tough nuts." Other interesting wood figurals include chimney sweeps, cavalier jumping jacks, snowmen, angels, roosters, rabbits, coal miners, bells, trees, and military figures. Soldiers and forest animals in wooden rings, angel musicians in stars, angels on crescent moons, and snowmen on sleighs were variations on single figures. Some of the most unusual forms included mushroom birdhouses, sewing machines, alarm clocks, phonographs, kitchen tool sets, and birdhouses.

Assortment of Steinbach nutcrackers imported by Midwest Importers in 1982.

0474 Angel Orchestra. 2", Germany, 20.50 set/6

2977 Angel Orchestra. 2", Germany, 19.00 set/12

2940 Angel with Sleigh. 2½", Germany, 6.25 ea., M-3

0468 Angel Carrying Basket and Tree. 3", Germany, 4.25 ea., M-2

2938 Margarita Angels. 1½", Germany, 15.50 set/6

0478 Angel with Letter. 2½", Germany, 4.25 ea., M-2

0553 Angel Pulling Wagon. 2½", Germany, 7.25

0414 Santa Pulling Sled with Angel. 3", Germany, 8.50

2801 Girl with Cradle. 2", Germany, 6.25

2942 Girl with Porridge and Birds. 2", Germany, 4.50 ea., M-2

0430 Angel Candleholder. 4", Germany, 3.75 ea., M-2

2941 Girl with Scissors. 2", Germany, 4.50 ea., M-2

0554 Angels Watching Over Cradle. 2", Germany, 11.50 set/4

0473 Santa with Angel. 3", Germany, 7.50 ea., M-2

2854 Bavarian Moving Van. 3", Germany, 21.50

2863 Children's Procession. 2½", Germany, 8.00 set/4

2843 Pied Piper with Children. 2"-4", Germany, 25.00 set/7

2908 Bavarian Dancing Couple. 2½", Germany, 4.75

2909 Bavarian Band. 2", Germany, 8.50 set/4

2907 Bavarian Beer Drinking Band. 2", Germany, 15.50 set/7

2812 Bavarian Band. 2½", Germany, 10.75 set/5

2827 Lady Bug with Umbrella. 2", Germany, 1.35 ea., M-6 asst.

2853 Bavarian Boy. 2½", Germany, 3.00 ea., M-4 asst.

2852 Flower Gardeners. 2", Germany, 3.00 ea., M-4 asst.

2958 Lady Bug Band. 1½", Germany, 5.75 set/6

TOLL FREE ORDER LINE 800-533-2075

Assortment of wooden ornaments manufactured in Germany and imported by Midwest Importers in the 1980s.

Andrzej

Andrzej was born and raised in Czestochowa, Poland. He learned how to blow ornaments as a boy in his father's workshop. Since the political system of the day gave very little hope for pursuing individual dreams, Andrzej nevertheless dreamed of one day owning his own business. Today, most all of Poland and Europe know of his artistic work. Many of his ornaments depicted life in the old world of Poland and other surrounding countries and appear on backgrounds of either brilliant royal blue or silvery gray.

The Sandor Collection

Established in 1988, the Sandor Collection, located in Hartford, Connecticut, has been providing ornaments rich in the cultural heritage of Hungary. Having fled communist Hungary in 1956, Leve Larvazy found that his native decorations were not available in the United States. With his wife, Carol, he started working with Hungarian artists to provide folk art decorations.

The Sandor Collection started including the handcrafts of artisans from neighboring Romania in 1997. Most recently, Leve and Carole have commenced work with Bosnian artists. In an effort to help women reclaim their dignity through meaningful work, the Sandor Collection became a part of the "Sarajevo Phoenix:" a project created by an American church group called "Hands Raised Together." These women are Croats, Muslims, and Eastern Orthodox Christians who have faith in a multiethnic Bosnia-Hercegovina.

Their entire collection spans the mediums and techniques in ceramics, hand-cut appliqué, doll making, embroidery, egg decorating, handmade lace, leather, wood, and bone carvings. But most intriguing and well recognized are the different egg-shaped ornaments they have provided for the American market. Artists such as Margit Jakab and Olga Lorant from Hungary, Maria Zinica from Romania, and Ileana Hotopila from Romania have gained the attention of many collectors who treasure the unusual and creative.

Christopher Radko

Radko's business offered over 700 styles starting in the early 1990s. From the lone glassblower who made the first ornaments, more than 1,000 people in the cottage factories of Germany, Italy, Poland, and the Czech Republic now are working to create these whimsical and delightful ornaments.

By 1993, his eighth year of being in business, Radko began to include other countries in his line. Remembering the Italian ornaments of the 1950s, which included annealed feet and hands, paint carefully applied with great detail, and characters now no longer produced, Radko investigated the possibility of recreating Italian ornaments as well. Armed with catalogs, photos of past lines, and samples of past ornaments, Radko met with Italian glassblowers and his first efforts were seen in his 1993 catalog.

Also blown for the first time was an entire new line of German-produced ornaments. However, Radko's creations take on a new dimension because his ornaments are not produced exactly as they were before World War II. These ornaments are new representations blending the past and the present as well as combinations of molds. Radko's designs often times include taking a doll's head fondly remembered from the past and a bell or pinecone mold and combining the two into a "new" creation. What is most fascinating about these new German-blown ornaments is the extraordinary detail of the paint. Bright colors accurately define pupils in eyes, blushing in cheeks, and countless other details which create a high quality, handcrafted ornament. Czechoslovakian beaded ornaments are also being created, but in larger sizes which make their appearance on the tree a truly spectacular one.

One of the most creative additions to the tree in this period was supplied by Radko through the introduction of glass-beaded chains like those used in Victorian times. In 1989, when Christopher Radko was on a tour of German and Austrian Christkind markets, he visited an antique store in Munich where he purchased some silver bead decorations. Even though they were tiny, each one was hollow and appeared to be individually mouth-blown. Inquiring as to their original source, Radko was referred by the antique dealer to "Gablonz," a small town in what was then East Germany. In 1991, he visited "Gablonz," which was really Jablonec in Czechoslovakia. While in Jablonec, he visited a century-old glass bead workshop where he found Mrs. Maria Turnovska who showed Radko an old hardbound notebook containing original designs for molds for hundreds of garland shapes, including a bishop, bear, champagne bottle, rolling pin, goldfish, and an Eskimo. All were designed by her mother, Irena, before 1915!

The craftsmen of the shop conducted an all out search of cellars and attics to locate these old molds. Within three months they had recovered enough molds to create over thirty new designs. Styles to be released in future years include a silver motorcycle, colorful carousel, Byzantine church, fancy purse, exotic dragonfly, sleigh, sail ship, tropical butterfly, and a Christmas spider in a golden web.

Radko ornaments have adorned Christmas trees in the Reagan White House, and the homes of Bruce Springsteen and Dolly Parton. His ornaments are made in the same painstaking way as ornaments of the past. Each takes a week to make. On day one, the glass is blown and allowed to rest over night. It should be noted that the glass is heavier, and more resistant to breakage, a quality that Radko reveres. Then the ornaments are lined with silver nitrate. After they are allowed to set for twenty-four hours, a base coat

of lacquer, for background color, is applied. On the fourth day, details are painted on. Finally, on day five, glitter and additional paint are applied.

Polish glass workshops are free to continue the once traditional course of creating more and more new designs each year, just as Germany had once done in the teens and twenties. The almost extinct art of mold making has now been revived in Poland. Expert glass blowers are currently producing difficult shapes that have not been available elsewhere in over forty years. In this way, the Christopher Radko Polish workshop is creating designs inspired by turn of the century designs that were thought to have been lost, with the successful result of making the new pieces look even better than the originals.

Christopher Radko has enjoyed outstanding success due to a high quality product which appeals to countless individuals interested in purchasing high-end ornaments which are destined to become family heirlooms in years ahead. In fact, ornaments recently retired are being avidly sought by those who found these very fine tree ornaments too late. Radko personally has toured the country autographing his exclusively designed ornaments and has acquired a strong following from countless collectors. Responding to countless requests from retail customers, Christopher Radko founded a collectors group, "The Christopher Radko Family of Collectors," whose members receive *Starlight*, a magazine offering historical Christmas information, ornament symbolism articles, and information regarding current and retired items. In addition, members are entitled to purchase ornaments sold only to members.

His earlier ornaments are extremely desirable and are highly collectible, as indicated by the secondary market which now exists for these past ornaments. It seems that once people start purchasing his recent ornaments, they start searching out those which have been retired or discontinued. From 1986 to 1989, there was no "RADKO" marking on the metal crown caps of his ornaments. In 1989, the very first "RADKO" appeared on the crown. After that, most all of his ornaments made in Poland bore that marking. But those ornaments made in Germany have a different cap history. For the year 1992 (first year of introduction), each of these ornaments had "West Germany" on the crown. Italian ornaments (first introduced in 1993) had only "Italy" on their crowns. Since 1994, almost every Radko ornament has "RADKO" on the crown. In 2000, the 14-carat gold dipped "Radko star" hangtag was phased into production. In addition to the familiar Radko metal cap, this star was hung on the spring inserted into the crown cap.

Radko balls elaborately painted with details and then glittered. $25-30 each.

Italian figural ornaments designed by Christopher Radko. Left to right: Duck, $75-85; Harlequin figure, $65-75; figure with two flags, $85-95; Comic figure, $75-85.

Italian figural ornaments designed by Christopher Radko in 1993. Left to right: Indian, $75-85; Napoleon, $70-80; Fountain, $100-110; Mermaid, $70-80; Alligator, $80-90.

German blown ornaments designed by Christopher Radko which combine the use of two molds to create a new, unique ornament. Left to right: Owl on bell, $60-70; Santa on heart, $45-55; Angel on leaf, $60-70; Clown on star, $55-65; Policeman on traffic sign, $75-85; Santa on berry, $50-60.

German blown ornaments designed by Christopher Radko and marketed in the 1990s in old traditional moulds. Left to right, top to bottom: Little snow baby on skis, $55-60; Indian head, $20-25; Clown, $15-20; Monkey with radio head phones, $20-25; Girl face in grape cluster, $20-25; Clown on quarter moon, $35-45; Girl breaking out of egg, $35-40; Wasps on grape cluster, $25-30.

Polish blown ornaments designed by Christopher Radko and marketed in the 1990s. Left to right: Mother Goose, $40-50; Madonna and child, $20-25; Santa face on blue ball, $55-65; German Kaiser, $15-25; Cat, $35-45.

Taz™ and Sylvester™ "Warner Brothers" ornaments designed by Christopher Radko in the 1990s. Taz, $100-110. Sylvester, $115-120.

Tweety Bird™ ornaments designed by Christopher Radko in the 1990s. Tweety angel, $60-70; Tweety in Sylvester's hat, $65-75; Tweety on twisted spiral, $95-105.

Mickey™ and Minnie Mouse™ ornaments designed by Christopher Radko in the 1990s. Mickey in stocking, $65-75; Mickey Mouse in wreath, $60-70; Minnie Mouse skiing down hill, $75-80; Mickey Mouse skiing down hill, $75-85.

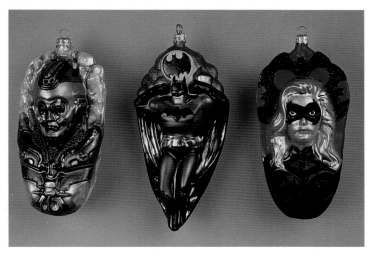

Batman™ series designed by Christopher Radko in late 1990s. Left to right: Mr. Freeze™, $65-75; Batman, $75-85; Batgirl™, $75-85.

Superman™ ornament designed by Christopher Radko in the late 1990s. $85-95.

Frankenstein characters designed by Christopher Radko in the late 1990s. $50-60 each.

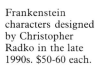

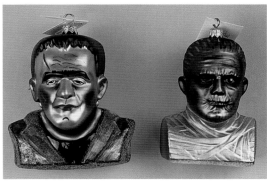

Patricia Breen Ornaments

In 1992 Patricia Breen and her husband Eric Shaikewitz traveled to Krakow, Poland as volunteers with the MBA Enterprise Corps., a volunteer organization for MBAs similar to the Peace Corps. Shaikewitz helped to privatize a large confectionery company while remaining focused on workers' rights' and Breen lectured at Krakow's Academy of Economics. After the pair fulfilled their two-year volunteer commitment, they decided to remain in Krakow, a medieval city.

They collected antique Christmas ornaments for many years, and in their spare time they scoured the farmers' markets, bazaars, and antique shops in Poland for some contemporary treasures to add to their collection. In an interview, Breen said, "We had heard about the resurgence of Polish glass ornaments—but there always seemed to be something missing. The forms were repetitive and lacked originality—the details were blurred and the painting was mechanical. We wanted to collect really beautiful Polish ornaments but everything we saw was marginal. We decided that the only way to get truly marvelous ornaments was to track down the blowers and become personally involved. We soon found ourselves in business—our ornaments tell the rest of the story."

Since founding their studio in 1994, Breen and Shaikewitz have raised the benchmark for collectible holiday glass ornaments. From two and three part ornaments linked by loop pins to ornaments connected by annealed glass hooks; from faces comprised entirely of fruits or flowers to the extensive use of calligraphy, from the hand mixed lacquers and custom created glitters to the introductions of highly detailed miniature versions of their ornaments—beauty and innovation are the hallmark of Patricia Breen Designs.

Patricia Breen Designs does not advertise nor does it have a sales force. When asked why her ornaments are so popular, Breen talks about details, "Lush, richly glittered beards, carefully painted eyes, sweet faces—these are the details I look for as a collector and these are the details that collectors recognize in our work. PBD collectors expect magic . . . season after season, we deliver that magic."

The couple credits much of their success to a lack of experience. Breen says, "We did not understand how to produce glass ornaments, we were not limited by convention. Our forms looked different because they were—no one told us what we could or should not do. We made lots of beautiful mistakes." The hands-on approach carries over to Breen's philosophy on painting. "From the outset we avoided the kind of 'assembly line production' that remains the industry standard" said Breen. "We do not have a factory, we have a studio. It is impossible for an ornament to have visual harmony when it has been painted by a series of people via an assembly line system."

In the mid-1990s, the Patricia Breen studio employed thirty full and part-time artists, many of whom were schooled at the Krakow Academy of Fine Arts. Breen and Shaikewitz were recognized for creating very modern working conditions that allowed their artisans to create in a bright, clean, cheery, safe atmosphere. The average age of the employees was the mid-twenties. Although the studio was open twelve hours daily, individual painters worked on flextime schedules that allowed them to accommodate their lifestyles.

Their Polish home is the former studio of the famous Polish portrait artist Jacek Malczewski. Their fluency in Polish increased with each passing year. Eric stated in an interview, "The different customs and just the day to day figuring out how to do things has really been the hardest part of living here." Eric goes on to tell the story from their early days. "When we first arrived, Patricia went to the market to buy food. She ended up at a very busy stall with a woman selling potatoes. When asked how many potatoes, she wanted, she replied, 'ten kilos.' Then the woman wanted her bag. Patricia didn't realize that she had to provide a bag for anything she bought. Patricia ended loading the ten kilos of potatoes in the front of her sweatshirt and walking home."

The Breen Studio is noted for some of the most elegant, artistic shapes of this decade. *Saint George and the Dragon; Saint Peter, Fisher of Men,* and *Planetary Santa* are just three of the hundreds of different shapes which earned the respect of collectors across the United States. Each ornament style is a unique design and created from an original PBD mould. Breen ornaments are produced in highly limited editions of 500 to 2,000 pieces per style—including all colorations and variations. Each year Breen and Shaikewitz introduce approximately fifty new styles, while at the same time retiring a comparable number of past designs. Watercolor renderings of new ornaments are featured in their artistically inspired catalog that debuts each year at Breen's first Autumn Signing Event.

Patricia and Eric Breen also reintroduced to the Christmas market the artistic two- and three-piece ornaments of times past so much treasured by collectors. The first linked two-part ornaments to be introduced were *Beeskeep with Bee, Spruce Goose Airplane,* and *Diving Santa.* The linked three-part ornament *Manhattan Ape* consisted of a large Art Deco style building, an ape clutching a damsel in distress, and a miniature Spruce Goose airplane. Ornaments such as *Night Flight Santa, Christmas in the Cosmos,* and *Three Wishes* cleverly connected two ornaments with an annealed hook. The first two-part ornament with an annealed hook was *Bacchus with Grapes* in 1995.

The Breen Studio had become known for bee-related ornaments. These included a fanciful *Queen Bee* with a woman's face and an annealed glass stinger, a full size and miniature *Beekeeping Santa,* a miniature bee hive finial; a bee garland; and numerous two-part linked beehives with bees. The inspiration for Breen's first beehive ornaments was a nineteenth century inkwell that her husband had given her. The Breen Studio introduced a new bee-themed ornament each year in this decade.

The Breen Studio was also recognized as the first modern glass producer to introduce highly detailed miniature versions of larger ornaments from their line. Just 2 1/2-inches tall, the first Breen miniatures were *Striped Santa*, *Saint Petersburg Santa*, and *Woodland Santa*. These were released in 1998.

Currently, Breen ornaments are accompanied by a cream-colored hangtag with a gold-foiled version of Breen's Clover Beeskeep marked "Patricia Breen Designs." This is the third hangtag to be introduced. Their original tag was used on less than 250 ornaments and featured the profile of an angel on a dark Greenfield accompanied by the words "Patricia Breen Design Group." The second tag features a similar angel printed in gold foil and is marked either "Patricia Breen Design Group" or "Patricia Breen Designs."

The Patricia Breen Collector's Society Review was begun in 1999 in an effort to make better communication possible between their studio in Poland and United States Collectors. Published in Las Vegas, Nevada, this quarterly newsletter highlights the latest designs, previews of ornament designs to come, and signing events in the U.S. by Patricia Breen.

Two-part ornaments for which Patricia Breen gained much attention on the collector's market. Left to right: St. Anthony with lost objects hanging at bottom, $75-85; Bacchus with grapes hanging below, $70-80; Golf bag with golf ball hanging below, $65-75.

Larger two-part ornaments by Patricia Breen. Icarus Flies, $95-110; Manhattan ape, $100-110.

Large elaborate two-part ornaments designed by Patricia Breen. Night Time Santa (one color variation), $95-105; Sweet Dreams, $120-135; Night Time Santa (one color variation), $95-105.

Madonna for Pablo, $120-135; Arcimbaldi Santa, $135-150; Adam and Eve, $120-130.

"A Walk in the Woods" Collection of vegetables including un chou rouge, les oignons nouveaux, une aubergine, les carrots, and un chou-fleur. $100-120 for set.

Patricia Breen ornaments. Left to right, top to bottom: Friends, $35-45; Henry's First Day of School, $75-85; Jack Frost, $40-50; Le Postal Cat, $40-50; Santa Paws, $55-65; Santa with package, $35-45.

Series of Bee Hive ornaments, the most unusual of which have a bee as an attached ornament. $65-85 each.

Series of Santa figural ornaments from Breen. Left to right, top to bottom: Making His List (purple coat), $65-75; White Father Christmas, $45-55; Snowflake Santa, $55-65; Workshop Santa, $45-50; Through Rain and Snow, $65-70; Making His List (red coat), $40-50.

Patricia Breen ornaments. Left to right, top to bottom: St. Ursula, $35-45; Our Lady of the Rosary, $35-45; Amor Angel, $30-40; St. Ursula, $35-45; Madonna of the Sun, $45-55; Bountiful Madonna, $40-50.

Breen Santa figural ornaments. Left to right, top to bottom: Advent Santa, $75-85; Striped Santa, $50-60; 'Round Midnight, $50-60; Gift of the Season, $45-55; A Santa for Thomas, $45-55; St. Louis Santa, $75-85.

Very detailed Patricia Breen ornaments. Left to right: Kris Kringle trunk to Fond du Lac, Wisconsin, $45-50; Letter to My Beloved (with authentic Polish stamp), $55-65; Valise, $40-50.

148

Extremely detailed Breen ornament. Left to right: City Santa (Midnight Version), $85-95; Harbor Santa, $65-75; A Santa for Anthony, $75-85.

Curtis Posuniak

Curtis Posuniak was playing the piano and organ by the age of seven and became Minister of Music at St. Joseph's Church in Dearborn, Michigan, at the age of twelve. Later he was to establish the Michigan Bach Festival. At one of its socials, he conceived the idea of creating ornaments which would honor the great classic composers of the world.

In 1996, he created four ornaments of his first music series: Bach, Brahms, Beethoven, and Chopin. All were busts of these personages in period costumes and powdered wigs. For 1997, his designs included busts of Mozart, Schubert, and Wagner. Most intriguing for 1997 was a full figure of J. S. Bach dressed in the traditional red and white costume, carrying a tree in his left hand, and a sack of musical instruments including a lute and French horn over his shoulder.

Slavic Treasures

Glenn Lewis, founder of Slavic Treasures, holds a degree in Design from the Clemson University School of Architecture. While he was completing postgraduate work with the head of the College of Architecture from the Technical University in Krakow, Poland, and formed a friendship that led Glen to Poland. There the two men founded a Polish-American architectural firm when Lewis moved to Krakow in January 1993. Their firm Wizja (Polish word for "vision") has been largely responsible for much of the restoration and modernization of buildings in Poland since the fall of communism.

While touring Krakow on his second day in Poland, he literally knocked down a young Polish lady, and profusely offered his apologies in English. What a surprise when she responded using fluent English. This young Polish lady, Basnia, married Glenn fifteen months later.

Basia Lewis, his wife, is co-president and principle designer for the company. Their daughter, Allyson, was born in July 1997. Basia constantly uses her abilities as a translator to coordinate and oversee the important language and cultural interaction among the various steps of production to ensure that everyone works together with one vision for the products' design, coloration, and overall quality. His life-long friend, Dave Wegerek, is the second vice-president, and third partner in this business endeavor. Dave provides the financial and business expertise necessary to run such a manufacturing business. Wegerek oversees the US headquarters, located in Charlotte, North Carolina. Almost 98.5-percent of Slavic Treasures' line is from original molds. Many of the ornament designs are a cooperative effort between several artists, but Glenn is the primary creative force and designer. Since he has studied art quite extensively and has even had one-man exhibitions of his art, his designs are quite creative, leaning toward abstract impressionism.

Ania and Marek Morawski also add to this partnership. Marek is a master glass blower and Ania oversees the economic issues involving factory personnel. Together, these five partners are in charge of creating some very fanciful designs, which attracted great attention from wholesalers, retailers, and consumers alike.

Some of his most captivating ornaments are those realistic animal designs such as an African elephant, a black rhinoceros, a lion, a Bengal tiger, and a zebra head. All of these animal designs display an inordinate amount of detail and molding, which have made them favorites of so very many collectors.

His "Glasscots" have taken the nation by storm. He debuted fantastic licensed glass figurals representing the major university mascots from across the country. Such ornaments included Bucky Badger from the University of Wisconsin-Madison; the wolfpack mascot from North Carolina State; and the cowboy mascot from Oklahoma State University. A later development was "Glasscots" of the professional sports teams in the United States.

However, Lewis' most outstanding and unique contribution to this decade was the production for the very first time of free-blown ornaments in the style of the Italian figural free-blown ornament. Up to this time, this was an Italian specialty. Working with expert glass artisans in Poland, Lewis was able to duplicate these quite well. Green

Kootie, Queen Bee, and other such large ornaments contained thin and elegant annealed appendages, intricate painting details, and expert proportions employing a single tube of glass.

Also of interest is their boxing of their ornament line. Lewis fabricated a box to protect his ornaments and prided himself on demonstrating this by dropping the box containing his ornament four to five times, sometimes from a height of over seven feet.

Full-bloom Irises. Slavic Treasures. 6.5". One of the detailed molded three-dimensional ornaments which came in series of flowers and animals in the late 1990s. $35-45 each.

Bengal tiger. 6" Slavic Treasures. One of the World Wildlife series in the late 1990s which also was produced in the shapes of an elephant, a monkey, black rhino, lion, and zebra. $40-45 each.

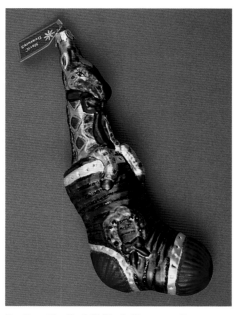

Geoffrey Giraffe. 9.5" Slavic Treasures. Late 1990s. $30-35.

Bucky Badger, 1997. One of the "Glasscots" line. Slavic Treasures. $Priceless for Badger's fans. For others, $35-45.

Assortment of Slavic Treasures ornaments from the 1990s. Left to right: Jeepers Creepers, $38-45; Zeke Zebra, $33-40; Fine Feathers-Gold Band, $37-45; Frosty Penguin skier, $45-55.

Komozja USA Limited

Svetlana Dymski was very well known on Fifth Avenue in New York City. She marketed contemporary art jewelry. The Artium, Ltd. was an elegant studio gallery in the Crown Building on Fifth Avenue. Long taking pride in offering high quality products for her customers, she commenced the sale of blown glass ornaments hand-crafted by Komozja artists from Czestochowa, Poland. Their ornaments were marketed in wooden boxes like those manufactured by Polonaise. The Komozja factory in Czestochowa, Poland, was founded in 1945 by three brothers who combined their names (Kozak, Mostowski, and Zjawiony) to create the company name. The trio was also the reason for the company logo of three dots forming an inverted triangle. Since 1945, they have been producing glass figural ornaments with just a few interruptions due to political upheaval. Komozja, USA was very receptive to custom designing ornaments per special request. They had the ability to transfer a design onto glass from a customer's picture or photograph.

Designer Anthony Ryan introduced breath-taking Faberge-inspired egg ornaments for their 1997 line. The smaller eggs averaged 3 1/2-inches with metal caps and loop pins while the large styles were over 5 1/2-inches with delicate hangers which were not annealed. They were blown from the same piece of glass as the egg. As a result the larger eggs were always see-through designs. One of their innovative shapes were double ball icicle shapes. Also quite intriguing were ornaments created by blowing the glass against a flat surface and then inhaling it quickly at the end of the process to achieve a concave bottom, giving the piece a lampshade shape. An annealed hook at the top finished each of the eight Tiffany lampshade styles in 1997.

Because of its close working relationship with the factory in Poland, the company has been able to develop some breathtaking commission pieces for such institutions such as the Metropolitan Museum of Art, the St. Louis Art Museum, and through the National Geographic Society.

Russia

While the production of Russian ornaments did start in the 1920s and was one of Russia's first cottage industries, they were not really made to any large extent and they seldom appeared for sale in markets. Interestingly enough, these earlier pieces are almost identical to those produced today. Popular subjects included Santa, figures from Russian folklore, and stories from Russian fairy tales. Moscow and St. Petersburg are the principal production areas. They are produced from a much "thicker" glass and are quite heavy in nature and invariably come connected to a spring-clip holder quite like the simple candleholders made in Germany in the 1920s. These ornaments are wired and spring-clipped into the holder and pinch onto the Christmas tree branches.

The finishes are shiny, matte, or have a frosted appearance and the glitter is almost crude compared to glitter applied in other Western European factories. There are animals, people, fish, angels, fruit, and vegetables galore. Many of the pieces have a painted finish, which blends from one color into the next. Their colors are also distinctively bright and almost garish to many who see them for the first time. It appears at this time that most all of the Russian ornaments appearing for sale are of recent vintage, being from the early 1990s.

Troika

Robert Sattler worked with Russian artisans to create his very elaborately detailed line. Russia has had a history of some very interesting figural ornaments created in the past. However, the old molds were not used to create ornaments in this decade. The antique molds, according to Sattler, required the glass blower to simultaneously blow out of the sides of the mouth, which is a difficult skill to master. When glass blowers died or retired, their skills went with them. Thus the Russian factories redesigned the old figural molds into new molds which required the glass blowers to blow from only one side of their mouth.

Troika was known for its elaborate painted spheres. Some very elegant examples were Water Bearer, Gingerbread House, Sleigh ride, and Gzhel Flower, reminiscent of a Russian pattern used on porcelain dishes and decorative items. The Troika line is famous for its ball ornaments, especially those that feature a clear opening in the silvering on the front of the ornament. This technique allows the collector to view the reflection from the painting on the front of the ball upon the silvery surface on the inside of the orb.

Varsovia Collection

Starting with a very modestly priced line of tear drops, balls, drops, and reflectors, Varsovia commenced mold blown styles as well. Thomasz Poddebski was president of the Eastern Europe Imports company which represented this line.

De Elena Collections

The De Elena Collections included ornaments created in Czechoslovakia. Originating in Cairo, Egypt, Ellen McGuire, owner of De Elena, began this ornament line in 1994 by importing perfume bottles. Once she saw them, she visualized them as decorative ornaments and her business took on a new direction. In 1995, the first catalog was printed, illustrating her mouth-blown, freeform-shaped ornaments. Blown in Czechoslovakia, each is hand etched, painted, and decorated with genuine gold imported from Germany. Originating in Egypt, it is somewhat difficult for the Muslim artisans to understand the concept of Christmas ornaments and a decorated tree. All of these ornaments have the distinctive look of a perfume bottle in various shapes and all of them are unsilvered and blown from different colored glass including red, blue, green, purple, and clear.

KO·KO·NA·MI & CO.

BASIA began her artistic career in 1988 with various art exhibitions in New York. She has worked both in front of and behind the camera as a fashion and food stylist, but she soon took her childhood love of Christmas and transcribed it into creating a designer line of ornaments. Her name for her company was derived from her daughter's childhood. When her daughter was about one, Basia was attempting to teach her to imitate rooster sounds. Her daughter's mispronunciation was so original that Basia named her company after it.

Her line began in 1994 with Kimona Girl, Teddy, Pixie Clip, Song on a Clip, and others. All of her ornaments were produced in Poland, with 1994-1996 tags looking like a contemporary tree mobile. From 1997 on, the hang-tags appeared with a modern tree logo. Her "Jackie Collection" was created after the April 1996, Jackie Onasis auction at Sotheby's. Her rationale for this line was to record the end of an era associated with the glamour of Jackie O., "where insane prices were paid for goods worthy and unworthy that belonged to an Icon." Basnia was one of the first artists to design blown glass eggs patterned after the works of Carl Faberge.

150

Represented by KO-KO-NA-MI & Co. are ornaments created by "Victor." Modern art style designs which could be used as tree ornaments or objets d'art are his signature product. Victor Chiarizia is a contemporary glassblower who created ornaments with futuristic forms. He was schooled in scientific glassblowing, starting his career in 1975 fabricating intricate scientific apparatus for the medical, environmental, and research industries. Later, Victor studied Venetian glassblowing with Maestro, Lino Tagliapietra. The average size of his ornaments was six-inches. Some of the most distinctive figural shapes were "The Visitor" (an extended legged space creature with an alien head), "TV: Drug of a Nation" (a television set with image in screen), and "Communication Vessel" (a satellite-shaped ornament).

The Potpourri Designs Collection of European Glass Christmas Ornaments commenced in 1995 and included various circus-themed ornaments. John Byron brought a fresh approach in 1998 with tree toppers including a large Madonna and Child perched atop a double ball base completed in great detail. A golden halo attached to the back of Mary's head and shoulder adds a unique distinction to this topper. A golfer, a Mrs. Santa, Springtime eggs, and three ball snowmen also added some very distinctive ornaments to this established line.

Roman, Inc.

Roman, Inc. was a leading producer and exclusive distributor of more than 15,000 giftware items. Its owner, Ronald T. Jedlinski, continued to guide its path in this decade. In the early 1990s, Jedlinski moved to form Seraphim Studios, a creative umbrella of world-famous artists and sculptors. Their singular assignment was to research and develop a collection of angels that would be modern interpretations of the world's most inspirational artworks. Seraphim Studios took advantage of 2,000 years of rich art. In 1994, the Seraphim Classics Collection was introduced. Based on the greatest achievements of Renaissance Masters, the collection became immediately popular with both retailers and consumers. Married since 1965, Jedlinski credits his wife, Diane, for invaluable assistance and moral support in his quest to build Roman, Inc. into the business that it is today. Dan Loughman, currently Bethlehem Lights Brand Manager at Roman, is married to Julie, their daughter. With the birth of their first grandchild, Emily Catherine, in 1996, and their second, Caroline Elizabeth, in 1998, they are sure to enter a fourth generation of business.

Romana Gugerbauer

Austrian ornaments also gained in considerable popularity during the 1990s. Romana Gugerbauer became quite famous for her mouth blown glass ornaments primarily due to the minute detail and exacting precision with which each sphere is painted. Established in 1985, it was not until 1995 that Gertrude began her widespread distribution of her Austrian tree ornaments across the United States. In Europe, this line of ornaments has been marketed under the Romana Gugerbauer name since 1973—same ornaments, same principal artisans, two different companies owned by two different people in two different countries. A third U.S. company has come upon the scene.

Romana Gugerbauer respects and works to preserve centuries-old Austrian traditions through her creation of hand-made ornaments from all-natural products. For example, a daisy with the same circumference as the cap on an ink pen might have as many as twenty-five individually painted petals, each presented in exquisite detail. Generally her pieces were not silvered. She is also known for the application of gold to her ornaments. Some of her pieces are astounding. One depicts the Holy Family walking down a winding road with expertly painted trees, hills, and stones along the road. Another has a bear swinging on rope tassels; another is of church in a wintry scene. There is even one scene which shows swaying flower spikes with butterflies and bees surrounding the plants and flowers.

Having lost her mother while a child, Romana was raised in humble surroundings by her grandmother. She started working while very young so that she could earn money to finance her education at the Academy of Arts and Traditional Folk Art in Graz. Her area of study was textile design. Married to a teacher, Romana remained house-bound with two children. In her spare time, she created traditional Austrian folk crafts. She started by selling her wares to small shops in the surrounding larger cities.

Already possessing the necessary art skills, Romana sought the advice of a friend who knew how to paint on glass. Women were hired from her village, and the Romana Gugerbauer line was debuted in Salzburg in 1973, making its first appearance in the United States at the New York Gift Show at the Javits Center in 1978. Romana's daughter, Sabina, who was the business manager, now shares partnership and responsibility in production. Many of her employed women have been with her for many years. Frau Kaiser has been with her since the start of the business.

Gertrude, the owner of the United States-based Austrian Christmas Tree Line, likened the work environment to an orchestra with Roman as the conductor and Sabina

as the first violin. Over the course of the years, over a thousands different designs have emerged from the Austrian studio. Usually no more than 1,000 to 1,500 ornaments are produced of any given design before they are retired. Romana does not blow her own ornaments, but rather purchases glass stock ornaments from German and Swiss glass blowers. True to the tradition of using only products derived from nature, Romana uses casein paints, derived from a mixture of milk powder and water. Sand and plant pods are occasionally used on egg ornaments to achieve three-dimensional effects.

Chase International

Susan Paolini, a Buffalo, New York, native was attending China's Peking University in 1985 when she met Larry Quek in Beijing, and they married. While living in China in 1990, they discovered two remote villages in the Hebei Province where the sons and daughters of local farmers spent their evenings painting the inside of snuff bottles and other small bottles. Paolini and her husband then conceived the idea of painting ornaments from the inside and established an artist's colony in Beijing to do just that.

A unique approach was taken by Chase International in its "Inside Art" line which painted ornaments on the inside. They used mouth-blown glass spheres manufactured at a light bulb factory quite nearby to their colony. Using Christmas cards and other pictures, they introduced Santas, angels, snowmen, and religious scenes to their employed artists.

The process is quite complex. The artist slips a fine brush into the narrow openings of the glass balls. The artist paints the outlines and then details on the inside of the glass. These elaborate masterpieces can take an entire day to complete, or even weeks, depending upon the intricacy of the design.

NYCO

While touring the Orient, Nicki Yassaman and her husband, Nassar, became fascinated with the technique of enameling, developed over 600 years ago. They immediately saw the possibilities of using this same process to create Christmas ornaments. Thus NYCO was born. Nicki designs the ornaments. The master designer adapts her drawings and makes a silver prototype, which is used to make an iron mold. Then liquid copper is poured into the mold and allowed to cool. After the ornament has hardened, an artist applies a delicate filigree copper or gold-plated wire onto the shape to create a pattern. Working with tweezers and glue, the artists applies the wire to the ornament, dusts it with epoxy, and fires it in a kiln to affix the wire. Then a base coating of white paint is applied, or the ornament is silver-plated. The thickness of the wire braid determines the layers of liquid enamel. An artist hand paints each piece, often applying one color over another to achieve a beautiful effect. Then a coal-fired kiln is used to heat the ornament to cause a chemical change in the paints—they become glass. The result is a copper ornament coated in glass.

Christina's World

Christina's World of Deer Park, New York, was founded in 1994 by Christina Mallouk. As Christina's mother was a dress designer, her earliest memories of home are being surrounded by beautiful fabrics, bolts of wool tweed, silk, and brocades. Her father, an entrepreneur, sold plastic and silk flowers. She studied dance and was a ballet teacher until the age of thirty. A divorce and subsequent work for her father, who headed Creative Arts Flowers, led her into her present business. As vice-president of marketing for her father, she decided that their business needed to import from Europe as well as Asia, specifically glass ornaments.

As a buyer and marketing director for Creative Arts Flowers, her employment required trips to Europe where she discovered European glass ornaments. She decided to start her own company, "Christina's World." Working with factories in the Czech Republic, Italy, and Poland, Christina and her very talented designer, Bill Lindemann, produced a great number of very elegant glass ornaments for the American market. Her collectors' club "Connoisseurs Circle" was extremely active in the latter part of this decade under the direction of the club manager, Mark Czapko.

At first her ornaments were copies of the old. However, it was the capacity of the factories to copy and interpret her ideas on glass that convinced her to design her own line. Christina has a very close working relationship with her production factories and, as a result, uses only two primary factories. The factories are given free reign to interpret her designs, even after she and the factory had created the original samples together. Complex silk screens are used to replicate the photos, textiles, and ribbon samples which are used as sources. Then, color is chosen from Kaiser Lacquers which imitate our US color standards PMS system. Each color has a number, which results in colors being consistent from year to year.

Christina's World themed "The Butterfly Zone" collection in 1999, one of many themed ornament collections.

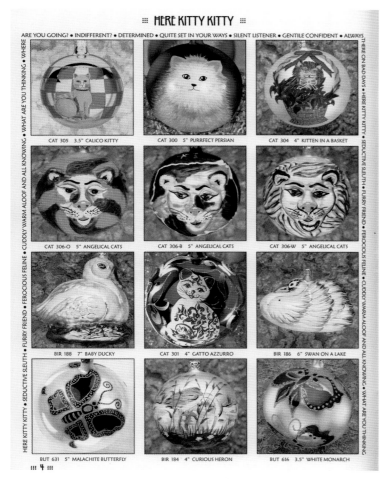

Christina's World themed "Here Kitty Kitty" collection for 1999-2000, also one of many themed ornament collections designed by Christina.

EuroVue, Inc.

EuroVue was established in Tucson, Arizona, in 1993 as a partnership among four original investors. The idea and the concept of the business were developed during a trip to Poland, a country with a long and renowned tradition of creating blown glass ornaments. At that time, market research in the United States indicated a growing awareness, demand, and appreciation for blown glass ornaments for collectible, aesthetic, as well as sentimental value.

In 1994, the company was incorporated under the name of EuroVue, Inc. and since November 1997 Jozef Biedermann has been its sole owner. Biedermann was born in Poland and currently resides in Tucson, Arizona. He designs and oversees all the aspects of the designing process, production, and marketing as well as management of the office and warehouse. Due to his multiple responsibilities, Biedermann divides his time, and travels frequently between the United States and Poland.

In 1998 EuroVue experienced significant growth, not only in the market arena, but also particularly within the collection. From a line of a few pieces in 1993, it has grown to a line of approximately 360 different designs in 1999.

EuroVue, Inc. is dedicated to the production and marketing of exclusive blown glass ornaments. It seeks to offer unique designs and updated versions of classic balls, reflectors, and shapes not found in other collections. Their ornaments are recognized for their quality, graceful and sometimes whimsical styles, exquisite colors, and fine glitters. As they are located in Arizona, their collection also includes southwestern designs. Their line is carried through out the United States by upper end gift stores, museums, catalogs, diverse organizations, zoos, aquariums, nurseries, and various other specialty shops as well as on line stores. With its current marketing strategy and the continuous development of novel designs, EuroVue should reach its goal of becoming one of the leading providers of blown glass ornaments in the United States. From its beginning, its logo had its signature heart as a symbol as they felt the heart embodied the sincerity of endeavor and, importantly too, the essence of holidays—giving.

EuroVue assortment of Spring and Easter-themed ornaments from their 1999 collection.

MIA

In 1990, Mia started her business and commenced the production of glass ornaments in 1993. Her family originates from Poland and was involved in the manufacturing of the wooden boxes for Polish ornaments. Her love for her native country, family, and glass ornaments drew her back to Poland in 1989, just at the twilight of Communism there, where she explored other business ventures at first. For several generations her family had been involved in the traditional Polish craft industry—making Polish boxes. However, she chose the production of glass ornaments to expand her business.

At first, the glass tree ornaments imported by MIA's were handcrafted by the Calik family and other small factories in Poland. Employing her own original molds, Mia used artists such as Van Gogh and Toulouse-Lautrec as inspiration for her designs. Such ornaments as "After Van Gogh—Vase with Pink Roses," "After VanGogh—Peasant Shoes," and "After Toulouse-Lautrec—Artistide Bruian" helped to establish her reputation as possessing wit and whimsy which she applied to designs such as this. However, in late 1996, she realized that they were not respecting the exclusivity of her designs and were also relaxing their standards of quality. Mia decided to start her own studio, and in April of 1997, she started her own production in Poland. Mia divides her time between her business and shipping headquarters in New York City and her design studio and retail store in Krakow, Poland.

In 1999, Mia was chosen to decorate the Vatican's large millennium tree. She used some of her exclusive museum commissions and some of her Krakow series ornaments which featured many of the city's landmarks. Special production ornaments for the tree included scenes of Wadowice, Pope John Paul II's birthplace, and reproductions of the stained glass windows and paintings by the turn-of-the-century Polish painter and writer, Stanislaw Wyspianski, which adorn the walls of the Church of the Franciscan Fathers, located directly across the street from the Krakow Archdiocese.

Rhyn-Rivet

Catherine Rhyner's ornaments have a distinctive Victorian style appearance. Ornament titles such as "French Long Holly," "Victorian Rose," and "Branded Floral" all employ floral patterns, sprigs of greens, and other such Victorian themes.

Sarabella Creations

Natalie Sarabella visited department stores with her family as a child. She recalls the fact that the ornaments appeared to be so huge on the trees. "But as I grew up, they seemed less special, less fine, and so little," according to Sarabella. In 1994 she introduced her first ornaments, which included some of the largest and most elegant ornaments on the market. Averaging more than six-inches in diameter, she used brilliant golds, reds, and aubergines. Using German-blown spheres, each ornament is subsequently hand painted in acrylics, then decorated with Swarovski crystals, cultured pearls, beads, and decorative brass accents. Then each glass ornament is crowned with a bow made from French wired ribbon interlaced with thinner complimentary colored ornaments. In the center of each of the ribbon bouquets is a surprise adornment which accentuates the design motif. Once her business grew, she was joined by her cousin Janet Mormile.

Larry Fraga Designs

The originator of this line is Larry Fraga, who some individuals might remember as a well-known model whose picture appeared on a poster in 1993 which sold all across America. After graduating from a junior college, he spent twenty years as a model, and kept gathering Christmas remembrances. Born and raised in Oakland, California, Fraga has been fascinated with decorating for Christmas from his early childhood onward. His father imported and sold rugs, and his mother worked as an inspector in a glass factory. Being the youngest of seven children, and the only boy, Fraga kept Christmas up all year, and ornaments were all he ever wanted for presents at Christmas. Thus, Fraga collected ornaments since he was a child.

As a teenager, he decorated historic buildings, churches, and nursing homes for the holidays. In his forties, he headed his own ornament company and became its chief artistic designer, starting the business in 1995. All of his ornaments are completed in Italy, Germany, and Poland. During the first few years, his ornaments were made from his original drawings as well as antique molds which were blown and painted to his specifications.

One of his innovations was to take existing two-part antique molds (front and back) which are of the same size, have the factory take them apart, and then switch the fronts and backs to create a fresh new look. Thus he made the transition to original creations, quite unlike the traditional ornaments of the past. Fraga's ornaments were painted with a matte-finish on the face and hands to give a porcelain look to the ornaments, unlike any others being produced at that time. Larry Fraga's ornaments mostly were designed with a soft matte-like finish to them that distinguished his glass figural ornaments from most others created in this decade.

In 1998, he introduced a large number of Victorian wire-wrapped ornaments which included antique paper scraps and spun glass. Capturing the look of the past in the Victorian era, these ornaments included zeppelins, balloons, swans, ships, and even chandeliers. At this time he also began producing more of his own designs from his original drawings and used fewer of the antique molds in his line. The "Glitter Series" burst upon the ornament scene in 1999. While Fraga had done all glittered ornaments in limited numbers for special signing events in 1997 and 1998, his innovative look and incredible sense of color gave the "Glitter Series" an appeal that would be quickly copied in the industry. The reaction of collectors was an immediate and resounding success. In 1999, a few designs were blown by Larry Fraga himself, and are very limited.

Larry Fraga designed ornaments for Christmas, 1998.

Millennium Ornaments

Christopher Radko provided some very stylish ornaments in celebration of the Millennium. These included an Art Deco Times Square, a wine bottle, a postcard complete with painted stamp, and a New Years baby.

Slavic Treasures provided a Millennium angel in a gold and red dress with white and red glitter trim. A 2000 Santa dressed in a red suit with white trim sitting on a gold moon that bears the number "2000" was the Polonaise Collection offering. EuroVue provided a Millennium Ball with an American flair. There was an image of North America on one side with a plane, a rocket, and car painted over it. An American flag was found on the other side. Old World Christmas produced "A Toast to 2000," a "Fin de Siecle" champagne bottle with the year 2000 in raised numbers above the label on the front of the bottle. Patricia Breen released a two-sided Santa: a 1900 representative on one side and a 2000 interpretation on the other.

Assortment of Millennium ornaments from Christopher Radko, Patricia Breen, and Old World Christmas. Left to right: Betty Boop (Adler), $75-95; Postcard (Radko), $50-60; Harold Lloyd with clock (Radko), $75-85; Times Square (Radko), $100-110; 2000 Boy with banner (Radko), $55-65; Millennium Santa (Breen), $125-135; 2000 champagne Bottle (Old World), $45-55.

Santa Claus Figures and Ornaments

Many folk artists continued to create Santa Claus figures for use in Christmas displays under the tree as well as smaller varieties for use as tree ornaments. But few have stood the test of time as well as Roberta Taylor of Jeromesville, Ohio, who started producing Santas as ornamental candy containers for the tree when she could not find a Santa for her son, Beck, one Christmas. Thirty years later, she continues to produce some of the most artistic and detailed Santa figures in the country.

What distinguishes her figures from many others is her very creative use of old fabric, toys, mica, and other antique materials to dress her figures and decorate their personages. A textile design college degree helped her gain an appreciation for using old wool and cotton to dress her Father Christmases. Her artistic design is especially evident in the faces of her Santas, which reveal almost a human appearance. With heads of plaster over composition, her love of detail is evident in facial expressions, even to the point of revealing an open-eyed Santa lovingly glancing off to the side. Finished with a beard of rabbit fur like the Germans used decades ago, her Santas are among the best.

Her longevity is evident as she now sells her figures to the children of parents who remember such Santas in their homes as children. Employing no advertising, she continues to attract countless followers who long to possess one of her beloved Santas. As she herself stated, "I don't need to just possess an item, but to get to the heart of the person who created the item in times past." Thus Roberta Taylor carefully studies historical accounts of Santa, pores over volumes of old images and illustrations of Santa, and speaks to all who will recall their personal memories of Santa as well as the European Father Christmas. Then she lovingly recreates a Santa today like one who no doubt existed in times past. Taylor's Santa figures now reside in countless collector's homes across America. While her production is somewhat limited (she insists on quality control and individuality, which she feels would be lost if she were to expand her production line), her Santa figures tower over much of her competition due to their miniscule details which set them apart. Such details as a jack-in-the-box, tiny wrapped presents in a woven basket, and mesh sacks of miniature glass vintage ornaments mark her pieces in a distinctive manner.

Canadian artist Kathy Paterson has also gained wide recognition recreating wonderful Father Christmas figures. Being a collector of German Santas, she began making her own molds. Made from a mixture of papier-mâché, polymer, and gypsum, her Santa figures are primarily candy containers. Individually hand-painted, and clothed in flannels, felts, and woolens; her figures range in size from 5" to 34". Situated in Paris, Ontario, her home studio continues to turn out wonderful figures, some made with glass icicle beards, some with nodding heads, and even some with rabbit fur beards. Each is marked with her initials and the year manufactured.

Even Mike Holmgren, former Green Bay Packer coach in the 1990s, appears as a Santa Claus figure among the hundreds of "one of a kind" figures designed and created by Eunice Hanson of New Berlin, Wisconsin. "I like to use old vintage clothing if I can get the material," Hanson stated in an interview. Santa's coat might be made from a nubby old coat purchased at a second hand store or a vintage fur coat gleaned from a local Milwaukee antique shop. It was actually a family illness in 1993 which caused her to begin her creation of such unique Santa figures. Her son Rod was diagnosed with a serious form of cancer. To help relieve her stress, Eunice took a hunk of clay she had purchased many years before and began sculpting Santa faces. She sculpted on breaks and during lunch hour while at work and even sculpted until she went to bed at night. Her son survived his bout with cancer, Eunice survived the stress, and she has been producing Santa figures full-time ever since.

Many smaller Santa figures were incorporated into Putz scenes. One very well recognized concern was Folk Art by May, American woodcarvings by Bruce and Dianne May of Madison, Iowa, which provided some very intriguing carved Santas. Bruce and Diane May began carving Santas for sale after carving one for a hobby and having a friend asking to buy it almost immediately. Started as a part-time business in Williamston, Michigan, it moved to Indiana in 1982. After being featured in *Early American Life* in 1985, they quickly became nationally recognized for their creative tree ornaments (carved from small pieces of wood picked up by the Ohio River) and their Father Christmas Santa figures. In the 1990s, it was, and continues to be, a family business run by their son Ted and wife Cynthia, son Matt, and daughter Cinda. Together, each artistic member of the family adds creative touches to their original work.

Candy Containers

Hershey Food Corporation marketed a set of Christmas tree ornaments in 1993, complete with strings, ready to hang. A box contained the twelve candies, each wrapped in gold foil decorated to represent one of the twelve days of Christmas. The last verse of this song was depicted on the reverse of the box.

Paper and Cardboard Ornaments

Bruce Catt continued his production of paper and cardboard ornaments, most of which were marketed through high-end department and gift shops. Some of the most remarkable in the late 1990s included a Nabisco cracker box ornament with lion inside,

a circus drum, and a wonderful hot air balloon with intricate gold braiding. His circus themes were indeed inspired by the animal cracker boxes! One elaborate rectangular box had a Dresden camel on the "inside," tiny gold Dresden paper bars, gold Dresden wheels, and top and bottom sections with a shiny blue foil paper. Each circus wagon piece is presigned by Catt himself. One other very unique piece was a Krampus appearing on cornucopias and barrels.

Many of his shapes were originally used as candy containers. Small baskets, pails, and cornucopias were created after such versions illustrated in *Godey's Lady's Book* and other ladies' magazines of the mid- to late 1800s. Predominant colors used by Catt included reds, blues (cobalt, peacock blue, ice blue), greens (including a vibrant emerald and soft celery green), royal purple, a "marbled" look, golds, pinks, and pale lavenders. His shapes are equally important to the colors; when his cornucopias come to a point, they come to a point! His ornaments are reminiscent of those early Dresden pieces, but appear in larger style sizes.

Clay Ornaments

Commencing in 1993, Carl Richard Rothe has been creating clay ornaments reminiscent of bakers' cookie ornaments. Rothe was a pastry chef and was an expert at edible "works of art." "Bread dough ornaments" appealed to him, but he wanted a more durable formula. He experimented and finally developed his own clay formula. He designed, produced, marketed, and sold his own ornaments which were freehand sculpted without molds. Each ornament came with its own tag attached by a gold thread strung through the metal wire securely embedded at the top of each piece. Each ornament took a full week to produce. After firing, each piece was hand painted with brightly colored acrylics, dried, glittered, and dipped three times to seal the ornament and add a high gloss.

Wooden Ornaments

In 1997, Tim Butner, a recognized artist, started the production of wooden ornaments quite like some of those created by German artisans, but being larger in size than the German counterparts. Tim's wife, Donna, applies the base coat of paint to the forms, glittering the pieces, inserting the gold hanging thread in the very small hole at the top if each ornament, sealing them into a package, and attaching the identifying "Flights of Fancy" tag to each. The wooden forms are 1/4" thick, vary in height up to nine-inches, and are painted a matching solid color on the reverse side, where the ornament is signed and labeled.

With the reunification of Germany, the bottom fell out of the East German nutcracker and wooden ornament market. Once these East German cooperatives attempted to survive in a capitalistic society, no longer protected and subsidized by the government, these businesses simply went under and ceased to exist. Some workshops did survive, including Franz Karl, Richard Glaesser, and Hodrewa.

After the reunification, both Steinbach and Ulbricht returned to Erzgebirge—Steinbach to the little town of Marienberg and Ulbricht to his home village of Seiffen.

Therefore, the Steinbachs and the Ulbrichts rose quickly to the top. The Steinbach Company further increased its visibility with the introduction of limited editions, which helped to create and foster a collectibles market for its nutcrackers. The first limited edition nutcracker was "King Ludwig," made for the House of Tyrol, a Georgia-based mail order company. Today Christian Steinbach is assisted by his daughter, Karla, the sixth-generation vice-president. Between them, they oversee product development and manufacturing and represent their company at collectibles shows around the world. Over 260 artists produce their almost 200 nutcrackers available for sale in the late 1990s. The Steinbachs are dedicated to preserving the production of wooden items for generations to come. One sign of this is their commitment to reforestation of trees in Germany and Poland since the wood used for their products may take as long as 200 years to age properly.

Christian Ulbricht quickly followed with a limited edition "Victorian Santa." Nearly all of the Ulbricht nutcrackers are designed by family members—Christian Ulbricht, his wife, Inge, daughter, Inzes, and son, Gunther. Inge designs most of the ornaments. The family employs around sixty workers in the Lauingen workshop, around eighty in the Erzgebirge factory, and another forty cottage workers who continue the tradition of working in their homes. Christian Ulbricht was born in Seiffen on February 15, 1933. His father, Otto, a professional wood turner who started his own business in 1928, built a new factory in 1934. After World War II, when the area became the East German Zone and private industry was taken out of the hands of individuals, Otto took his family across the border to the West where they settled in Lauingen, near Augsburg. Once settled, with his Erzgebirge wood-turning traditions transplanted to Bavaria, Otto began again. When Otto died in 1968, Christian continued in charge. In 1978, Christian expanded his thinking, and developed a new company which he named Holzkunst Christian Ulbricht. When Germany reunified, Christian brought back original factory in Seiffen to his family business.

E. M. Merck of Old World Christmas in Spokane, Washington, designed nutcrackers during this decade. These nutcrackers were made by KWO in Olbernhau in the heart of the Erzgebirge. During the early 1990s, she merely designed nutcrackers for general production. In the late 1990s, she commenced the design and release of limited edition nutcrackers which have received quite a warm reception from many collectors.

Tinsel Icicles and Garlands

Santa's Best of Manitowoc, Wisconsin, is one of the few American-based companies producing tinsel garlands for our trees. Originally known as National Tinsel Manufacturing Company, this business merged in 1991 with Rennoc of Vineland, New Jersey. Currently in its third generation of a family-owned business, Santa's Best is headed by William F. Protz, Jr. and John P. Protz, both sons of William F. Protz, Sr., who headed the firm for many years after the death of his father-in-law, William C. Stoltz, who originally founded the firm in an old Lutheran school house on Hamilton Street. In the early 1920s it moved to new headquarters on 16th Street, where it still operates today. Heavy tinsel roping is one of its principal products.

Some of the more innovative colors of this decade for tinsel roping included imperial purple, bright magenta, and teal. Traditional red and green, however, remained as the most popular colors. Garlands far outsold icicles, those tinsel stands that for years have divided users into two categories: those who lovingly placed each strand across the branches one by one with each hanging perfectly and those who merely threw the tinsel on the tree losing patience quickly. This decade of trimmers more than ever never removed the tinsel from the tree after Christmas. They merely threw the tree on the curb for recycling, tinsel and all.

While many Americans continued to follow the tradition of garland roping on their tree, the traditional tinsel type declined somewhat in sales, losing sales to ribbons, beads, and also dried flowers used to decorate trees in place of tinsel garlands. But by the mid-to late 1990s consumers used both traditional and newer styles. Bead-and-star garlands were among the most popular.

Under Our Trees

Nativity Scenes

When Germany reunited, the tradition of producing elegant papier-mâché creche figures was revived when Renate Weigelt, the granddaughter of Richard Mahr and niece of Julius Weigelt, regained Marolin, the original producer of such items before World War II. Today, Renate, with her husband, Walter Greiner, and their daughter, Evelyn Forkel, carry on the family craft using their own family heirloom molds. Since 1991 the material of papier-mâché is going through a renaissance. Being loved by collectors of traditional handcrafted papier-mâché items, the Marolin figures quickly regained their former status on the international market.

It all began in Steinach, a little town in the Thuringian Forest nearly 100 years ago, when Richard Mahr created nativity figurines made of papier-mâché at his parents' home. The first figurines were in a strict Nazarene style. Later, in 1920, a new style arose when the young and talented designer Julius Weigelt joined the company. His style can be seen even today on all Marolin products.

Richard Mahr was always open for new talents and designers. He supported his new employees in every way he could. His instinctive sense for business advanced the company even during the years before World War II. Marolin became known world-wide as a company for handcrafted Christmas items made of papier-mâché until the start of World War II. After World War II, Marolin started out very promisingly, but the division of Germany stopped most of these developments.

The creation of each piece takes about seven days, with some larger pieces taking up to one-half year to dry. First, their special type of papier-mâché formula is blended in a large vat. This formula includes water, porcelain, plant resin, slate, karolin, paper pulp, and other "secret ingredients."

The liquid is poured into such forms, they suck up the moisture in the liquid, and push it against the walls of the forms. After six to twelve hours the form is opened and the figurine is dried.

The putt type (a heavier papier-mâché formula much like the consistency of soft clay) is hand pressed into molds to form small and delicate features such as hands and legs. Often times, wires and pins are fixed into the center of these items to ensure durability.

Their version of papier-mâché is more durable, being produced in both dough and liquid consistency. For figures with a height taller than 4.9-inches, the liquid is poured into a form to create a hollow body. Liquid papier-mâché is poured into plaster of Paris molds, which, when heated extract water from the material. This causes the hardening of the outside of the figure first, enabling the extra to be poured off. This is the method using for creating the hollow figures. Then these figures are placed in a drying room. The drying process takes place in a heated drying furnace at 70 degrees C.

Once figures are dried and assembled, they are primed with a thin coat of plaster which smoothes out the surface. Then each figure is individually hand-painted, shellacked, antiqued, and glittered. So it takes two types of artisans to create on Marolin figurine: the pourer and the "handpress" artisan. The two create the figurine step by step. Lastly, the most important step in the creation of a papier-mâché figurine is completed with the delicate skills of the painter. The figure should gain depth, shine, and everlasting impressions when the coat of a solution called "Patina" is attentively applied. Every figure gets the same artisan attention as it was given in the past. The cottage industry of Thuringia is proud that the company never lost its original methods established by Richard Mahr and continues to preserve the art of creating papier-mâché handicrafts.

France's tradition of providing dressed nativity figures continues to grow in popularity with each passing year. With international travel, the Internet, and the publicizing of European Christmas traditions, many Americans have turned from the Italian and German crèche figures to those manufactured in France. The French counterpart of the nativity figures include Santons, or "little saints." One very well known maker of these came to the forefront in this decade. Michele St.-Alexis Scott was born in the south of France. At the age of twenty-four, she moved to the United States, finding work in Beverly Hills, doing the makeup for Hollywood stars. After a 1990 move to Maine, she decided to begin designing driftwood Santas. She opened a gift shop and imported gift items from France. When she couldn't get enough Santons to fill her orders, she decided to create them herself. Today, she is one of few artists in the world who still designs, carves, and hand-paints Santons—who bring gifts to the newborn Jesus. Sold under the name of Saint-Alexis Santons, the figurines, some of which represent the Arcadians (the first settlers in North America), are 3 1/2" high.

Roman, Inc. continued to supply some very elegant crèche scenes through this decade. In 1994, they introduced "The Fontanini Golden Edition Nativity," by master sculptor Elio Simonetti. The fourteen-piece set was limited to an edition of 2,500 and retailed at about $375. The figures were 6 1/2-inches high; the stable about 10 1/2-inches high and 24-inches long.

Evelyn Forkel (great-granddaughter of Richard Mahr) and her daughter in Marolin factory in Steinach, Germany.

Working with the putte type papier-mâché figures to be used in crèche scenes at Marolin.

Painting details on the large papier-mâché crèche items at Marolin.

Large nativity scene complete with figures and crib on display in the Marolin showroom in Steinach, Germany.

Evelyn Forkel placing the patina to give that old world look to her crèche figures produced at Marolin.

Setting in museum in Steinach illustrating the home and workshop of Richard Mahr, the founder of Marolin.

Close-up of large papier-mâché molds in Marolin factory.

A few representative examples of the type of papier-mâché items produced by Marolin in the period just after World War II.

French Santons mixed in with Holy Family made in Germany in a museum in Southern France where the history of creating Santons is very rich.

"Le Vitrier" glass window repair person Santon figure. Southern France.

"Le Berger" shepherd Santon figure. Southern France.

Mica for Sprinkling Under the Tree

"Old German Mica Hoarfrost" or "Rauhreif" mica flakes from the 1940s was merchandised through B. Blunchen & Company in this decade. In 1994, Blumchen's offered mica snow, once again being manufactured in Germany.

Village Houses

Department 56 Village Scenes

In 1990, Department 56 introduced "The North Pole." This series included "Santa's Workshop," "Reindeer Barn," and "Elf Bunkhouse." This series combined fantasy and humor and was intricately detailed. In "The Reindeer Barn," for example, each reindeer has its own personalized door by which to enter the barn. By 1990, it was obvious that Department 56 had attracted a lot of collectors with their various village series. This series particularly appealed to young collectors who could get in on the ground floor, rather than starting a set and having to obtain the retired pieces on the secondary market.

In an effort to better communicate with collectors, Department 56 created a quarterly magazine, *Department Quarterly,* in 1991. Articles on new and retired village pieces, snow babies, and other Christmas items are blended with historical Christmas information which helps to educate enthusiasts as to various Christmas customs and decorating schemes. In October 1992, Department 56, Inc. was acquired by Forstman Little & Co. In June 1993, a public stock offering of the company's stock sent many collectors to their stockbrokers. In 1994, Department 56 added "The Disney Parks Village" series, a set of classic Disney characters and theme-park buildings, to its "Heritage Village" collection. This series was a result of a licensing agreement with The Walt Disney Company. The first pieces in the series included "Mickey's Christmas Shop," "Old World Antiques," "Fire Station," a Disney park family grouping, and "Old World Antiques Gate."

Animals and Figures

The Fontanini Collection by Roman, Inc. introduced the Bristol Falls Carolers Society. This Victorian-era village collection is set in the New England town of Bristol Falls. This was a storyline-themed collection designed by Elio Simonetti. Figures included townspeople and three resin building facades. Accessories such as a park bench, old-style mailbox, evergreen trees, and a welcome sign add charm to this series.

Department 56 continued its production of snow babies into this decade as well.

Indoor Electric Lighting of Our Trees

Manufacturers of midget lights became more innovative in this decade. The M & M Mars Division, Hackettstown, New Jersey, introduced M & M Happy Lights packaged together with a six-ounce bag of chocolate candies. The string of twenty Christmas tree lights had bulbs in the shapes of M & M candies, with a smiling face and "M" printed on them plus hands and feet attached to make happy little people-like objects out of the candy. A special warning said, "Keep away from children. This light set is not a toy."

Chasers and multifunctional lights were used indoors as well as outdoors. Star, angel, snowmen, and cluster candle lights were among the novelty lights which attracted lots of attention in this decade. Lower priced miniature lights propelled the sales of these lights to new heights, with the most inexpensive lights being under $2 a set. The best seller in 1994 was the 100-light string of blinkers. While clear lights continued to be the most sold, families started to turn more and more to solid colors such as blue, green, red, and even purple. These monochromatic color schemes appealed to those who tired of the same thing year after year. Multi-colored sets diminished in popularity as Americans turned to trendier fashions.

Another factor which helped sell lights was the elimination of the eight percent tariff on light sets. Decorative light sets intended for holiday use were now exempt from this tax. Interestingly, Americans started to turn back to the C-7 (CANDELABRA) size light in the last part of this decade. No doubt motivated by historical references and photographs of trees from the 1940s and 1950s, families purchased these lights. Sometimes they were combined with the midget lights for a special effect, but most often, those seeking a nostalgic look placed only these larger size bulbs on their tree. This sparked an interest in older style replacement lights. Americans remembered the soft reds, blues, and greens of older days. They even remembered the wonderful pink color from the 1950s. Therefore, there was renewed interest not only in the newer sets, but the collecting of older replacement lights as well, especially those of different hues.

Outdoor Electric Lighting

If there was a decade in which outdoor lighting exploded, it was the 1990s. More than any other decade, Americans homeowners put lights into their shrubs, hung lights in their deciduous trees, and created countless themed and color displays across the United States. Many Americans now started as early as Thanksgiving to put up their displays and usually lit them well into the second week of January. It almost became competitive in neighborhoods to see who could outdo their neighbor's display. Countless neighborhoods then became pilgrimage sites for others to visit during the Christmas season.

Outdoor wire sculptures of deer, Santa Claus, and Nativity figures were popular sellers in this decade. Icicle lights were one of the most trendy customs of this decade; introduced in 1997, they sold out every year for the first three years of their existence. Almost every block had a home roof or porch from which these icicle lights were hung.

Thirty million sets were sold in 1998 with sixty million being sold in 1999. While the idea had been around for a while, it just was not marketed. The first years these lights were clear, with blue becoming quite popular for those who wished for a softer effect.

Another trend was using mesh or net lighting which draped over shrubs and bushes, once again facilitating quick outdoor lighting. Sue Scott, President of Primal Lite, Richmond, California, noted in 1999 that the lights category "just continues to grow, and it's a year-round category now." John Rinehimer, president and owner of Arizona Light Creations, which produced Light Scamps, also noted the popularity of outdoor lighting. His Scamps could be hung from an outdoor tree to give an effect much like a clump of grapes. The fiber optic look appeared in a line of fiber optic string lights by GKI. LED lights in red, yellow, and green which were longer-lasting, cooler, and more intense than conventional bulb lighting also appeared in the late 1990s. Also available in net lighting were sets where the lights flicked on and off to show an expanding and contracting design. The designs included a heart, a star, and a tree.

Americans also returned to large plastic figures like those employed in the 1960s. Americans sought big outdoor figures such as candy canes, lollipops, and toy soldiers due to their generic, non-religious style and their appeal to children. But the most popular continued to be Santa Claus figures sold in sizes from 24-inches to an eight-foot-tall, 200-pound model retailing for over two thousand dollars.

Underwriters Laboratories, Inc. seized and destroyed 270 shipments of electrical products, including millions of dollars worth of imported Christmas lights with counterfeit UL labels in 1997. UL's switch to a holographic label two years previous made counterfeiting the UL label more difficult. Although the UL certification is not required by law, most retailers refused to stock non-UL-listed Christmas lights. Some shipments had lights with no fuse protection and 30-gauge wire wrapped around the blades rather than soldered to them. UL implemented a new, tougher standard in effect for lights manufactured after January 1997. There is no doubt that as Americans closed out the decade and went into a new Millennium, they more than ever turned to outdoor lighting to express their Christmas spirit.

Lighted Santa head from late 1980s into early 1990s. American plastic. $10-15.

GE "Gala" midget lights intended to look like the larger candelabra base bulbs of earlier decades. $5-8 in original box.

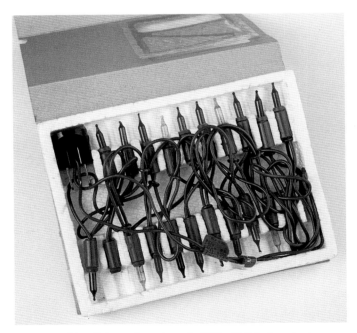

Common midget light set from the early 1990s. $2-3 for boxed set.

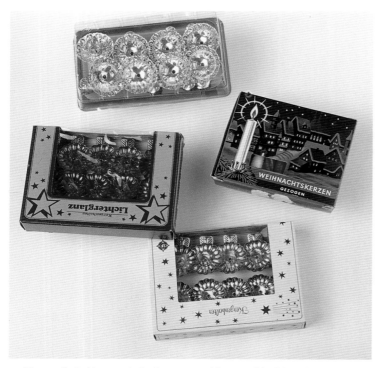

Tin candle holders made in Germany and imported by Blumchen's in the early 1990s. Very common in Germany, and gained some popularity with Americans who sought to recreate the old-fashioned Victorian tree with candles. $5-10 for boxed set.

"Swinging Santa" novelty toy from Hong Kong, late 1980s into early 1990s. Adult toy, not for giving to little children. $20-25.

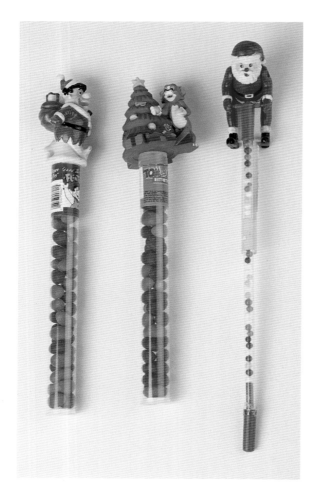

1993 candy containers with familiar characters. Very popular as a stocking stuffer. $3-5 compete with candy.

Action toy Santa which reveals power ranger underneath. $20-25.

Accessory pieces for Department 56 villages. Brush trees. $3-5 each.

Felt Santa of the type so popular throughout this decade. Made in China. $5-10.

Large collection of Santa Claus figures from the 1940s through the 1990s.

References Cited

Brenner, Robert. *Christmas Past.* (3rd edition) Exton, PA: Schiffer Publishing, 1996.

Brenner, Robert. *Christmas Revisited.* (values updated) Exton, PA: Schiffer Publishing, 1998.

Brenner, Robert. *Christmas Through the Decades.* (values updated) Exton, PA: Schiffer Publishing, 2000.

"Christmas hasn't changed—It's just more Plastic." *Oil, Paint and Drug Reporter.* 19 December 1960: 3+.

Country Home: An old-fashioned Christmas. Des Moines, IA: Meredith Books, 1992.

Dezso, Douglas M., J. Leon Poirier, and Rose D. Poirier. *Collector's Guide to Candy Containers.* Paducah, KY: Collector Books, 1998.

"A Disney Christmas at Kurt S. Adler." *The Antique Trader Weekly.* 6 December 1993: 83-84.

Early, Ray and Eilene. *Snow Babies.* Ohio: Newark Leader Printing Co., 1983.

Ehernberger, Jerry. *Keeping Christmas, Collecting Memories.* Chicago, IL: Jerry Ehernberger, 1997.

Hillier, Bevis. *Greetings from CHRISTMAS PAST.* Great Britain: The Herbert Press, 1982.

Iwamasa, Robert. *Antique Christmas Figural Light Bulbs.* York, PA: Shuman Heritage Printing Co., 1996.

Johnson, George. *CHRISTMAS Ornaments, Lights, and Decorations* (values updated). Paducah, KY: Collector Books, 1995.

Johnson, George. *CHRISTMAS, Ornaments, Lights, and Decorations Volume II.* Paducah, KY: Collector Books, 1997.

Johnson, George. *CHRISTMAS, Ornaments, Lights, and Decorations Volume III.* Paducah, KY: Collector Books, 1997.

Jones, Diane Carnevale. "Village Tidings." *Collectors Editions.* December 1994: 71-5.

Kaufman, J. G. and Jerry Ehernberger. *THE HISTORY AND CATALOG OF ELECTRIC CHRISTMAS LIGHT BULBS.* Prospect, KY: Christmas Antiques, Inc., 1978.

Lasansky, Jeanette. *HOLIDAY PAPER HONEYCOMB.* Lewisburg, PA: Oral Traditions Project, 1993.

McTammany, Theresa. "Trees of a Feather." *Colonial Homes.* December 1999: 24-8.

Moore, Connie A. and Harry L. Rinker. *SNOW GLOBES.* Pennsylvania: Running Press, 1993.

Neuwirth, Waltraud. *Glasperlen Christbaumschmuck.* Vienna, Austria: Selbstverlag, 1995.

Perlez, Jane "In ornaments from Poland, reflections of an art." *New York Times.* 24 December 1994: 41.

Pinkerton, Charlene. *Holiday Plastic Novelties: The Styrene Toys.* Atlgen, PA: Schiffer Publishing Ltd., 1999.

Rinker, Harry L. "Let it snow, let it snow, let it snow." *Antique Week (Central Edition).* 20 December 1993: 1+.

Rintz, Don. "Christmas Greetings from Racine." *The Golden Glow of Christmas Past Newsletter.* August 1995: 61-62.

Rittenhouse, Judith A. *ORNAMENTAL AND FIGURAL NUTCRACKERS.* Paducah, KY: Collector Books, 1993.

Snyder, Phillip V. *The Christmas Tree Book.* New York: Viking Press, 1976.

Segeth, Uwe-Volker. *Nostalgischer Weihnachtsschmuck.* Augsburg, Germany: Battenberg, 1994.

Stille, Eva. *Christbaumschmuck.* Nuremberg, West Germany: Rinehardt & Company, 1979.

Stille, Eva. *Chrisbaumschmuck des 20. Jahrhunderts.* Munich, Germany: Klinkhardt & Bierman, 1993.

Stille, Eva. *Ulter Christbaumschmuck.* Nuremberg, West Germany: Rinehardt & Company, 1972.

Warning, Don. *Memories of Santa Collection.* New York: Christmas Reproductions, Inc., 1992.

Whitmyer, Margaret and Ken. *CHRISTMAS COLLECTIBLES.* Paducah, KY: Collector Books, 1994.

Index

Acorn, W. German ornament, 90
Action toy Santa, 1990s, 158
Adam and Eve, Breen, 1990s, 146
Adler, Clifford, 138
Adler, Kurt S., 1960s, 21
Adrian Taron & Sons, 1990s, 137
Advent calendars, 1970s, 51
Advent Santa, Breen, 1990s, 147
Advertising, 1960s 10-2
Advertising, 1970s, 50
African-American Christmas, 105
Alice in Wonderland, Italian ornament, 85
Alligator, Radko, 1990s, 144
Althoff, Kenneth W., 141
Aluminum tree, 1960s, 16-7
Aluminum trees, 1970s, 52
American Tech. Machinery Corp., 16
American Greetings Co., 13
American ornament, 1970s, 56-7
American Tree & Wreath, 52
Amor Angel, Breen, 1990s, 147
Andrzej, 143
Angel hair, 1960s, 37
Angel on leaf, Radko, 1990s, 144
Angel w/wings, Italian ornament, 127
Angel's Flight, Blumchen, 1990s, 112
Angels, plastic, 1960s, 34
Apple, German, ornament, 1960s, 24
Arabian lady, Italian ornament, 127
Arcimbaldi Santa, Breen, 1990s, 146
Armstrong, Mary Lou, 98
Artificial snow, 1960s, 37
Artificial trees, 1980s, 77-9
Artificial trees, 1990s, 107-8
Astronaut, Italian ornament, 127
ATI, 16
Austria, 1960s, 26
Austrian ornament, 1970s, 61
Aztec bird, Radko, 1980s, 91
Bacchus, Breen, 1990s, 146
Baker's pig, Italian ornament, 58
Baldwin, Linda, 112
Ball w/bird, German ornament, 1960s, 24
Banks, 1970s, 68
Banks, 1980s, 101-2
Barclay figures, 1960s, 38-9
Barclay figures, 1970s, 66
BASIA, 149-50
Batgirl, Radko, 1990s, 145
Batman, Radko, 1990s, 145
Bauer, Dennis & Joyce, 108-9
Bauer, Karen, 108
Bauer, Sharen, 108
Bead garlands, 1960s 32
Beaded ornament, Czech, 1990s, 129
Bear w/cymbals, Italian ornament, 58
Bear w/fiddle, Italian ornament, 58
Bear w/heart, Italian ornament, 84
Bear w/horn, Italian ornament, 58

Bear/chenille tail, Italian ornament, 58
Beatle, Italian ornament, 20
Beehive ornament, Breen, 1990s, 147
Bengal tiger, Slavic, 1990s, 148
Berry, German, ornament, 1960s, 24
Betty Boop, Polonaise, 140
Biedermann, Jozef, 151
Bird on clip, German, ornament, 1960s, 24
Bird w/tail, E. German ornament, 90
Bird, Italian ornament, 77
Black Forest trees, 1980s, 78
Blum Boyce, Beatrice, 93
Blumchen, 1980s, 93-4
Blumchen, D. & Co., 1990s, 112-3
Books, children, 1960s, 13-5
Books, children, 1970s, 51
Books, Children, 1980s, 79
Bountiful Madonna, Breen, 1990s, 147
Boy w/cloth sack, Italian ornament, 20
Boy/gold suit, E. German ornament, 90
Boyce, Deborah L., 93
Boyce, Diane S., 93
Bradford Novelty Co., 96
Breen, Patricia, 1990s, 145-8
British man, Italian ornament, 127
Brogowski, Filip, 128
Bronner family, 1990s, 136
Bronner, Wally & Irene, 1990s, 135-6
Bronner, Wally, 1970s, 56
Bronner, Wally, 83
Bronner's, 1970s, 56, 57
Bronner's, 1980s, 98
Bronner's, 1990s, 135-6
Bronson Imports, 96
Brush trees, 1960s, 37
Brush trees, 1990s, 159
Bubble lights, 1960s, 41-2
Bubble lights, 1970s, 70
Bucky Badger, Slavic, 1990s, 149
Bug's Life, Italian ornament, 128
Bugle, German, ornament, 1960s, 24
Bush, George, 1980s, 75
Business, 1960s, 7
Butner, Tim, 153
Byron, John, 150
Calik, Ewa, 130
Candle holders, 1990s, 158
Candles, figural, 1960s, 40
Candy cont., 1960s, 28-9
Candy cont., 1970s, 61-2
Cardboard ornament, 1980s, 98
Cardboard ornament, 1990s, 153
Cards, 1960s, 13-5
Cards, 1970s, 50
Cards, 1980s, 79
Cards, 1990s, 110
Carey-McFall Co., 16
Carlson, Rob & Dianna, 108

Carry-lite, 1970s, 66
Carter, Jimmy, 48
Cat rattle, Radko, 1980s, 91
Cat, Italian ornament, 58
Catt, Bruce, 1980s, 98
Catt, Bruce, 1990s, 153
Celluloid Santa, 1960s, 39
Ceramic décor, 1970s, 53-5
Ceramic décor., 1970s, 17-9
Ceramic décor., 1980s, 80-1
Chalkware, Vaillancourt, 137
Chanukah, 105
Charlie Brown, Italian ornament, 57
Chase International, 150
Chaser lights, 1990s, 156
Chef w/apron, Italian ornament, 58
Chiarizia, Victor, 1970s, 57
Childhood Memories, OWC ornament, 133
Christborn, 1960s, 21
Christian Ulbricht, 1990s, 153
Christina's World, 150-1
Christmas mouse, Italian ornament, 83
Christmas Reproductions, 1990s, 138
Christmasphiles, 97
Christopher Radko, 1990s, 143-5
Church indent, German, ornament, 1960s, 24
Cinderella's sister, Italian ornament, 127
City Santa, Breen, 1990s, 148
Clay ornament, 1990s, 153
Clear inserts, German ornament, 1960s, 25
Clock, German ornament, 1960s, 24
Clown head, German ornament, 1960s, 25
Clown head, ribbon, Italian ornament, 20
Clown on ball, German ornament, 1960s, 25
Clown on block, Italian ornament, 127
Clown on star, Radko, 1990s, 144
Clown w/hat, Italian ornament, 84
Clown w/paper collar, Italian ornament, 20
Clown w/red hair, Italian ornament, 57
Clown w/wine flask, Italian ornament, 57
Clown, fat, German ornament, 1960s, 25
Clown, German ornament, 1960s, 24
Clown, Radko, 1990s, 144
Clown, red, German ornament, 1960s, 25
Clown, W. German ornament, 90
Coburg museum, 111
Coca-Cola, Polonaise, 139
Colonial lady, Italian ornament, 84
Colonial man, Italian ornament, 84
Combs, Janet, 1980s, 98
Comic figure, Italian ornament, 127
Comic figure, Radko, 1990s, 143
Corning Glass, 1960s, 20
Corning Glass, 1970s, 56-7
Corning ornament, 1980s, 82
Cottage, German, ornament, 1960s, 25
Cotton ornament, 1980s, 98

Cotton ornament, Blumchen, 1990s, 113
Cowboy Santa, Radko, 1980s, 91
Cowboy, Polonaise, 140
Crackers, Christmas, 1980s, 76
Crèche scenes, 1960s, 34-6
Crèche scenes, 1970s, 66
Crèche scenes, 1990s, 154-8
Curtis Posuniak, 148
Czech figural ornament, 1990s, 139
Czechoslovakia ornament, 1990s, 128-9
Daisy boy, Italian ornament, 84
Daisy girl, Italian ornament, 84
Dancing pig, Italian ornament, 84
Dancing pirouette, Italian ornament, 58
De Carlini family, 1990s, 123
De Carlini Soffieria, SNC, 1990s, 123-5
De Carlini, 1970s, 57
De Carlini, 1980s, 83-5
De Carlini, Enrico, 124
De Carlini, Maria Luisa, 57
De Elena Collections, 149
De Gilardoni, Fausto, 126
De Gilardoni, Fiorenzo, 126
De Gilardoni, Iris, 126
Debbie Thibault, 113
Decorating trends, 1960s, 17
Decorating trends, 1970s, 53-5
Decorating trends, 1980s, 75
Decorating trends, 1980s, 79-81
Decorating trends, 1990s, 110-11
Dennis Bauer feather trees, 108-9
Dept. 56 villages, 1980s, 101
Dept. 56, 1990s, 156
Dinosaur, Italian ornament, 84
Dolphin, Italian ornament, 84
Dow Chemical Co., 1960s, 32
Dow Chemical, 16
Drama figure, Italian ornament, 58
Duck, Radko, 1990s, 143
Dutch Love, Blumchen, 1990s, 112
Dwarfs, 1980s, Italian ornament, 84
Dwarfs, Italian ornament, 59
Dymski, Svetlana, 149
East Germany, 1970s, 59-60
East Germany, 1980s, 85-6
Easter Basket, Blumchen, 1990s, 112
Eckardt, Max & Sons, 20-1
Eggert, Carol, 78
Egyptian ornament, Polonaise, 140
Eichhorn, Brigit, 85-6
Eichhorn, Erwin Jr., 85-6
Einstein kite, Radko, 1980s, 91
Electric bells, 1960s, 45
Electrical advertising, 1960s, 12
Elephant Uncle Sam, Italian ornament, 84
Elephant, pink, Italian ornament, 57
Elf w/red cap, Italian ornament, 20
Elf, Italian ornament, 20
Elliot, Sandy, 1990s, 107-8

Empire Plastics, Co., 1960s, 46
Empire Plastics, Corp., 1970s, 73-4
Energy crisis, 1970s, 48
Enesco, 1970s, 54
ENESCO, 1990s, 137
Erzgebirge, Germany, 141
EuroVue, Inc., 151
Evening Cathedral, Blumchen, 112
Evergreen Press, 96
Face w/moon, German ornament, 1960s, 24
Feather Tree Co., 1990s, 108
Feather trees, 1980s, 78
Feather trees, 1990s, 107-8
Felt covered ornament, 1970s, 64-5
Felt Santa, China, 1990s, 159
Fences, 1960s, 36
Ferraresi, Luca, 122
Fine Feathers, Slavic, 1990s, 149
First Frost, Blumchen, 1990s, 112
Fish, Polish ornament, 130
Fish, silver, German ornament, 1960s, 25
Flaner, Tenna, 113
Flapper girl, Italian ornament, 85
Foil ornament, 1960s, 31
Folk Art by May, 153
Fontanini Collection, 156
Football player, Italian ornament, 83
Forkel, Evelyn, 153
Fountain, Radko, 1990s, 144
Fraga, Larry 152
Frank, Paul, 16
Franke, Edward, Jr., 82
Frankenmuth, MI, 1990s, 135
Frankenstein, Radko, 1990s, 145
Friends, Breen, 1990s, 147
Frog, German ornament, 1960s, 25
Frog, Radko, 1980s, 91
Frosty Penguin, Slavic, 1990s, 149
Fruit, ornament, OWC, 1990s, 132
Fruit, W. German ornament, 91
Fruits, Italian ornament, 83
Garland, glass, 1960s, 32
Garland, tinsel, 1990s, 153
Garlands, tinsel, 1980s, 99
GDR, 60
GEDANIA cooperative, 130-2
Gedania, 1990s, 130-2
General Electric, 1970s, 73
General Electric, 17
General Foam Plastics, 104
Gentleman/hat, Italian ornament, 1990s, 127
Geoffrey Giraffe, Slavic, 1990s, 148
George Franke & Sons, 82
Gerlach, Bob & Sylvia 94-5
Gerlach's of Lecha, 94-5
German figural ornament, 1990s, 139
German Kaiser, Radko, 1990s, 144